The Vietnam War:
Confidential Files
On the
Siege and Loss
Of
Khe Sanh

Volumes in the Top Secret series by
New Century Books:

World War Two:
U.S. Military Plans for the Invasion of Japan

The FBI Files on Elvis Presley

The Vietnam War:
Confidential Files on the Siege and Loss of Khe Sanh

TOP SECRET:

The Vietnam War: Confidential Files On the Siege and Loss Of Khe Sanh

Thomas Fensch, Editor

New Century Books

Copyright © 2001 Thomas Charles Fensch

New Century Books
P.O. Box 7113
The Woodlands, Texas, 77387-7113

Library of Congress Number: 2001117310
ISBN #:   Hardcover   0-930751-07-8
            Softcover   0-930751-08-6

*. . . for Charles and Arleen,
the west Texas side of the family . . .*

Contents

Introduction 1

Confidential Files
On the
Siege and Loss
Of Khe Sanh 9

Appendix 311

Bibliography 326

Index 329

About the Editor

Introduction

Khe Sanh remains, to this day, an extremely controversial and emotional aspect of the war in Vietnam. The U.S. armed forces fought to defend Khe Sanh in early 1968, and then abandoned the combat base there after a 77-day siege was over. Khe Sanh was the largest joint effort of the allied forces in Vietnam.

In *The Hidden History of the Vietnam War*, John Prados writes:

> Khe Sanh became important precisely because of its location on Route 9 near the Latian border. In the early years of the war . . . Military Assistance Command Vietnam (MACV — ed.) followed a strategy of border surveillance and denial, using detachments of U.S. Army special forces to organize and train Vietnamese montagnard tribesmen. The Khe Sanh border camp, opened in 1962 at a time when the CIA ran this program, actually predated the assumption of command responsibility by MACV. It was still in place in 1965 when the U.S. Marines came to the northern provinces of South Vietnam, the I Corps Tactical Zone (I

TOP SECRET

CTZ), making that area a Marine preserve. There was the little fighting at Khe Sanh in those years. Only in January 1966 was the camp subjected to a heavy mortar barrage by the enemy for the first time. (Prados 166)

As the relatively-nearby Ho Chi Minh Trail brought increased traffic in supplies and materiel, it also brought additional North Vietnam Army units to defend it, and brought these units close to Khe Sanh.
And thus Khe Sanh came into play.
By 1966, U.S. command planners had recognized that Khe Sanh was not only a key area to defend, but it was also a key staging area, should the allied command receive orders to invade Laos, in pursuit of the North Vietnamese Army.
By early 1968, allied planners saw evidence that the North Vietnamese Army was planning an offensive thrust in the general area of Khe Sanh; and it became equally obvious that to close Khe Sanh would be a major disaster for the U.S. and South Vietnamese Army and a major victory for the North Vietnamese forces.
The battle of Khe Sanh began January 21, 1968. And although U.S. military forces, and officials as high as President Lyndon Johnson refused to call it a siege, it was, in fact, exactly that.
And they were well aware of the French defeat at Dien Bien Phu, in 1954.
Lyndon Johnson is quoted as stating, "I don't want no damned Dinbinphoo!" (Prados 170) and,

he demanded daily briefing reports and also received a table-top sand model of the Khe Sanh area, provided by the Pentagon.

These daily briefing reports, from General William C. Westmoreland, and others, passed along through General Earle G. Wheeler, chairman of the Joint Chiefs of Staff, and reports and memos sent through the offices of W.W. "Walt" Rostow to the President form the core of this book.

Forty B-52s were designed for the Khe Sanh area, and an electronic sensoring system code-named Muscle Shoals was established in case visual patrols could not be undertaken.

Then the massive Tet offensive erupted throughout South Vietnam, but Khe Sanh was largely untouched. When the Lang Vei Special Forces camp was attacked — and by armor, which was the first time the enemy had used armor — officials believed the concluding element of the war had begun — and also assumed that Khe Sanh would be the key area.

Former Joint Chiefs of Staff chairman General Maxwell D. Taylor voiced his opinion that Khe Sanh could not easily be defended. "My present opinion is that Khe Sanh probably can be held but that it will be at a heavy price in causalities and in terms of other ground troops necessary to support and reinforce it. I have real doubt that we can afford such a defense," Taylor said. (Prados, 173).

Khe Sanh *was* a something of a technological victory for the allied and southern Vietnamese side as more than 14,000 tons of supplies plus 85,000 tons of ordinance was flung at the enemy from Khe Sanh, with only 205 Americans killed, 852

TOP SECRET

medivaced to safety and 816 others wounded.

Yet, it was a victory for the North Vietnamese as well. While Saigon and Washington officials were transfixed on the battle at Khe Sanh that never came, the North Vietnamese were relatively free to pursue the Tet offensive throughout South Vietnam, which they did.

And, the siege and loss of Khe Sanh has been compared to the much earlier French loss at Dien Bien Phu. But in *Vietnam: A History,* Stanley Karnow disputes the comparison:

> The Dienbienphu analogy was preposterous. The French had been trapped in an inaccessible valley with only a few artillery pieces, while the Americans had a formidable array of howitzers and mortars at Khesanh as well as long-range guns capable of blasting the enemy positions from outside the perimeter. In contrast to the French, who lacked aircraft, the U.S. force could rely on a formidable fleet of helicopters and cargo planes to carry in supplies and replacements as well as evacuate the wounded. Above all, the besieged Marines were able to count on the B-52s, which would drench the surrounding North Vietnamese and Vietcong troops with explosive over a nine-week span — the deadliest deluge of firepower ever unloaded on a tactical target in the history of warfare.
>
> The ratio of American to Communist causalities was also to highlight the difference between Dienbienphu and

Khesanh. Approximately eight thousand Vietminh and two thousand French Army soldiers died at Dienbienphu. But the struggle for Khesanh cost the Communists at least ten thousand lives in exchange for fewer than five hundred U.S. Marines killed in action. In Hanoi, after the war, a Communist veteran of the battle recalled the carnage inflicted on his comrades, disclosing to me that some North Vietnamese and Vietcong units suffered as much as 90 percent losses under the relentless downpour of American bombs, napalm and artillery shells. (Gen.) Giap, who as rarely troubled by heavy human tolls, flew to the front in January 1968 to inspect the situation personally — and he nearly became a casualty himself when a flight of thirty-six B-52s dropped a thousand tons of bombs near his field headquarters. Westmoreland had ordered the air strike after his electronic experts suspected, from intercepting enemy radio traffic, that a prominent communist figure might be in the area. (Karnow, 553)

Karnow suggests that the attacks at Khe Sanh were a ruse by the North Vietnamese to force Washington to defend an area not really worth defending. (Karnow, op. cit., 555)

And so this volume.
The messages in this volume were formerly-

TOP SECRET

secret files retrieved from the archives of Lyndon Johnson Presidential Library, in Austin, Texas. They were photocopied from the originals; then commentary and analysis by the editor was added, then the manuscript was retyped and recoded for electronic storage and publication in book form.

Every effort has been made to reproduce all the messages accurately. In some cases, the photocopies are too faint to be accurately read; thus, the editor does not guarantee complete reproduction of this material.

In sum, however, the flow of the siege and loss of Khe Sanh is all too evident in these dispatches — many marked TOP SECRET or EYES ONLY for the President.

Readers are also offered the *caveat* that some of these formerly-secret files have been "Sanitized" prior to their release; and some contain *redactions*, material edited out, prior to their release. Additional documents may still be classified secret on this topic.

In contrast to almost all nonfiction books, the editor has exercised an editorial prerogative *not* to arbitrarily break up this material into chapters; in many cases, the break between chapter three and chapter four in some book, for instance, and then between chapter six and chapter seven, may indicate a break in time; the editor has chosen to publish all these documents without chapter breaks to show the *continuous flow* of the story, as a *cohesive narrative*.

Readers may make up their own minds about the wisdom or folly of Khe Sanh by reading these reports from Khe Sanh, and from Saigon to Washington, DC, and messages and memos from Washington, DC to Saigon and then to Khe Sanh.

These are, I believe, the roughest drafts of history; the raw evidence of how decisions are made.

And what of the outcome? And what of those who had to leave after the war ended? And what about the Americans after the end of the conflict? And what of the scars and the ethics and the pathos of the war in Vietnam?

Perhaps one of the most eloquent summaries is by Michael Maclear. In *The Ten Thousand Day War: Vietnam — 1945–1975*, he writes:

> The 230,000 South Vietnamese who left in 1975 to settle in North America are now citizens or eligible citizens of the US and Canada, and could safely revisit families in Vietnam if the diplomatic channels were opened. Tran Van Don says he has kept his Vietnamese citizenship and 'we have to hope that one day we'll be back — if not our children, our grandchildren'. The former Defense Minister opened several Vietnamese restaurants and then settled in Florida. Bui Diem also started a restaurant — in Washington where he was once Ambassador — and also feels the same. 'We thank the United States for welcoming us but deep in our heart we would like to go back,' he says, and 'looking back I cannot afford not to feel sad; all

the sacrifices were in vain.' Former Vice-President Nguyen Cao Ky chose California and the liquor business and says if America was at fault it was 'in doing too much for us'. Ex-President Nguyen Van Thieu puts a different nuance on that: America wanted to control the Vietnamese but had not the patience to see it through. Thieu finally settled in a grand mansion outside London which he elected to call The White House. He preferred to be known by the alias 'Mr. Martin'.

Graham Martin, the last US Ambassador in Saigon, abandoned his dream farm in Tuscany — choosing a Tudor-style mansion in North Carolina. The envoys, all rich and venerable, retired sumptuously: Ellsworth Bunker to Vermont; Henry Cabot Lodge to the family estate at Beverly, Massachusetts; General Maxwell Davenport Taylor to a Washington apartment full of mementos of different wars. Bunker now feels that 'maybe in hindsight one would say that we shouldn't have been there'. Lodge believes 'we could have done something that cost less, took longer and would have had lasting results'. Taylor unequivocally regrets the war: 'We didn't know our ally. Secondly, we knew even less about the enemy. And the last, most inexcusable of our mistakes was not knowing our own people.' (pp. 416–417)

Confidential Files
On the
Siege and Loss
Of Khe Sanh

TOP SECRET

The Khe Sanh files begin January 10, 1968; Walter "Walt" Rostow, Lyndon Johnson's National Security Affairs advisor cables Johnson that he had visited with, and tried to convince columnist Joseph Alsop to ally himself more closely with the Johnson administration. It seems clear in the cable that Alsop didn't believe in the Johnson formula for success in Vietnam.

FROM: WALT ROSTOW
TO: THE PRESIDENT
CITE: CAP82252

LITERALLY EYES ONLY

JANUARY 18, 1968

At his urgent request, I had lunch today with Joe Alsop at his house. I thought I wold use the occasion to encourage him to write thoughtfully about the inadequacies of the Trinh negotiating formula; underline the elements in San Antonio; and discourage false optimism, I found myself confronted with an hour's monologue in which I could barely get a word in edgewise.

The monologue was, however, of sufficient interest for me to report it precisely.

There were three subjects: negotiations; Senator Robert F. Kennedy; and Khe Sanh.

Negotiations. In his best gloom-and-doom manner, Joe, said we are about to lose a war we are well on the way to winning. He has been talking to McNamara and Bill Bundy. He says

Confidential Files on the Siege and Loss of Khe Sanh

McNamara's idea that we can fight a more effective war without bombing the north is "tragic nonsense," even if the DMZ is quiet. There are, in Joe's judgment, 800,000 North Vietnamese tied up in dealing with our bombing. They will pour south via the Ho Chin Minh trail into Laos. We shall have a new massive war as the result of living with the San Antonio formula as he understands it is now being interpreted. When I pointed out that we did not intend to engage in Panmunjom-type endless negotiations, he then said that the evidence required to demonstrate an increase in infiltration would be so obscure that we could never persuade the British, etc., that infiltration had increased. The pressure to continue the talks on Hanoi's terms would be very great. Once the president had accepted the talks and then was forced back to bombing, he would lose ground. He would appear weak and vulnerable.

He then went on, with some relish, to say: "I told the president he should make a statement that would fend off any negotiations. He refused to take my advice. Now he is in a great dilemma which could be mortal. What he should do is to get on the air and tell the people: 'I am responsible for 525,000 of our men in southeast Asia. It will not accept negotiations which will release the manpower in the north for a much expanded war. In the south, I will not have that bloodshed on my hands. Let those who are prepared to accept this cost step forward.' "

Putting the emotion aside, what Joe is saying is that:

TOP SECRET

It will be very difficult to monitor an increase in infiltration;

It will be very difficult to demonstrate an increase in infiltration persuasively;

It will be hard, therefore, to make a public case for resuming bombing if talks are protracted and they begin to release manpower from the north to the south;

And, therefore, we must interpret the San Antonio formula as requiring a total cessation of infiltration.

In short, Joe puts a very high premium on the pinning down in the north of what he now estimates to be 800,000 North Vietnamese by our bombing; and believes that if we put Hanoi in a position to release these people for movement to the south, we could gravely prolong the war.

Senator Robert J. Kennedy. Joe says he saw Bobby Kennedy yesterday. Bobby is under great pressure from all his advisers except Ted Sorensen to challenge you for the nomination: "All that is stopping him is his own sense of political reality." He says that President Kennedy had advisers stretching from Ted Sorensen on the left to his father on the right. Senator Robert Kennedy has Ted Sorensen on the right and God knows whom on the left. In his own judgment, the only way for the president to deal with Senator Kennedy is to assert tough leadership. Uncertainty might lead him to jump, even though he told Bobby, he says, that the only result would be to destroy himself and the democratic party and put the republican right wing into power for twenty years. Joe linked how the negotiation issue is handled to now Senator Kennedy will move. If we get into a negotiating situation and then have to resume bombing on inadequate evidence, we shall look weak and uncertain. That will be the signal for Robert Kennedy to get into the ring.

Khe Sanh. Joe said that in his judgment the military campaign is going exactly as the documents said it would. They are using up their assets in the south. He is, however, worried about the concentration of forces in Laos against the Marine outpost of Khe Sanh. He said that if he were the president he would ask Westmoreland for a statement of the pros and cons of our getting out of Khe Sanh. He understands the road to Khe Sanh is already cut. He believes the airfield at Khe Sanh can be commanded by the North Vietnamese from nearby hills. He feels that Westmoreland is inherited in that area by the traditional, somewhat distant relations between the Marine commander in I corps and himself. He feels the president must be assured that Westmoreland is absolutely confident he can deal with the Khe Sanh problem: it is the best opportunity for a Dienbienphu. And the enemy is looking for a Diebienphu.

FYI. I have for some time been asking questions about Khe Sanh. It is clear that Westmoreland has it very much on his mind. I shall look further into our contingency planning.

TOP SECRET

The next day, January 11, Rostow, warns of an enemy build-up of "20,000 should they decide at some point to commit all personnel from the elements of the four divisions now in the general area. This is considerably more than they would need merely to take Khe Sanh."

FROM: WALT ROWSTOW
TO: THE PRESIDENT
CITE: CAPR5254

January 11, 1968

Herewith a CIA summary of a longer text on the enemy threat to Khe Sanh.

In the past several weeks there have been a number of indications that the enemy is building up its forces in the Laotian Panhandle west of the demilitarized zone.

The target primarily threatened by these forces appears to be the allied base at Khe Sanh in western Quang Tri Province of South Vietnam. Enemy reconnaissance and probing activity near Khe Sanh has increased markedly in the last few weeks. [Redacted] The communists could be using the time between now and the Tet holidays to complete their concentration around Khe Sanh in preparation for an offensive after Tet.

[Redacted]

The communists could muster a total force of over 20,000 should they decide at some point to commit all personnel from the elements of the four divisions now in the general area. This is considerably more than they would need merely to take Khe Sanh. Their primary objective in attacking Khe Sanh would be to draw US reinforcements into the area, tie them to static defensive positions, and inflict maximum casualties on US forces, over a period of time.

The buildup of forces in Laos and western Quang Tri Province also strengthens North Vietnamese defense of the Laos corridor. [Redacted]

TOP SECRET

General William Westmoreland also warns of the necessity of troop build-ups in the Khe Sanh area: "... contingency plans for augmenting this force with an additional United States Marine Corps battalion on eight hours notice, followed by a second battalion on twelve hours notice ..."

CITE: MAC 00547
DTG: 1214227
FROM: GENERAL WESTMORELAND COMUSMACV SAIGON
TO: GENERAL WHEELER CJCS WASH DC
 ADMIRAL SHARP CINCPAC HAWAII

SUBJ: KHE SANH (8)
REF: A. JCS 00343/111546Z JAN 68 (TS)
B. MAC 00276/01723OZ JAN 68 (TS)
C. MAC 00321/081259Z JAN 68 (TS)

I have just returned from a visit with General Cushman during which we discussed contingency plans for reinforcing Khe Sanh and the I CTZ which is pertinent to tour inquiry in ref. A. General Cushman has two USMC BNS (Reinf) in Khe Sanh now and contingency plans for augmenting this force with an additional USMC BN on eight hour notice, followed by a second BN on twelve hour notice, and by SLF forces. Additionally, and as a result of the above discussion, I have directed him as a matter of first priority to alert a brigade of the Americal division to move into the Hue/Phu Bai area. This can be done quickly with fixed wing or rotary wing aircraft.

As a second priority we are prepared to reinforce I CTZ in the Hue/Phu Bai, Danang, or Chu Lai areas in that priority with another BDE, either from the 101st airborne division or from the ST Cav div (Am).

Additional actions underway include the following:

As the ROK Marine brigade moves into the Danang Taor, elements of the 1st Marine division are being released for deployment north of AI-Van pass. This in turn is releasing elements of the 3D Marine division for movement into Quang Tri Province, two BNS of the ROK Marine BDE have completed their movement and four BNS of the 1st Marine Div are now north of A1-Van Pass. This move will be complete by 31 Jan with four ROK BNS in the Danang Taor and five 1st Marine Div BNS north of the pass.

The JGS has agreed to deploy a TF of two ABN BNS to 1 CTZ O/A 15 Jan 68 bringing to four the number of Arvn ABN BNS in I CTZ.

We are developing priority targets (OPN Niagara, Ref b) for a sustained Air Light campaign, augmented by Tac Air, beginning not later than 18 Jan. We plan to concentrate on targets in Rvn prior to Tet with approximately 75 percent or more of our total effort. During and following Tet cease fire we will strike targets in Laos. This operation (Niagara) also includes a slam type operation in the Khe Sanh area by 7th AF. In conjunction with our sustained Air Light campaign I am requesting by front channel A further step up in the B-52 accelerated program now scheduled to begin 20 Jan.

TOP SECRET

We are requesting a carrier be alerted to be brought in to augment Tac air, and the prompt return of the SLF for commitment to either the 3D or 1st Mar Div areas.

Maximum number of MGF support ships will be concentrated in the I CTZ.

Regarding view number one in Ref A: My concept and a time frame for operations in Laos are outlined in a proposed operation (El Paso) Ref. C. Preempting a Khe Sanh area assault by an offensive into Laos is neither logistically nor tactically feasible at this time. Significant considerations include the following:

To be effective a Laotian assault should be launched in the near future.

With the NE monsoon upon us, launching and supporting the magnitude of force envisioned is not within our current capability. An air LOC is essential and flying weather is marginal. Additionally, our airlift capabilities are inadequate to support both this concept and an acceptable tactical posture in other run threat areas at this time.

We estimate sizable enemy forces to be in the Tchepone area and to the north thereof; thus a brief successful campaign there may not be possible.

Air assaults into Laos west of Khe Sanh will most probably encounter heavy AA fire which we might not be able to neutralize in a short time frame.

With respect to view number two Ref A; the following paragraphs are keyed to your message:

Khe Sanh Road: True, it is not now open. It

can be opened, and defended; though with considerable difficulty during the NE monsoons. Route 9 is not, however, a decisive element in our defense of Khe Sanh. We can supply and reinforce by air.

Control of commanding highground: At this time, we control the following key hills at Khe Sanh: Hill 881 (XD777438), Hill 861 (KD803443), and Hill 950 (AD843455). Those that are tactically essential will be defended.

Enemy artillery: We have only one report of artillery threatening Khe Sanh; and this report notes the presence of 75MM pack artillery. The enemy is faced with great obstacles in the movement of heavy equipment in the western Quang Tri terrain. However we do anticipate great quantities of mortar and rocket fire.

Withdrawal from Khe Sanh: Although this area is critical to US from a tactical standpoint as a launch base for SO as flank security for the strong point obstacle system, it is even more critical from a psychological view point. To relinquish this area would be a major propaganda victory for the enemy, its loss would seriously affect Vietnamese and US morale. In short, withdrawal would be a tremendous step backwards.

COMUSMACV — LTG Cushman relationship: We have no problem here and I reject out of hand any implications to the contrary. This is absurd.

In summary with respect to REF A I regard the non-military expressions as tantamount to desperation tactics on the one hand, and defeat on the other. Needless to say such action would favor the enemy who himself is desperate.

TOP SECRET

Although there are those in non military circles who favor the concept of retreating into enclaves, I must reiterate this strategy merely returns the center of violence to the midst of the RVN people in the populated centers. On the other hand, a massive assault into Laos is not feasible in the near time frame.

In view of the enemy capability to initiate a major offensive in Quang Tri Province before Tet I would prefer to defend with force deployment and combat support as indicated above. I will submit additional support requirements by front channel for Air Light, carrier and NGF support.

As I file this message, another thought occurs to me which I tag on. I believe the time has arrived to declassify and employ COFRAM.* I recommend that the JCS act on this matter and that it be authorized for use in the unpopulated areas of I Corps.

Warm regards.

* Anti-personnel explosives — ed.

Rostow continues briefing Lyndon Johnson on the situation in flux:

Thursday, January 18, 1968
11:00 a.m.

MR. PRESIDENT:
Your judgment is needed on the following problem:

As you know, it was agreed sometime ago that there would be a 48-hour stand-down for Tet — January 30.

Apparently Generals Westmoreland and Vien, without evidence of consultation with Ambassador Bunker, went to Thieu and, against his better judgment, persuaded him to cut the 48 hours to 36 hours. There are perfectly good military grounds for this, given the behavior of the Viet Cong during the Christmas and New Year's stand-downs.

Secretaries Rusk and McNamara believe that it is unwise to cut back from 48 to 36 hours, for two reasons:

— Hanoi could regard it as our changing rules of the game in the middle of a tense period of communications;

— We could be criticized further for toughening up our behavior in a delicate, potentially pre-negotiation situation. (There is apparently some criticism of your State of the Union message along these lines.)

Therefore, Secretaries Rusk and McNamara would like to go back to Bunker and Westy and reverse the decision, reinstalling the 48-hour Tet

TOP SECRET

truce. Both do this reluctantly out of respect for Westy, and having whipsawed Thien once already on this matter.

January 21, 1968: Westmoreland briefs Naval operations in Hawaii and the Joint Chiefs of Staff in Washington DC regarding the "anticipated enemy attack on Khe Sanh . . ."

CITE: MAC 00992
DTG: 210945Z
FROM: GEN WESTMORELAND, COMUSMACV, SAIGON
TO: ADM SHARP, CINCPAC, HAWAII
INFO: GEN WHEELER, CJCS, WASHINGTON

21 JANUARY 1968

Ref: A. Comusmacv Mac 00797 DTG 180009Z Jan
B. Cincpac Dtg 18 2231Z Jan

The anticipated enemy attack on Khe Sanh was initiated last evening. Khe Sanh military installation has been under constant rocket and mortar fire since early morning, and Hill 861 has been under ground attack. Ammunition and Pol dumps have been hit, with fire and explosions reported by air force Fac. 7AF is maintaining an airborne command post and Fac's in the area. There is a build-up north of the DMZ and in base areas 101 west of Quang Tri and 114 west of Hue. The next several weeks are destined to be active.
The following actions have been taken:
On 6 Jan a coordinated intelligence collection effort was initiated on the Khe Sanh area (Niagara I) using maximum available resources.
On 6 Jan, I directed Gen Momyer to prepare a

TOP SECRET

plan to concentrate all available air resources into the Khe Sanh area (Niagara II).

On 17 Jan the 1st air cavalry division minus one brigade began to deploy to Hue/Phu Bai, and will close tomorrow.

On 18 June two additional Vietnamese airborne battalions deployed to Hue, making a total of four in the area.

On the 19th, I diverted all B-52 strikes to the area.

Based on my visit to III Maf on 19 January, I sent my J2 to Khe Sanh on 20 January to insure coordination of reconnaissance activities in and around Khe Sanh.

On the 19th, I directed Gen Cushman to deploy the 3D brigade of the 1st air cavalry division as soon as practical from the Wheeler-Wallowa area to Hue/Phu Bai to join its parent division.

On 20 January, I instructed LTG Weyland to deploy the 2D brigade of the 101st airborne division to Hue/Phu Bai for attachment to 1st cavalry division as soon as air lift becomes available, probably about 23 January.

Based on plans initiated last week, I directed en Momyer on 20 January to divert any useful "dump truck" assets from the Muscle Shoals project to the Quang Tri area.

On 20 January, I instructed Ltg Cushman to defer any further work on the trace involved in the dye marker project to as to keep maximum troops available to react to enemy initiatives.

Today, I am sending Gen Abrams to III Maf to assess the situation. Also I have directed en Momyer to station an liaison officer at Khe Sanh.

It has never been my intention to in any way interfere with the close air support so essential to the Marines on the ground or to upset the system at this critical time. On the other hand, I intend to do all possible to bring to bear in the most efficient and coordinated way all weapons that can support our fight during the important period at hand. I urgently need authority to delegate to my deputy commander for air, the control that I deem appropriate over the air assets in my command. The following are my instructions to him and CG III Maf which I plan to issue as a matter of operational urgency and which I believe you will find fully satisfactory. Quote.

I consider it imperative that we use the maximum air firepower available to meet the enemy threat in I Corps. This was the issue which prompted my message (copy being relayed to you) Mac 00791 171206Z Jan 68.

In order to effect detailed application of my air resources in I corps, the following directive will apply:

7th Air Force will be responsible for the air support of the 1st air cavalry and Americal divisions now deployed into I Corps. Policy of having 7th Air Force support Army and ARVN units in I Corps will constitute guidance for future deployments.

To meet the threat in the Quang Tri-Thua Thien area, I have directed my deputy COMDR MACV Air, Gen Momyer, to develop a plan to concentrate all available air resources (in the battle area). The initial area of concentration will be around Khe Sanh (Niagara II). Depending upon the tactical situation the area will be shifted.

TOP SECRET

Deputy COMUSMACV for air operations will coordinate the details of this air plan with the 1st Marine air wing and III MAF as appropriate. I have charged him with the overall responsibility for air operations for the execution of this plan. He will coordinate and direct the employment of Tac air, Marine air, diverted air strikes from out of country air operations and such naval air that may be requested. B-52 strikes will be coordinated through him.

Until further notice, it is directed that III MAF make available to the 7th Air Force all tactical bomber sorties not required for direct air support of Marine units. These sorties will be initially committed to the Niagara II operation.

(S) I wish to stress the absolute necessity for coordination of all elements of the command to bring our firepower against the enemy in the most effective manner. The serious threat we face in I Corps and Khe Sanh in particular, demands this. I have directed my air deputy to insure in my name that these air resources are applied to this end. Unquote.

A similar directive now under study with respect to the efficient utilization of airlift may be necessary due to the critical nature of this resource.

January 22, 1968: Westmoreland continues to advise of developments after the first 48 hours of enemy attacks north of Khe Sanh:

EYES ONLY

Copy of MAC 01049 from General Westmoreland Jan. 22, 1968

1. The following is my assessment of the situation as it has developed over the past 48 hours.

2. The initial attacks of the expected enemy offensive in northern I Corps began on 20-21 January with assaults on 26th Marine positions north of Khe Sanh and on the Huong Hoa subsector. These were repulsed by the Marines and the Regional and Popular Forces in the area. Attacks by fire destroyed some ammunition and fuel and cratered the runway on the airfield. (3,000 feet of runway is still usable, however.) There was also a heavy attack by fire on Camp Carroll, with no significant damage or casualties resulting. The enemy broke contact around Khe Sanh at about noon the 21st and his activity subsided.

3. These actions were probably preliminary to a full-scale attack on Khe Sanh. [Redacted]

4. The [Redacted] will probably conduct supporting attacks against friendly installations along Highway 9, particularly Camp Carroll. [Redacted] Indicate that an attack on Camp Carroll may occur within 24 hours.

TOP SECRET

5. [Redacted]

6. The two-week general lull in country-wide activity that was interrupted on the 20th indicates preparations for a widespread effort. The presence of high echelon representatives near tactical units in all corps areas strengthens the probability. I believe that the enemy will attempt a country-wide show of strength just prior to Tet, with Khe Sanh being the main event. In II Corps, he will probably attack around Pleikn and Kontum cities, and I expect attacks on the Special Forces camps at Dak Seang, Duc Co, and Dak To. In III and IV Corps, province towns are likely targets for renewed attacks by fire. Terrorism will probably increase in and around Saigon.

EYES ONLY

The next entries were the unofficial memo, and the formal memorandum, by Lieutenant General A.J. Goodpaster, who briefed former President Dwight Eisenhower on the Vietnam war.

DEPARTMENT OF DEFENSE
THE NATIONAL WAR COLLEGE
OFFICE OF THE COMMANDANT
WASHINGTON, D.C. 20115

22 January 1968

MEMORANDUM FOR THE PRESIDENT:

I met with General Eisenhower for 2 hours at Palm Desert on Thursday. He is in excellent health and spirits, and was most appreciative of being brought up to date. After a brief report on the war, I covered the recent "peace feelers". His principal observations and comments are contained in the last 4 paragraphs of the attached Memorandum for Record.

A. J. GOODPASTER
Lieutenant General, USA

DEPARTMENT OF DEFENSE
THE NATIONAL WAR COLLEGE
OFFICE OF THE COMMANDANT
WASHINGTON, D.C. 20315

22 January 1968

TOP SECRET

MEMORANDUM FOR RECORD

SUBJECT: Meeting with General Eisenhower, Palm Desert, 18 January

I met with General Eisenhower for two hours at his office and his home at Palm Desert on 18 January.

I began with a report on the progress of the war. In recent weeks, the VC and NVA have been making an unusual military effort, and taking very heavy losses — 3,000 and 2,200 in the last weeks. Documents have been captured which call for an immediate or "final" effort by all units. The general pattern continues to show Communist losses more than 5 times as great as the losses to U.S., Allied and ARVN forces combined.

Next I gave a resume in some detail of the principal US/ARVN operational efforts now going on and envisaged for the near future, including ground/air operations in SVN (by Corps area), ground activities relating to Laos and Cambodia, naval operations in the Vietnam area, B-52 operations, Air operations against NVN, Air operations in Laos, the anti-infiltration system, and revolutionary development operations in SVN.

Next I covered a few points of special note. There is an enemy concentration which may total 3 NVA divisions in the Khe Sanh area which is being closely watched. Also there is enemy preparation for possible renewed action in the Dak To area. Next, I reported recently obtained VC reports that in Quang Tri and Quang Nam, the Communist organization is being "stunted" by

US/SVN military operations, and that in areas of Phu Yen, cadre and infrastructure are disintegrating; also an NVN report indicates that North Vietnam is hurting from the bombing attacks and suffering losses, some of which are irreplaceable.

I then passed on a report that the NVN has conducted a remarkably well coordinated supply operation during Christmas week. Trucks observed in Route Package 1, other than Christmas Day, ranged from 3 to 95 (averaging 44) and waterborne logistic craft from 0 to 43 (averaging 17); on Christmas Day 547 trucks and 325 waterborne logistic craft were sighted. On the same day between Thanh Hoa and Dong Hoi 900 trucks were sighted, 888 moving south (carrying an estimated 4,000 tons). General Eisenhower thought these were extremely significant figures and asked why these figures are not better known. I told him that figures like these had been made public, and there had been some press coverage, although not with the emphasis he had in mind. (I indicated that I could not speak about TV coverage.) He said he thought that photographs should be taken and publicized in case of any future suspension. I told him this has been done in the past, and that in the discussions I have heard concerning possible future bombing halts there was strong insistence on the need to provide photo reconnaissance.

I next reported on Chieu Hoi returnees in 1967. The number — some 27,000 — was less than had been estimated when the year began, but was 34% over 1966. Of the 27,000, some 17,000 were military, the equivalent of 2

TOP SECRET

Communist divisions or about one-fifth of the total VC/NVA killed or captured in 1967 (91,000). Political returnees numbered nearly 8,000 of whom 4,700 were infrastructure or party organizers. General Eisenhower asked whether some of these may be VC agents. I told him that they are screened, and that in fact some of the returnees are used with patrols that seek out, propagandize, and call in air and artillery strikes on the units from which they came.

General Eisenhower commented that the TV coverage of our bases that are hit by mortar fire is damaging to our people's understanding of the war. The presentations are highly dramatic and shocking in their effect. I told him that a great deal of patrolling, which is often successful, goes into protecting our bases against mortar fire, and that some attacking groups have been detected and attacked by air and artillery. This, of course, cannot be shown as graphically on TV and in the press as the attacks on our bases.

I next reported upon the widespread SVN concern over "coalition", as the background for General Thieu's recent statement. Ambassador Bunker had reported rising concern in SVN that the U.S. might be shifting to favor coalition, and had suggested that this should be scotched. Also, Mr. Rostow told me that there was a great deal of talk and worry about this in SVN, much of which seemed to be starting with the VC. The latter, according to captured documents, is pushing the coalition issue in its propaganda (and linking the U.S. to the idea) while calling for a special round of combat effort. I said Mr. Rostow had told me that our government does not favor coalition; this is simply VC propaganda. General Eisenhower said that an coalition would be undesirable and dangerous and we should oppose it. I also mentioned that Mr. Rostow believes there is some evidence of a shift in the view the Communists have held that time is on their side. General Eisenhower thought such a shift would be highly significant.

Next I took up the status of the possible NVN "peace feeler" involved in the shift from "could" to "will", covering points provided to me by General Wheeler. We do not know what the NVN objective may be — whether they are serious, want a respite, seek a psychological coup, etc., or whether their shift on "permanent" cessation is somehow an indirect assurance they will not take advantage of a bombing halt.

During discussion, General Eisenhower cited his experience first with the Italian surrender and later with the German surrender. He advised not to rely on "iffy" favorable interpretations, but to insist upon more frank and clear-cut statements (which may, of course, be made privately). Even then, he said, we must not put ourselves in the position of depending upon believe in what a Communist says. Whatever is worked out must be self-enforcing. I told him that these questions, and others like them, are being very carefully studied within the government, and that a great deal of thought is being given to them. There seems to be considerable recognition that the key issue is whether the NVN is ready, or can be led, to give up its efforts at take-over of SVN by force.

TOP SECRET

Also, that if bombing is stopped, it could prove very difficult to start up again. This underlies the cautious and careful approach that is being made.

Next he said that if the NVN is in fact weakening its position, now is the time to hit them harder. He mentioned B-52 attacks on enemy forces and bases in SVN, and I told him that an expansion of effort is envisaged currently. Also, he thought we should hit the enemy with our ground forces, and should encourage the SVN to go after him with special aggressiveness at this time. The enemy might, as suggested, be making a great military effort in order to impose losses on us, and advance his advantages in going into negotiations. We should do much the same.

He said he hoped that we could get an effective armistice. To that end, now may be the time to increase our combat effort. He commented that this will be a partisan and political year, but that there is nothing partisan in his views when the lives of U.S. military men are involved. He said he wants to see the president win the war.

A. J. GOODPASTER
Lieutenant General, U. S. Army

Confidential Files on the Siege and Loss of Khe Sanh

Rostow suggests a 36-hour military stand down:

Friday, January 19, 1968 — 10:15 a.m.

Mr. President:

Herewith the argumentation which led Gen. Westmoreland and Gen. Vien to recommend a 36 hour rather than 48 hour standdown. As you can see (page 3), the argument has JCS support. These points could be made as follows:
 — Present rules of engagement permit strikes against "abnormally great resupply activities" during a standdown. These rules are meant to protect against the kind of resupply our people in Saigon fear. The argument in the attached paper is really for no truce rather than a 12-hour reduction.
 — There is a strong case for excluding the Khe Sanh area from the truce. It is relatively unpopulated. Given the evidence that the North Vietnamese are assembling forces for a massive attack, I believe it would be unwise for us to give them even 36 hours of free moment of forces and supplies in the Khe Sanh area.
 With the Khe Sanh exception and the freedom of action Westy already has to deal with abnormal supply movements, I don't think the 12 hours matter much one way or the other.

W. W. Rostow

TOP SECRET

The following memo analyzes how much difference there would be, for the North Vietnamese, between a 36-hour and a 48-hour cease fire, to resupply their forces:

In any standdown period in North Vietnam a major logistic effort takes place. This effort involves truck and waterborne logistic craft (WBLC). WBLC come into prominence whenever the length of the ceasefire period is sufficient to allow this relatively slow transportation a round trip opportunity. Prearms truce periods which involved WBLC to any significant degree were 48 hours or more in length. The WBLC activity starts as far north as Thanh Hoa (19° 45'N) and usually has a southern terminus near Dong Hoi (17° 30'N). The larger and faster craft can make the maximum distance round trip in about 48hours while smaller and slower boats can make the delivery and then achieve dispersed positions to avoid attacks when hostilities recommence.

During the 48 hour Christmas truce in 1966, US forces observed a 20 fold increase over daily average craft sightings along the southern coastal areas of NVN. During the 96 hour Tet truce in 1967 WBLC moved about 20,000 tons southward indicating a capability to move about 10,000 tons during a 48 hour period. This past Christmas and New Years ceasefire periods of 24 and 36 hours duration respectively exhibited no significant WBLC activity although the 36 hour period was more active than the 24 hour pause.

Truck Activity.

During the most recent Christmas and New Years truce periods, truck activity in NVN was eight to ten times normal daily estimates. It wold appear that about 2,200 tons of material was moving southward in NVN during an average 24 hour period. This amount of material was estimated to be destined for southern NVN, the DMZ, Laos and SVN. Should the total 2,200 tons be delivered to SVN, it would represent about a 95 to 120 day supply of external requirements provided by NVN to Viet Cong-NVA forces in SVN. In other terms 2,200 tons represents approximately a 22 day supply of material to a NVA division in moderate combat conditions.

Summary.

It can be estimated that the logistic difference to the North Vietnamese between a 36 hour and 48 hour ceasefire period could be as much as 10,000 tons of material. This difference being represented by the ability or lack of ability to employ WBLCs to any great degree.

TOP SECRET

January 29, 1968: Vietnam Roundup, *a fact-sheet publication for United States Information Agency personnel reprints an article by Joseph Alsop, headlined:*

Battle for Khesanh
Major Turning Point

His lead — his beginning — stated (the Vietnam Roundup *reprinted the entire 14-paragraph article):*

AT KHESANH, the Marine outpost on the western end of the DMZ, the enemy's heavy artillery began landing in the perimeter last week. The civilians fled from the little nearby villages. The battle had started.

It is a battle that has been expected since mid-December. At that time, as then revealed in this place, the single Marine regiment holding the outpost was already threatened by two enemy divisions. Since then, three more North Vietnamese regiments have moved up, bringing the total in the area to nine — a formidable force.

Beyond doubt, too, the long interval since mid-December has been used by the North Vietnamese troops to dig bunker systems and artillery redoubts into the nearby heights; for Khesanh is an isolated hill with still higher hills all round about. And despite its airfield, Khesanh can be cruelly difficult to resupply and reinforce.

January 29, 1968: General Earle G. Wheeler, Chairman, the Joint Chiefs of Staff, Washington, briefs President Lyndon Johnson on "The Situation at Khe Sanh":

THE JOINT CHIEFS OF STAFF
WASHINGTON, D. C. 20301

MEMORANDUM FOR THE PRESIDENT

Subject: The Situation at Khe Sanh

1. You will recall that on 12 January 1968 General Westmoreland informed me that the Khe Sanh position is important to us for the following reasons: (a) it is the western anchor of our defense of the DMZ area against enemy incursions into the northern portion of South Vietnam; (b) its abandonment would bring enemy forces into areas contiguous to the heavily populated and important coastal area; and (c) its abandonment would constitute a major propaganda victory for the enemy which would seriously affect Vietnamese and US morale. In summary, General Westmoreland declared that withdrawal from Khe Sanh would be a tremendous step backwards.

2. At 0910 hours this morning I discussed the Khe Sanh situation by telephone with General Westmoreland. He had just returned from a visit to northern I Corps Area during which he conferred with senior commanders, personally surveyed the situation, and finalized contingency plans. General Westmoreland made the following points:

TOP SECRET

a. The Khe Sanh garrison now consists of 5,000 US and ARVN troops. They have more than a battalion of US artillery supporting them, and 16 175 MM guns which can fire from easterly positions in support of the Khe Sanh force.

b. Among other reinforcing actions, he has moved a full US Army Division into northern I Corps. Within a few days the equivalent of an ARVN airborne division will also reinforce this area.

c. He has established a Field Army Headquarters in the Hue/Phu Bai area to control all forces, both US and ARVN, in northern I Corps. This headquarters is commanded by General Abrams.

d. General Momyer, Commander 7th Air Force, is coordinating all supporting air strikes in the NIAGRA area which constitutes the locale of enemy buildup around Khe Sanh.

e. Air action since 17 January has been remunerative. About 40 B-52 sorties per day and some 500 tactical air sorties per day are being conducted in the NIAGRA area. There have been numerous secondary explosions. It appears that air strikes and our artillery fire have disrupted the enemy's logistic buildup and troop concentration.

3. General Westmoreland stated to me that, in his judgment, we can hold Khe Sanh and we should hold Khe Sanh. He reports that everyone is confident. He believes that this is an opportunity to inflict a severe defeat upon the enemy. Further, General Westmoreland considers that all preparatory and precautionary measures have been taken, both in South Vietnam and here, to conduct a successful defense in the Khe Sanh area.

4. The Joint Chiefs of Staff have reviewed the situation at Khe Sanh and concur with General Westmoreland's assessment of the situation. They recommend that we maintain our position at Khe Sanh.

For the Joint Chiefs of Staff:

EARLE G. WHEELER
Chairman
Joint Chiefs of Staff

TOP SECRET

The Khe Sanh files continue with two pages of press clippings, dated 31 January, 1968. The clippings, under the banner:

EARLY BIRD EDITION
CURRENT NEWS

Which were part of a Department of Defense (DOD) service:

"PREPARED BY THE AIR FORCE (SAF—AA) AS EXECUTIVE AGENT FOR THE DOD TO BRING TO THE ATTENTION OF KEY DEFENSE DEPART- MENT PERSONNEL MATTERS WITHIN THEIR OFFICIAL RESPONSIBILITIES. NO OTHER USE OF THIS PUBLICATION IS AUTHORIZED."

The CURRENT NEWS dated Wednesday morning, 31 January, 1968 consisted of the articles "Navy to Aid Hunt For Four H-Bombs" by Evert Clark, published in The New York Times, 31 January, 1968, pp. 13; "New Tonkin Inquiry To Call McNamara" published in The New York Times 31 January, 1968, pp. 1; "U.S. Recaptures Embassy In Saigon In 6-Hour Siege," an Associated Press article published in The Baltimore Sun, 31 January, 1968, pp. 1; "U.S. Reports Saigon Was In Contact," by Charles W. Corddey, published in The Baltimore Sun, 31 January, 1968, pp. 2 and "U.S. Keeping Close Tab on Enemy Drive," (no by-line) published in The Washington Post, 31 January, 1968, pp. 11.
    The article headlined "U.S. Reports Saigon Was in Contact" referred to outbreaks of Vietnam

attacks in Saigon. The first three paragraphs read:

Washington, Jan. 30 — The White House tonight described as "serious" the outbreak of Viet Cong attacks in Saigon but said there had been no loss of contact with the American Embassy, invaded briefly by raiders.

General William C. Westmoreland, American commander in Vietnam, was understood to have reassured President Johnson that the savage guerrilla fighting that erupted throughout South Vietnam could be dealt with.

Military sources have said the offenses, which reportedly struck more than 40 towns, could be expected to have the effect desired by the Communists of embarrassing the United States and South Vietnamese Governments and showing that combined forces of more than 1,100,000 troops could not prevent attacks on population centers.

TOP SECRET

February 3, 1968: General Wheeler, continues to brief Lyndon Johnson on the situation at Khe Sanh:

THE JOINT CHIEFS OF STAFF
WASHINGTON, D. C. 20301

MEMORANDUM FOR THE PRESIDENT
SUBJECT: KHE SANH

In response to your telephone call to me last evening, I asked General Westmoreland to provide me his views as soon as possible on our reinforcement capability in the Khe Sanh area. His reply to me is presented in the following paragraphs for your information.
"1. I agree with (General Wheeler's) response on the question of our Khe Sanh reinforcement capability and would add the following amplification.
"2. Our situation at Khe Sanh as compared with the French at Dien Bien Phu is different in three significant respects. We have supporting air (tactical air and B-52's) for all-weather attack of enemy forces by orders of magnitude over that at Dien Bien Phu. We have reinforcing heavy artillery within range of the Khe Sanh area from USMC positions east of the mountains. We have multiple and vastly improved techniques for aerial supply and we are within helicopter support range for troop reinforcement, logistic support, medical evacuation and other requirements.
"3. We now have four Marine Corps battalions and one ARVN ranger battalion with combat and combat service support in the Khe Sanh area. We

currently have two brigades of the 1st Air Cavalry Division (Airmobile), plus one brigade of the 101st Airborne Division, with appropriate light and medium artillery support, located north of the Ai Van Pass, within prompt reinforcing distance of Khe Sanh. We have plans to further reinforce this area on short notice if required.

"4. We have a significant capability to reinforce Khe Sanh by fire in all weather conditions by artillery, tactical air, and B-52's. There are 18 105MM howitzers and 6 155 MH howitzers within the Khe Sanh defensive system. Additionally, 16 175MM guns are with the 3d Marine Division forces east of Khe Sanh positioned at the Rock Pile and at Camp Carroll. These guns are within range of Khe Sanh and their fires can be massed as required through the use of the centralized fire direction facility at Dong Ha. In addition to this heavy artillery support, and in contrast to the French situation at Dien Bien Phu, we have a highly effective tactical air and B-52 capability. Radar or "SKY SPOT" technique allows us direct tactical air strikes either at night or in zero visibility conditions throughout the Khe Sanh area. In addition to tactical air, our B-52 strikes are also weather independent. During adverse weather in the Khe Sanh area there are frequent breaks of three or four hours, in which we could intensify the air strikes, and insert helicopter gun ships into the area for additional fires as required. If the enemy masses to attack, he will be extremely vulnerable to the massed B-52's against his supporting forces and destructive power of tactical air, gunships and artillery

TOP SECRET

against his infantry. This capability of reinforcement by fire alone could have changed the course of battle at Dien Bien Phu.

"5. Although logistical support will present a major problem, I am satisfied we can resolve it by our multiple means of resupply. Enemy interdiction of the airfield at Khe Sanh will not deny our reinforcement and support capability by helicopters. As pointed out in (General Wheeler's) response to the President, we could also re-open Route 9 for a land line of communication. This would take 22 company days of engineer effort, but with considerable cost in security.

"6. Although not ideal, the tactical situation at Khe Sanh as well as our improved combat techniques and capabilities are considerably different from those at Dien Bien Phu.

"7. Addressing the President's query on additional help required, with the current level of activity we need an additional squadron of C-130 aircraft, complete with ground handling and maintenance crews, for immediate usage. In addition, I recommend a second squadron of C-130's be alerted for immediate movement if unforeseen contingencies arise. Admiral Sharp may wish to address these requirements from the standpoint of assets available elsewhere in the theater. Additionally, it would be prudent to have heavy air drop equipment in reserve which can be called forward if we need it. We currently have a capability of delivering 600 tons per day for 14 days with no recovery. I would like at least an equal quantity ready for immediate air shipment forward if required. These requirements are also being submitted separately. Acceleration of the issue of M-16 rifles, M-60 machine guns and M-29 mortars to South Vietnamese Army (ARVN) units would improve our posture in economy of force areas. The importance of helicopter assets in the pending battle cannot be overstated. To achieve the necessary helicopter lift for forces deployed to Northern Corps Tactical Zone, I plan drawing on Rosson's (Commander I Field Force) and Weyand's (Commander II Field Force) assets to a major degree. Expediting the rate of delivery of replacement helicopters for assault helicopter companies and assault support helicopter companies would aid in maintaining our situation in the south during the battle in the north. We are also experiencing high loss rates of O-1 observation aircraft and replacements are urgently needed to maintain our observation and surveillance capability over our newly opened LOC, new areas under pacification, enemy routes of infiltration and enemy base areas. The northern I Corps Tactical Zone has greatly increased our engineering requirements. Construction of a logistical base, the maintenance of Route I in that area, construction of DYE MARKER obstacle/strong point system, plus the need of opening Route 9 to Khe Sanh will tax severely our construction capability. Providing the Naval Mobile Construction Battalion yet to be furnished as part of Program 5 would significantly improve our buildup in the north. With regard to Republic of Korea Forces, action should be taken to oppose any thought of withdrawing elements of Republic of Korea forces in Vietnam and returning them to

TOP SECRET

Korea. In addition, every effort should be made to re-open negotiations regarding the proposed ROK light division deployment as soon as the situation in Korea will allow. Expedited deployment of the Thai light division, within practical limitation, is most desirable and would permit greater flexibility in the employment of our ready reaction forces in RVN.

"8. The use of tactical nuclear weapons should not be required in the present situation in view of the authority to use COFRAM. However, should the situation in the DMZ area change dramatically, we should be prepared to introduce weapons of greater effectiveness against massed forces. Under such circumstances I visualize that either tactical nuclear weapons or chemical agents would be active candidates for employment."

EARLE G. WHEELER
CHAIRMAN
JOINTCHIEFS OF STAFF

General Wheeler requests an up-date of the situation from Gen. William Westmoreland to advise Lyndon Johnson:

CITE: JCS 01272 3 FEBRUARY 1968
DTG: 0303327
FROM: GENERAL WHEELER, CJCS
TO: GENERAL WESTMORELAND, COMUSMACV
INFO: ADMIRAL SHARP, CINCPAC

SUBJ: KHE SANH
REF: JCS 01147 JAN 68

1. I sent you earlier a message regarding presidential concern relative to reinforcement and resupply of Khe Sanh during bad weather with the highway closed and the airfield interdicted. I reported to you that my response was that helicopters can fly when fixed wing aircraft cannot and that helicopters do not need an airstrip. Also, weather so bad that helicopters cannot fly some part of the day is most unusual. Moreover, in extremes, road can be opened but at a cost.

2. I have just had a phone conversation with the president in which he reiterated his concern that the situation could become so serious in the Khe Sanh area he could be confronted with a decision [Redacted] which he does not want to be forced to make. I repeated my foregoing assessment to him and told him of my conversation with you this morning in which you stated your belief that an attack would soon be made at Khe Sanh (perhaps tonight), that it would be a bloody fight but that you are confident that the position can be held.

TOP SECRET

As to reinforcements, I pointed out that you have the bulk of the 1st cavalry division available and that you have authority to use COFRAM and the assent to do so.

3. In response, the president asked me if there is any reinforcement or help that we can give you.

4. I recall that I told you in my earlier message that no early reply was needed. However, since I will be seeing the president tomorrow at noon, I need a response from you by about 0900 Washington time, in order to discuss intelligently with him the situation, your views, and any request which you see fit to put forward.

5. I recognize that this is short notice; on the other hand, the president is concerned all the more because of the happenings of the last four days in Vietnam and the tempo of VC/NVA action against Vietnam and US forces and installation. Request, therefore, that you furnish me your judgments as to the problems set forth above by the time specified. Warm regards.

Confidential Files on the Siege and Loss of Khe Sanh

National Security Council advisor General Robert H. Ginsburgh ("whom LBJ trusted implicitly" (Prados, 171), encourages Johnson, after Ginsburgh toured the area:

THE WHITE HOUSE
WASHINGTON

    Sunday, February 4, 1968
    8:25 P.M.

Mr. President:
As we wait for some word about what may be happening at Khe Sanh, it helps to remember that these are always trying periods for Commanders (or Commanders-in-chief).

General Eisenhower, after refusing to allow Prime Minister Churchill to accompany the D-Day invasion forces expressed his thoughts: "Nevertheless, my sympathies were with the Prime Minister. Again, I had to endure the interminable wait that always intervenes between the final decision of the high command and the earliest possible determination of success or failure in such ventures.

"I spent the time visiting troops that were to participate in the assault. . . . I found the men in fine fettle, many of them joshingly admonishing me that I had no cause for worry since the 101st (one brigade of the 101st is now at Hue in the I Corps) was on the job and everything would be taken care of in fine shape."

ROBERT N. GINSBURGH

TOP SECRET

The following is the first major daily report from General Earle G. Wheeler, concerning the Khe Sanh situation. Wheeler would make 55 major reports (counting the Feb. 3, 1968 memo), on these dates:

KHE SANH

    3 Feb 68 — Wheeler Memo to President, Khe Sanh
    5 Feb 68 — 1st Report
    6 Feb 68 — 2nd Report
    7 Feb 68 — 3d Report
    8 Feb 68 — 4th Report
    9 Feb 68 — 5th Report
    10 Feb 68 — 6th Report
    11 Feb 68 — 7th Report
    12 Feb 68 — 8th Report
    13 Feb 68 — 9th Report
    14 Feb 68 — 10th Report
    15 Feb 68 — 11th Report
    16 Feb 68 — 12th Report
    17 Feb 68 — 13th Report
    19 Feb 68 — 15th Report
    20 Feb 68 — 16th Report
    21 Feb 68 — 17th Report
    22 Feb 68 — 18th Report
    23 Feb 68 — 19th Report
    24 Feb 68 — 20th Report
    25 Feb 68 — 21st Report
    26 Feb 68 — 22d Report
    27 Feb 68 — 23d Report
    28 Feb 68 — 24th Report

Confidential Files on the Siege and Loss of Khe Sanh

(Not quite all of these situation reports now exist in this archive.)

29 Feb 68 — 25th Report
 2 Mar 68 — 27th Report
 3 Mar 68 — 28th Report
 4 Mar 68 — 29th Report
 5 Mar 68 — 30th Report
 7 Mar 68 — 32d Report
 8 Mar 68 — 33d Report
10 Mar 68 — 35th Report
11 Mar 68 — 36th Report
12 Mar 68 — 37th Report
16 Mar 68 — 41st Report
17 Mar 68 — 42d Report
18 Mar 68 — 43d Report
21 Mar 68 — 46th Report
22 Mar 68 — 47th Report
24 Mar 68 — 49th Report
26 Mar 68 — 51st Report
29 Mar 68 — 44th Report
30 Mar 68 — 55th Report

INFORMATION

THE WHITE HOUSE
WASHINGTON

      Monday, Feb. 5, 1968
      12:00 noon

Mr. President:
Herewith Bus Wheeler's first daily report on Khe Sanh.

TOP SECRET

"Gravel munitions," in para. 7, are the small antipersonnel mines developed for the barrier.

W. W. Rostow

THE JOINT CHIEFS OF STAFF
WASHINGTON, D.C. 20301

>GM-2968-68
>5 February 1968

MEMORANDUM FOR THE PRESIDENT

Subject: Situation in the Khe Sanh Area

1. At the present time, the situation in the Khe Sanh area is quiet. No enemy contacts have been reported in the area since the attack on Hill 861 ended yesterday at 6:25 PM EST, the details of which are described in the succeeding paragraphs.
2. At 3:00 PM EST yesterday, the Khe Sanh combat base began receiving heavy concentrations of enemy rocket, artillery and mortar fire. Twenty minutes later a force of from 200 to 300 enemy, supported with rocket and mortar fire, launched a ground attack against the US Marine company position on Hill 861, three and one-half miles northwest of the Khe Sanh airstrip. As the fighting grew in intensity, the Khe Sanh combat base provided artillery support, which included the delivery of chemical munitions (CS tear gas) on the enemy. At 4:20 PM EST a small group of the enemy succeeded in penetrating the defensive

wire on the perimeter of the position, but the Marine defenders held their positions and drove the enemy off. Approximately thirty minutes later the enemy resumed the assault on Hill 861 while continuing to deliver mortar fire on the Khe Sanh combat base. Approximately one hour later the mortar fire on the Khe Sanh base ended and the attack on Hill 861 began to diminish in intensity. At 6:25 PM EST all action had ended and the Khe Sanh airstrip was open. In the attack on Hill 861, the enemy lost approximately 108 killed; eight of the dead were found inside the perimeter and numerous enemy dead were hanging from the barbed wire on the perimeter of the Marine company position. US Marine casualties, all from the company on Hill 861, were placed at seven killed and 44 wounded. Marine units in the Khe Sanh area expended a total of 2,800 rounds of various calibre artillery and mortar rounds in response to enemy shelling of the Khe Sanh base and surrounding area.

3. Yesterday, US Air Force B-52 bombers flew 45 sorties against enemy targets in the Khe Sanh/DMZ area. This brings the total number of B-52 sorties flown in that area since 15 January 1968 to 566, with approximately 16,980 tons of bombs delivered on the enemy. In these strikes a total of 426 secondary explosions have been observed.

4. US tactical aircraft flew 216 strike sorties in support of US Marine units at Khe Sanh during the past 24 hours (79 US Air Force, 94 US Marine Corps, and 42 US Navy). Bomb damage assessment of the foregoing sorties included

TOP SECRET

three structures destroyed, seven bunkers destroyed and three secondary explosions. Weather prevented complete bomb drainage assessment.

5. Air landed resupply during the period amounted to 328 tons.

6. No COFRAM was used during the period; however, these munitions are available and will be considered for use at the appropriate time.

7. General Westmoreland told me this morning at 9:30 AM EST that gravel munitions were emplaced yesterday in areas north of Khe Sanh.

8. The weather observation at 3:00 AM EST today in the Khe Sanh area reflects cloudy conditions with visibility at 15 miles. The outlook for the next 15 hours is cloudy with low ceilings, poor visibility, drizzle and fog. From 10:00 PM EST today until 7:00 AM ET tomorrow the outlook is improved; cloudy, but with higher ceilings and visibility at seven miles.

9. Planned operations in support of Khe Sanh:

a. During the next 24 hours, a total of 45 US Air Force B-52 aircraft are scheduled to bomb six targets near the Demilitarized Zone. Four of the targets are in the vicinity of Khe Sanh while two targets are adjacent to the Demilitarized Zone approximately 20 miles northeast of Khe Sanh.

b. For the period ending 11:00 PM EST today, 156 tactical sorties are planned in the Khe Sanh area. Some 192 additional sorties are available on call to augment the planned effort. Should the situation require it, additional sorties up to a theoretical total of 623 could be diverted. The actual number which could be employed depends upon the weather in the area and the ability to control the strikes. In addition, the aircraft carrier KITTY HAWK has been alerted to provide additional close air support when requested.

10. Enemy units in contact are unknown at this time, but it is believed that the 95C Regiment is targeted on Hills 881 and 861 and the 101st Regiment on Khe Sanh. The exact location of other enemy units believed to be in the area is unknown.

EARLE G. WHEELER
Chairman
Joint Chiefs of Staff

TOP SECRET

The Economist *magazine published an article/editorial "This Is It," February 5, 1968, indicating the major north Vietnam offensive of the war was coming. The first two paragraphs appear below (the files contained the entire article):*

This Is It

General Giap has set it rolling. This is the big battle, at last. Beautifully synchronized, and timed for the middle of the truce, the action he opened this week should settle the Vietnam war one way or the other. General Giap is one of the best tactical commanders of our generation. He seizes the local initiative by moving his troops faster than anyone has a right to expect given the other side's control of the air. And he is a master of the surprise diversion. This week's attacks by the Vietcong on eleven South Vietnamese cities unmistakably bear his stamp: though the Vietcong is nominally an independent Army, its last known commander was a North Vietnamese general and it does not plunge in like this unless General Giap gives the word. In all these things — and in the way he cannot stop himself jumping in to take tactical control at the key moment in the fight — General Giap is remarkably like another great tactical commander: Erwin Rommel.

But he may resemble Rommel in another way too. Rommel in north-west Europe in 1944 was a master-tactician trying to cope with what he knew as in the long run a strategically hopeless situation. The more one looks at the offensive General Giap has been running since the autumn, and which led to the attacks on the towns this week, the more it looks as if its real aim is not a military one at all. Its aim is political: if possible, to shake American public opinion into electing a peace-making president in November; failing that, to get negotiations going on relatively favourable terms before the Americans' firepower eats deeper and deeper into the communists' hold of the back-country. General Giap might have preferred to hold his hand until closer to November, but he is obliged to strike now because the weather will turn against him in the spring. It is an attempt, conducted with brilliant tactical dash, to force a settlement before it is too late.

INFORMATION

THE WHITE HOUSE
WASHINGTON

    Tuesday, February 6, 1968
    9:50 a.m.

Herewith Gen. Wheeler's daily Khe Sanh summary. The handwritten note on Abrams' assessment is encouraging.
In fact, there are now two solid conclusions:
— the people didn't rise;
— the government and the South Vietnamese functioned under maximum surprise, shock, and strain.

W. W. Rostow

TOP SECRET

GM-2970-68
6 February 1968

THE JOINT CHIEFS OF STAFF
WASHINGTON, D.C. 20301

    CM-2970-68
    6 February 1968

MEMORANDUM FOR THE PRESIDENT

Subject: Situation in the Khe Sahn Area

1. There have been no major enemy contacts reported in the Khe Sanh area since the enemy attack on Hill 861. An updated report on US Marine casualties during the attack on Hill 861 shows 14 killed and 32 wounded.
2. Marine units in the Khe Sanh area received sporadic small arms and mortar fire. The enemy fire increased as supply missions to the outlying outposts and Hill 861 were conducted. However, there were no reports of casualties during the period. Marine units in the Khe Sanh area expended a total of 7,788 rounds of various caliber artillery and mortar ammunition in response to the sporadic harassment fire by the enemy forces.
3. During the past 24 hours, US Air Force B-52 bombers flew 55 sorties against enemy targets in the Khe Sanh/DMI area. On 4 February (5 February South Vietnam time), 33 B-52 sorties, not previously reported, were flown against enemy targets in the Khe Sanh/DMZ area. The B-

52 sorties flown in that area since 15 January 1968 now total 654, with approximately 19,000 tons of bombs delivered on the enemy.

4. US tactical aircraft flew 213 strike sorties in support of US Marine units at Khe Sanh during the past 24 hours (88 US Air Force, 90 US Navy, 35 US Marine Corps). Bomb damage assessment of the foregoing sorties included fifteen bunkers destroyed, seven gun positions destroyed, three trucks destroyed, three secondary fires, and one secondary explosion.

5. Air landed resupply during the period amounted to 214 tons.

6. No COFRAM was used during the period.

7. The weather observation at 3:00 AM EST (4:00 PM, 6 Feb, South Vietnam time) today in the Khe Sanh area reflects cloudy conditions with visibility at 10miles. The outlook for the next 14 hours is cloudy with low ceilings, poor visibility, drizzle and fog. From 9:00 PM EST, 6 Feb. (10:00 AM, 7 Feb. South Vietnam time) until 7:00 AM EST, 7 Feb (8:00 PM, 7 Feb, South Vietnam time) the outlook is improvised: cloudy, but with higher ceilings, and visibility at seven miles, with occasional light showers.

8. Planned operations in support of Khe Sanh:

a. During the next 24 hours, a total of 33 US Air Force B-52 aircraft are scheduled to bomb five targets near the Demilitarized Zone. Two of the targets are in the vicinity of Khe Sanh, two targets are near the Laotian border approximately 10 miles southwest of Khe Sanh, and one target is adjacent to the Demilitarized Zone approximately 20 miles northeast of Khe Sanh.

TOP SECRET

b. For the period ending 11:00 PM EST today (12:00 Noon, 7 Feb, South Vietnam time), 175 tactical sorties are planned in the Khe Sanh area. One hundred thirty-four additional sorties are available on call to augment the planned effort. Should the situation require it, additional sorties up to a theoretical total of 646 could be diverted into the area.

There have been no changes reported in enemy troop dispositions in the Khe Sanh area.

EARLE G. WHEELER
Chairman
Joint Chiefs of Staff

P.S. I talked to Gen. Westmoreland at 0830 hours. He had nothing spectacular to report. However, he stated that Gen. Abrams has now visited all ARVN divisions except the 1st and 2nd I Corps. Gen. Abrams is highly pleased by alertness, aggressiveness and steadiness of all division commanders.

Confidential Files on the Siege and Loss of Khe Sanh

General Westmoreland updates Wheeler, the White House, the C.I.A. and the State Department on the current status at Khe Sanh, effective Feb. 4 to Feb. 5, 1968:

FM GEN WHEELER CJCS
INFO WHITE HOUSE
STATE DEPT
CIA
O 051131Z ZYH ZFF-3
FM GEN WESTMORELAND COMUMACV SAIGON
TO GEN WHEELER CJCS
INFO ADM SHARP CINCPAC
AMB BUNKER SAIGON
ZEM
MAC 01666 EYES ONLY
SUBJ: DAILY REPORT ON KHE SANH/DMZ
    SITUATION

This is my initial reply to your request for a summary of activity in the Khe Sanh/DMZ area. The period covered is 041200H to 051200H Feb 68: During the initial 17hours of the period Khe Sanh combat base and Marine units in the Scotland area reported a total of approximately six rounds of rocket fire and 70 rounds of mortar fire resulting in three USMC KIA evacuated. An artillery mission was fired resulting in a reported 10 NVA KIA. In addition, at 050400H, Khe Sanh combat base began receiving rockets, arty and mortar fire and at 050400H Marines on Hill 861, NW of Khe Sanh, came under ground attack by an estimated 200 enemy (8N minus) using Bangalore torpedoes, satchel charges and mortars. The mor-

TOP SECRET

tar attack on Khe Sanh combat base terminated at 0630H but resumed again at 1100H. The ground attack on Hill 861 had diminished at 0645H, with initial casualty reports listing an estimated 100 enemy KIA and friendly losses of seven KIA and 24 KIA evacuated. During the period, 39 B-52's ran six strikes delivering 975 tons of ordnance in support of the Khe Sanh combat base and the Scotland area.

Marine units in the Khe Sanh area expended a total of 2819 rounds of various caliber Arty/mortar in response to the enemy shelling of the Khe Sanh combat base and environs. The Marine aircraft wing flew 94 sorties in support of the third Marine division during the period, 81 of the sorties were TPE's in direct support, 13 sorties were in close support. SOHB damage assessment of the foregoing sorties included three structures destroyed, seven bunkers destroyed, and three secondary explosions. Weather conditions prevented a complete bomb damage assessment. 43 of the total sorties flown, delivering a total of 100.7 tons of ordnance, were flown in support of the immediate Khe Sanh area. USAR supplies amounted to 79, while the USN flew 43 sorties. Total tactical sorties flown were 203.

Airlanded resupply during the period amounted to 128 tons.

No COFRAM was used during the period.

For the next 24 hour period, FMAW plans 50 strike sorties in the Khe Sanh area in direct support of the 25th Marines. These sorties will be flown throughout the 24 hour period and consist of a variety of ordnance.

An additional 12 strikes sorties will be available on hot pad alert for scramble as required. Due to damage sustained by Marine aircraft on ground during recent rocket attack on Chu Lai, there has been a reduction in available Marine air sorties. Fifty eight 7th AF strikes sorties are planned to augment the FMAW effort in the vicinity of Khe Sanh combat base. The USN will fly 43 sorties, five Air Light strikes will be flown for the 5-6 Feb period. There are currently 32 additional AF tactical support aircraft on call in support of Khe Sanh which could produce 180 sorties in a 24 hour period. Should the situation require, additional sorties could be diverted up to a theoretical total of 623. The number that could be employed would depend upon the weather and our ability to control the strikes.

Enemy units in contact are unknown at this time, but we believe that the 95C Regt is targeted on Hills 881 and 861 and the 101st Regt on Khe Sanh. The exact location of other enemy units believed to be in the area is unknown.

SSO Note: Deliver immediately. Cas "Pass to Mr Chillemi" for AMB bunker.

FM GEN WHEELER, CJCS. WASH DC
INFO GEN JOHNSON, CSA, WASH DC
GEN MCCONNELL, CSAF, WASH DC
GEN CHAPMAN, CMC, WASH DC
ADM MOORER, CMC, WASH DC
RIROSTON, WHITE HOUSE, WASH DC
MR RUSK, STATE DEPT, WASH DC

TOP SECRET

MR HELMS, CIA
O 2610297 ZYH ZFF
FM GENERAL WESTMORELAND, COMUMACV, SAIGON
TO GENERAL WHEELER, CJCS, WASHINGTON
INFO ADMIRAL SHARP CINCPAC HAWAII
AMBASSADOR BUNKER, SAIGON (PASS TO MR CHILLEMI)
ZEM
HAC 01595 EYES ONLY

This is the second report on the Khe Sanh area and covers the period 051200ST to 061200 February 1968.
 During this period the Khe Sanh combat base and Marine units in the Scotland area continued to receive sporadic small arms and mortar fire. The enemy fire increased as supply missions to the outlying OP's and Hill 861 were conducted. However, there were no reports of casualties during the period. Marine units in the Khe Sanh area expended a total of 7788 rounds of various caliber artillery and mortar ammunition in response to the sporadic harassment fire by the enemy forces. No COFRAM was used. During the period, 43 B-52 aircraft and five strikes in the Niagara area. Air support in the Khe Sanh (Niagara) area was provided by 35 USMN sorties, 38 USAF sorties and 90 USM sorties for a total of 213 tactical sorties. Although complete bomb damage assessment was prevented by adverse weather, the following was reported: one secondary explosion, three secondary fires, seven gun positions destroyed, three trucks destroyed, and 15

bunkers destroyed.

Air resupply was effected in the Khe Sanh area during the period with the delivery (air landed) of 214 short tons.

For the period 261200T to 271200H February, the Marine air wing plans to fly 69 tactical air sorties in support of the Khe Sanh area while an additional 14 aircraft will be on call during the period. USAF sorties planned for the next period in Niagara amount to 54, while the USN will fly 52 sorties, for a grand total of 175 planned sorties. The USAF will have 120 sorties on call for the Niagara area. Also, an additional 395 USAF sorties and 250 USN sorties could be diverted into the Khe Sanh area, for a theoretical total of 646 additional sorties. Thirty-six Air Light strikes are scheduled in the Niagara area. Enemy unit identifications remain the same as reported yesterday, and the threat to Khe Sanh remains unchanged.
GP-4

SSO Note: Deliver during duty hours.
400

The Associated Press released a bulletin (high priority story) that a Special Green Beret camp was overrun by Communist Troops. The President received a memo that the story was not true.

183
Bulletin
    Camp

TOP SECRET

Saigon (AP) - South Vietnamese headquarters said a special forces-green beret-camp in the northwest corner of South Vietnam was overrun and occupied early Wednesday by Communist troops using tanks and armored cars.
GG816P 6

MEMORANDUM
THE WHITE HOUSE
INFORMATION

    Tuesday, February 6, 1968
    8:30 p.m.

MR. PRESIDENT:
Based on a telephone call to MACV, the Pentagon says the attached AP bulletin is _not_ true. The camp has _not_ been overrun and occupied.
South Vietnamese forces and our forces at Lang Vei are in their bunkers.
Bromley Smith

Walt Rostow files a confidential response to the President concerning the thrust of the Economist *article.*

INFORMATION CONFIDENTIAL

Wednesday, February 7, 1968 — 3:30 p.m.

Mr. President:
With respect to the ECONOMIST article:
1. I agree with the basic conclusion: This Is It.
2. Exactly as the document said, they have, for whatever reasons, decided to win or lose the war in the weeks and months ahead.
3. We do not know how much they have left after the first attack on the cities, but it is my feeling at the present time that they will continue to use whatever assets they have to continue to attack the cities with two objectives:
— To try to exhaust the Vietnamese military and civil apparatus which has taken the first shock well but has little depth;
— To force Westy to commit to the battle in the cities the reserves needed to hold Khe Sanh.
In short, the ECONOMIST may assume that the battle of the cities, as a serious diversionary operation, Is more nearly over than, in fact, it will prove to be.
4. In this connection, I must tell you that I found Bus Wheeler's statements at the NSC meeting like a fireball in the night; that is, a most serious warning. Westy has been forced to commit some of his units from the Air Cav Division and the 101st Airborne to support the battle for the

TOP SECRET

cities. Meanwhile, the North Vietnamese units opposite Dak To and elsewhere along the western frontier have not been committed.

The captured documents indicate that Hanoi's generals are very conscious of the limit to Westy's own reserve forces.

5. Since this is a battle which may determine the shape of Asia for a very long time — as well as the U.S. position on the world scene — it is a battle that must be won. Therefore, I am inclined to think, as of this afternoon, that we are close to the time when we should:

— Fly the 81st Airborne out to Vietnam;
— Extend enlistments in Vietnam and elsewhere;
— Call up reserves; etc.

6. We may be able to wait a day or so because it is possible that we have so damaged the Viet Cong main force units that attacked the cities that they will not have the capacity to extend for long the flight in Hue, Cholon, Danang, and Dalat. But for what it is worth, my gut feeling is this is one where we had better be safe than sorry.

Having said that, I would underline that my military qualifications consist in once having risen as high as the rank of Major in the planning of bombing operations.

W. W. Rostow

Two additional news releases in the files indicate the A.P. bulletin apparently was true:

FBIS 13 FOR OFFICIAL USE ONLY
PARIS AFPIN SPANISH 0428 GMT 7 FEB 68 E

(Text) Saigon — The Lang Vei Camp has been destroyed and occupied by the North Vietnamese, it was officially announced here this morning.

7 FEB 0457 AN/RS

(175)
(SUBS PREVIOUS)
VIETNAM
BY EDWIN Q. WHITE
(Saigon)—North Vietnamese infantrymen supported by nine medium tanks and flame-throwers made repeated assaults on the Lang Vei (Lahng Vay) special forces in the northwest corner of South Vietnam early Wednesday and penetrated the barbed wire perimeter.

The U-S command says radio contact with the American green beret troopers inside the camp was lost for more than an hour but was re-established and it appeared the Montagnard militiamen in the camp and their American advisers are still holding out.

The command said five of the enemy's Russian-Kobel T-34 tanks were destroyed. It was the first time the enemy has been reported using tanks in the Vietnam War.

South Vietnamese military headquarters had reported earlier that the camp four miles west of

TOP SECRET

the Laotian border and about 23 miles south of the de-militarized zone had been over-run.

A government spokesman says a reconnaissance plane flying over the camp at dawn saw North Vietnamese troops moving inside it. He added that the pilot reported making radio contact with members of the camp's garrison who said they had withdrawn from the camp.
OS123CAES FEB. 7

INFORMATION

THE WHITE HOUSE
WASHINGTON
    Wednesday, February 7, 1968
    10:45 a.m.

Mr. President:
Herewith Gen. Wheeler's Khe Sanh daily — key passages marked.

W. W. Rostow

TOP SECRET

THE JOINT CHIEFS OF STAFF
WASHINGTON, D. C. 20301

    CM-2971-68
    7 February 1968

MEMORANDUM FOR THE PRESIDENT
Subject: Situation in the Khe Sanh Area

Confidential Files on the Siege and Loss of Khe Sanh

1. The enemy has renewed his efforts against US and South Vietnamese forces in the Khe Sanh - Lang Vei area. During the early morning hours yesterday (approximately 3:00 PM on 6 February, South Vietnam time) the Khe Sanh Combat Base and US Marine units in the surrounding area received 58 rounds of mixed mortar fire and an undetermined number of rockets resulting in five US Marines wounded. At 11:45 M EST yesterday (12:45 AM on 7 February, South Vietnam time), the Khe Sanh Combat Base began receiving a heavy volume of rocket and mortar fire. At approximately the same time, the Lang Vei Special Forces Camp came under a heavy ground attack by an estimated enemy infantry company supported by nine armored vehicles believed to be Soviet PT 76 Amphibious tanks (description attached). By 1:50 PM EST (2:50 AM on 7 February, South Vietnam time) five of the tanks were reported to have been damaged or destroyed. The attacking enemy also directed heavy supporting mortar and artillery fire on the Lang Vei defenses, and an aerial observer saw the enemy employing flame-throwers in the assault on Lang Vei. Despite poor weather conditions US tactical aircraft provided continual close air support during the heavy fighting and the Khe Sanh Combat Base delivered a large volume of supporting artillery fire throughout the battle. The supporting fire included 28 rounds of 105-mm COFRAM ammunition, but no report of its effectiveness has been received. The intensity of the fighting began to diminish at 10:00 PM EST last night (11:00 AM

TOP SECRET

on 7 February, South Vietnam time). US tactical aircraft continued to strike enemy concentrations throughout the Khe Sanh - Lang Vei area during the day (7 February, South Vietnam time). A reaction force was en route to Lang Vei at 3:30 AM EST this morning (4:30 PM on 7 February, South Vietnam time). Latest reports indicate fighting still prevails, but on a limited scale. There are no reports as yet of the exact extent of enemy or friendly casualties, but a preliminary report states

6. Planned operations in support of Khe Sanh:

a. During the next 24 hours, 39 US Air Force B-52 sorties are scheduled against targets in the Khe Sanh/DMZ area. Four of the targets are in the vicinity of Khe Sanh, and one target is adjacent to the Demilitarized Zone, approximately six miles north-northwest of Camp Carroll.

b. For the period until 11:00 PM EST today (12:00 noon 8 February, South Vietnam time) 152 tactical air sorties are scheduled into the Khe Sanh area. 16 additional sorties are available on immediate call to augment the scheduled sorties. An additional 396 US Air Force and 250 US Navy sorties could be diverted into the Khe Sanh area, for a total of 646 additional sorties.

7. US Marine units defending the Khe Sanh area have a vast amount of fire support available to them from external sources (16 175-mm guns, all-weather tactical aircraft, armed helicopters, and B-52 bombers). These units also have considerable fire power from their own assigned weapons, which, in addition to a large number of automatic weapons, include 102 mortars (60-

mm, 81-mm, and 4.2 inch), 32 106-mm recoilless rifles, and 24 howitzers (105-mm and 155-mm). Also available are two vehicles which mount four .50-caliber machine guns (quad 50s) each and two track-type armored vehicles with two 40-mm guns (twin 40s) on each vehicle. The quad 50s and twin 40s are dual-purpose and can be used either for air defense or against ground targets. In addition, there are five M48 tanks (90-mm guns) and ten light track-type vehicles (ONTOS) on each of which are mounted six 106-mm recoilless rifles. Because of the significant fire power of the units defending Khe Sanh and the reinforcing fires immediately available from the heavy artillery east of Khe Sanh along with the supporting strikes of tactical aircraft, armed helicopters and B-52 bombers which can be delivered against the enemy, it is not considered necessary to employ additional supporting weapons and forces to the Khe Sanh Combat Base. Moreover, additional weapons and units within the Khe Sanh defensive perimeter would inordinately increase the concentration of our resources in a relatively confined area, correspondingly increasing the risk of losses to enemy fire, and would add a significant amount of logistic support requirements. It is considered preferable to retain additional fire support means for employment in concert with counter-attacking and exploitation forces when they are committed.

EARLE G. WHEELER
Chairman
Joint Chiefs of Staff

TOP SECRET

A rough situation report is forwarded from the Khe Sanh area toward Saigon and from there to Washington, DC. General Earle G. Wheeler, Chairman of the Joint Chiefs of Staff, continues his series of reports to President Lyndon Johnson:

FM COMUSMACV
TO NMCC
CINCPAC
INFO ZEN/CG III MAF DA NANG
ZEN/CG I FFORCEV NHA TRANG
ZEN/CG II FFORCEV LONG BINH
ZEN/SN IV CTZ CAN THO
ZEN/CDR 7TH AIR FORCE SAIGON
ZEN/COMNAVFORV SAIGON
ZEN/CO 5TH SFGA NHA TRANG
ZEN/MACV FORWARD
BT
FROM MACCOC3
Subj: Special Telecon (Khe Sanh/Lang Vei) (U)

1. Situations as of 071200H Feb: The enemy controlled the camp above ground with an undetermined number of CIDG and an estimated 14 USASF personnel holed up in bunkers (underground). Artillery and air was delivered against the enemy and an element of BV 33 battalion advised by a USASF Sgt attempted to penetrate the camp to assist in the extraction of the friendly personnel on site.
2. As of 071630H Feb: A heliborne relief force led by USASF personnel from the Khe Sanh combat base was dispatched with the mission of joining

with the BV 33 unit in a raid on the camp. Gunships and tactical air from the 1st Marine air wing fired suppressive fire on the TOC of the camp in preparation for the raid. Under cover of this fire and prior to the arrival of the relief force, the friendly personnel on site took escape and evasion action.

3. The relief force put down at "old" Lang Vei (XD 794357) and moved overland to the New Lang Vei Sixt (XD 786356), enroute the relief force encountered 13 of the 20 US personnel who were in the camp at the time of the initial attack. One additional US personnel was subsequently recovered. A total of 14 of 20 US personnel were recovered, six US personnel remain unaccounted for, since no reentry of the campsite was make by the relief force, the exact status of the six is not known.

4. There are unconfirmed reports that approximately 70-100 of the 450 indigenous forces originally in the camp have been picked up, an additional unknown number of these personnel are assumed to be in an escape and evasion status.

5. Three destroyed tanks were observed in the area (one inside the perimeter, two on the road outside the perimeter). It is believed that an estimated enemy company now controls the camp site.

6. The foregoing constitutes a preliminary report. Further information and refinement will be provided as available.

GP-4

BI

TOP SECRET

THE JOINT CHIEFS OF STAFF
WASHINGTON, D. C. 20301

    CM-2971-68
    7 February 1968

MEMORANDUM FOR THE PRESIDENT
Subject: Situation in the Khe Sanh Area

1. The enemy has renewed his efforts against US and South Vietnamese forces in the Khe Sanh - Lang Vei area. During the early morning hours yesterday (approximately 3:00 PM on 6 February, South Vietnam time) the Khe Sanh Combat Base and US Marine units in the surrounding area received 58 rounds of mixed mortar fire and an undetermined number of rockets resulting in five US Marines wounded. At 11:45 AM EST yesterday (12:45 AM on 7 February, South Vietnam time), the Khe Sanh Combat Base began receiving a heavy volume of rocket and mortar fire. At approximately the same time, the Lang Vei Special Forces Camp came under a heavy ground attack by an estimated enemy infantry company supported by nine armored vehicles believed to be Soviet PT-76 (Amphibious tanks (description attached). By 1:50 PM EST (2:50 M on 7 February, South Vietnam time) five of the tanks were reported to have been damaged or destroyed. The attacking enemy also directed heavy supporting mortar and artillery fire on the Lang Vei defenses, and an aerial observer saw the enemy employing flame-throwers in the assault on Lang Vei. Despite poor weather conditions US

tactical aircraft provided continual close air support during the heavy fighting and the Khe Sanh Combat Base delivered a large volume of supporting artillery fire throughout the battle. The supporting fire included 28 rounds of 105-mm COFRAM ammunition, but no report of its effectiveness has been received. The intensity of the fighting began to diminish at 10:00 PM EST last night (11:00 AM on 7 February, South Vietnam time). US tactical aircraft continued to strike enemy concentrations throughout the Khe Sanh - Lang Vei area during the day (7 February, South Vietnam time). A reaction force was en route to Lang Vei at 3:30 AM EST this morning (4:30 PM on 7 February, South Vietnam time). Latest reports indicate fighting still prevails, but on a limited scale. There are no reports as yet of the exact extent of enemy or friendly casualties, but a preliminary report states that 16 US Special Forces advisors, who had been wounded, were evacuated from Lang Vei at 2:00 AM EST today (3:00 PM on 7 February, South Vietnam time). Fourteen wounded South Vietnamese were also evacuated at the same time. A preliminary report also indicates that all buildings in the Lang Vei camp were destroyed. The military population of the Lang Vei Special Forces Camp included 18 US Army Special Forces advisors, 494 members of the South Vietnamese Civilian Irregular Defense Group organized into three companies and a mobile strike force, and 29 other South Vietnamese personnel. The Khe Sanh Combat Base continued to receive enemy fire throughout the night and early morning hours (South

TOP SECRET

Vietnam time) until it ceased completely at 9:47 PM EST last night (10:47 AM on 7 February, South Vietnam time). The runway at Khe Sanh airfield was cratered, but it was repaired and the airfield was fully operational at 9:30 PM EST last night (10:30 AM on 7 February, South Vietnam time). In another action at 9;40 AM EST yesterday (10:40 PM on 6 February, South Vietnam time), the US Marine company on Hill 861 was hit by a light ground attack from the southeast. The attack ended about one hour later. The results of the attack have not yet been reported.

2. During the past 24 hours, US Air Force B-52 bombers flew 30 sorties against enemy targets in the Khe Sanh area. The number of B-52 sorties flown in the Khe Sanh/DMZ area since 15 January 1968 now totals 684 with approximately 19,900 total tons of bombs delivered on the enemy.

3. US tactical aircraft flew 199 strike sorties in support of units at Khe Sanh during the past 24 hours (83 US Air Force, 67 US Marine Corps, 49 US Navy). Bomb damage assessment of the reported air sorties was somewhat hindered by weather, however, one very large explosion and 15 other secondary explosions were reported by tactical support aircraft.

4. During the period, 136 short tons of supplies were delivered to the Khe Sanh Combat Base by air, over half of which was ammunition.

5. The latest weather observation at 5:00 AM EST (6:00 PM 7 February, South Vietnam time) today in the Khe Sanh area reflects cloudy conditions with visibility at five miles in fog. The forecast for

the next 14 hours is cloudy with low ceilings, poor visibility, drizzle and fog. From 9:00 PM EST, 7 February (10:00 AM, 8 February, South Vietnam time) until 7:00 AM EST, 8 February (8:00 PM, 8 February, South Vietnam time) the outlook is improved: cloudy with intermittent light rain, higher ceilings and visibility at seven miles.

6. Planned operations in support of Khe Sanh:

a. During the next 24 hours, 39 US Air Force B-52 sorties are scheduled against targets in the Khe Sanh/DMZ area. Four of the targets are in the vicinity of Khe Sanh, and one target is adjacent to the Demilitarized Zone, approximately six miles north-northwest of Camp Carroll.

b. For the period until 11:00 PM EST today (12:00 noon 8 February, South Vietnam time) 152 tactical air sorties are scheduled into the Khe Sanh area. 16 additional sorties are available on immediate call to augment the scheduled sorties. An additional 396 US Air Force and 250 US Navy sorties could be diverted into the Khe Sanh area, for a total of 646 additional sorties.

7. US Marine units defending the Khe Sanh area have a vast amount of fire support available to them from external sources (16 175-mm guns, all-weather tactical aircraft, armed helicopters, and B-52 bombers). These units also have considerable fire power from their own assigned weapons, which, in addition to a large number of automatic weapons, include 102 mortars (60-mm, 81-mm, and 4.2 inch), 32 106-mm recoilless rifles, and 24 howitzers (105-mm and 155-mm). Also available are two vehicles which mount four

TOP SECRET

.50-caliber machine guns (quad 50s) each and two track-type armored vehicles with two 40-mm guns (twin 40s) on each vehicle. The quad 50s and twin 40s are dual-purpose and can be used either for air defense or against ground targets. In addition, there are five M48 tanks (90-mm guns) and ten light track-type vehicles (ONTOS) on each of which are mounted six 106-mm recoilless rifles. Because of the significant fire power of the units defending Khe Sanh and the reinforcing fires immediately available from the heavy artillery east of Khe Sanh along with the supporting strikes of tactical aircraft, armed helicopters and B-52 bombers which can be delivered against the enemy, it is not considered necessary to employ additional supporting weapons and forces to the Khe Sanh Combat Base. Moreover, additional weapons and units within the Khe Sanh defensive perimeter would inordinately increase the concentration of our resources in a relatively confined area, correspondingly increasing the risk of losses to enemy fire, and would add a significant amount of logistic support requirements. It is considered preferable to retain additional fire support means for employment in concert with counter-attacking and exploitation forces when they are committed.
Earle G. Wheeler
EARLE G. WHEELER
Chairman
Joint Chiefs of Staff

THE WHITE HOUSE
WASHINGTON

February 8, 1968

Mr. President:
Herewith Westy reports minor operations at Khe Sanh.
Weather operational for both resupply and tactical air support.

W.W. Rostow

Thursday, February 8, 1968

Following is the text of a cable sent by General Westmoreland at 5:22 AM this morning.

This is the fourth report on the Khe Sanh area and covers the period from midnight EST February 7 to midnight EST February 8.

During this period the Khe Sanh combat base continued to receive sporadic shelling from mortar and rockets throughout the afternoon and night. By 3:00 am February 7 thirty two persons had been helilifted from the Lang Vei special forces camp, including 14 Americans. Three helicopters received enemy fire in the extraction resulting in one pilot being wounded. Three enemy tanks are reported to have been destroyed in the Lang Vei area.

At 4:25 pm the Marine outpost southwest of Khe Sanh started receiving rocket and mortar fire, followed by a ground attack. The attack continued until 5:45 pm. The enemy penetrated the

TOP SECRET

wire of the platoon outpost but was repulsed. The enemy broke contact by 6:30 pm.

At 8:00 pm a Marine reinforcing element moved into position at the outpost. The position continued to receive sporadic incoming fire throughout the morning (last evening Washington time). The enemy fire was returned but with unknown results. During the period one Marine was reported killed, and two Marines were wounded and evacuated.

At 10:45 pm EST an air observer reported four enemy tanks southwest of Khe Sanh. Air strikes were run and it is believed that two of the tanks were disabled. An air observer also reported siting 20 vehicles moving in a westerly direction five kilometers west of Lang Vai. Air strikes were conducted with unknown results.

During the period Marine tactical air flew 44 sorties in support of the area, the Air Force flew 98 sorties, the Navy 37, for a total of 179 sorties. Four Arc Light strikes (35 sorties) were flown against targets in the Niagara area. Reported bomb damage assessment as the result of the Arc Light strikes included three secondary fires and numerous secondary explosions.

The logistics status remains satisfactory in the Khe Sanh area. Airlift resupply provided 127 short tons of supplies, 94 tons of which was ammunition. Individual combat rations were increased from 15 to 26 days.

No COFRAM type ammunition was expended during this period.

For the period encompassing the 24-hours of February 8 EST, seven Arc Light strikes (45 sorties) will be flown in the Niagara area. Tactical sorties include 44 Marine, 48 Air Force, and 52 Navy, for a total of 144 sorties. The Marines will have 16 aircraft on call for the Khe Sanh area while the Air Force will have 120 sorties on alert. Additional sorties that could theoretically be diverted into the Khe Sanh area total 406 Air Force, 250 Navy, for a grand total of 656.

Enemy unit identifications in the Khe Sanh area remain the same as previously reported.

The weather on the afternoon of February 7 was marginal for flying with a ceiling of 1,500 feet. The period from 7:00 am to 7:00pm was poor with low ceilings and visibility as low as one third to one half miles in fog. Weather conditions improved to marginal at 7:00 pm, with ceilings of 2,000 feet and good visibility.

The forecast is for marginal to good conditions in the afternoon and evening of today, with ceilings carrying from 2,000 to 3,000 feet. Early tomorrow the weather will become poor, with low clouds and visibilities restricted to one quarter to one mile in fog. By morning the weather should improve again to marginal, with ceilings of 1,500 feet.

INFORMATION

THE WHITE HOUSE
WASHINGTON

    Thursday, February 8, 1968
    2:00 p.m.

TOP SECRET

Mr. President:
Herewith a supplementary from Gen. Wheeler on Khe Sanh.

W.W. Rostow

THE JOINT CHIEFS OF STAFF
WASHINGTON, D. C. 20301

CM-2972-68
8 February 1968

MEMORANDUM FOR THE PRESIDENT
Subject: Situation in the Khe Sanh Area

You have received General Westmoreland's fourth report on the Khe Sanh area, covering the period through 11:00 PM EST, 7 February 1968. I have received additional information from General Westmoreland and Admiral Sharp which is reported in the succeeding paragraphs.

General Westmoreland informed me that he has issued instructions to General Weyand (Commanding General, II Field Force) to arrange for a US unit to be brought into the race track area of Saigon. This will release Vietnamese troops to put more pressure on enemy elements in the city. Although General Westmoreland is reluctant to take this step, he feels that it is essential to push ARVN to greater action to cleanup Saigon. Additionally, as I told you yesterday, he plans to move a battalion of the 101st Airborne Division to Hue/Phu Bai. Also, a Vietnamese Marine Battalion will be moved to

Hue/Phu Bai to replace one of the depleted Vietnamese airborne battalions in that area. He indicates that he may follow these deployments with two more Vietnamese Marine Battalions into that area.

You may be interested to know that, yesterday, as a result of an ambush of an enemy party by US forces west of Saigon, a North Vietnamese passport containing a Cambodian visa, stamped Phnom Penh, and a baggage claim check from Phnom Penh, were taken from one of the bodies. The party had a sophisticated radio, believed to be single sideband. It was reported that this appeared to be a most important group.

Regarding the North Vietnamese air threat, Admiral Sharp has assured me that all concerned have been watching this activity closely and that all forces have been alerted to this potential threat. In this regard, air strikes are being conducted daily at Vinh and Bai Thuong airfields to preclude their being used as forward staging bases for MIG operations. These airfields are being seeded with 500 pound bombs with influence fuzes (Mark 36s) as necessary to harass and disrupt repair operations. Additionally, fighter cover is being provided for B-52s operating in the DMZ and Mu Gia Pass areas. A full report on the air threat will be provided separately as requested by you.

EARLE G. WHEELER
Chairman
Joint Chiefs of Staff

TOP SECRET

THE JOINT CHIEFS OF STAFF
WASHINGTON, D. C. 20301

CM-2993-68
9 February 1968

MEMORANDUM FOR THE PRESIDENT
Subject: Situation in Vietnam

You have received General Westmoreland's fifth report on the situation in Khe Sanh through 11:00 PM EST, 8 February 1968. I talked to General Westmoreland at 8:30 AM EST this morning and obtained some additional information which is contained in the succeeding paragraphs.

Yesterday was fairly quiet. The enemy appears to be tired. However, General Westmoreland expects the second cycle of attacks to begin soon and he has been getting ready for these attacks.

In Khe Sanh, B-52 and tactical air strikes continue to pound the area. The weather is marginal in that area and bad along the coast.

In Hue/Phu Bai, three ARVN Airborne Battalions are down to the approximate strength of 160 men each. General Westmoreland is reinforcing with three Vietnamese Marine Battalions — one to be airlifted into Hue today, one tomorrow, and one the day after. In addition, one battalion of the 101st Airborne Division will be deployed to Hue/Phu Bai tomorrow. A second battalion of the 101st will be moved to Hue by landing ships. There have been reports out of I Corps that the Citadel in Hue has been cleared of enemy; however, General Westmoreland can neither confirm nor deny this yet.

February 8, 1968

<u>Questions Related to the Military Situation in Viet-Nam.</u>

1. What are the problems confronting General Westmoreland if the enemy continues the attacks on the cities and, at the same time, opens up one or more border fronts (e.g., Khe Sanh, DMZ, Darlac-Kontum)?
a. What mobile reserve forces does Westmoreland have to meet these frontier attacks? Can he sustain them concurrently in action? IN particular, will he have enough airlift to support and supply all of the actions?
b. With respect to Khe Sanh, what will be the supply problem if the airstrip is kept under artillery and rocket fire?
2. How have the Marines organized Khe Sanh for defense? How many days of supply, particularly ammunition, are in the perimeter? Are these supplies protected from enemy fire?
3. How is weather likely to affect the action along the border? When does it favor us, when the enemy?
4. What is the enemy air capability if he elects to use his IL-28's, MIG's and AN-2's in South Viet-Nam or against U.S. naval targets? Are there any other surprise weapons with which we should be concerned?

5. If we decided to send additional forces to Viet-Nam, what ones are available? How soon could they be deployed and become operational in South Viet-Nam? What would be the effect on our strategic readiness world-wide?

6. In case of an affirmative decision to reinforce, what actions should be taken with regard to extension of tours and terms of service, call-up of reservists, and requests of Congress? Should we reconsider the question of a declaration of war?

7. What would be the domestic and international impact of the foregoing actions?

8. In the light of the foregoing considerations and our estimate of the probable course of events during the next few months, are we satisfied with the military resources presently available in Southeast Asia or should we make a drastic effort to rush additional forces to the area?

Confidential Files on the Siege and Loss of Khe Sanh

President Lyndon Johnson addresses the nation. In this speech he reacts to the Tet offense, during the lunar New Year, which is Vietnam's holiday. Toward the top of his speech he states that "200,000 men, women and children have been left homeless" during the Tet offense. He also forecasts a battle at Khe Sanh, and refers to Khe Sanh as the American equivalent of the much earlier defeat of the French at Dien-Bien-Phu - but says that will not happen.
(In retrospect over the years, it seems this is a very poignant and painful speech coming from Lyndon Johnson. . . .)

My fellow Americans:

Nine days ago, the Communist enemy in Vietnam launched the biggest attack of the war. He chose to strike during the heart of the lunar New Year's celebration, which is Vietnam's major holiday. It was as if a wide-spread assault had been launched against American cities in the early morning hours of Christmas Day. Undoubtedly, the Vietnamese defense forces in the stricken cities were somewhat relaxed. Certainly, the civilian population of the cities was totally unprepared for the savage assault of which they were the victims.

We should remember that this coordinated and long-planned attack came during the middle of a cease-fire which the communists themselves had announced. We should remember that — because it

TOP SECRET

tells us so much about the nature of the enemy we are facing.

I feel that I should report to you on the events of the past nine days — what the cost has been to us and to our friends — what the enemy was able to accomplish — what he was not able to accomplish — and what we should expect in the days ahead.

The cost in terms of American lives and those of our friends and allies has been grievous. Since January 30, 614 telegrams have gone from this city to American citizens informing them of the death of their son or their husband. The toll among our Vietnamese allies has been even higher — 1,500 Vietnamese soldiers have died since January 30 defending their cities and their homes. Very many Vietnamese civilians have died and been hurt, although we do not yet know the numbers. The damage in the cities and towns of Vietnam has been heavy, so heavy that we now believe some 200,000 men, women and children have been left homeless as a result of the Communist assault.

There is no gain saying the fact that we have sustained a heavy blow. I do not wish in the slightest to suggest otherwise. No one, I think, is more aware than I am of the grisly statistics by which we must measure the past few days and their meaning in terms of human grief. I have followed these developments almost hourly— and with an increasingly heavy heart. The enemy set out to bring home to us the heavy cost of defending freedom. He set out to give us a grim week — and he has succeeded.

He has also done something else during the past few days. He has learned the cost of aggression. The communist forces which attacked the cities of Vietnam have paid an appalling cost for their boldness. Over 22,000 communist soldiers died since January 30. Another 5,000 have been taken prisoner. In one week, the communists have lost many more soldiers than we have lost during the entire Vietnam war. I take no joy in this carnage. But I think that our sadness about the past week should be mixed with deep pride at the magnificent performance of our men in Vietnam, and of the performance of our allies.

The communist attack was, of course, an assault upon the will of the Vietnamese and American people to continue the fight. Apart from that, the communist attack appears to have had three primary purposes. First, they hoped to cause a general uprising in their favor among the inhabitants of the cities and towns of Vietnam. They told their own troops that this would happen. Their propaganda broadcasts called upon the Vietnamese people to rise up and end the

TOP SECRET

war. That they were serious in this hope seems clear, for they did not provide any orders to their troops for withdrawal, apparently believing that withdrawal would not be necessary.

They could not have been more wrong. Nowhere did the Vietnamese civilians come to the aid of the communist troops. Nowhere was there an uprising. To the contrary the civilian population of Vietnam's cities appears to view the Communist assault as exactly what it was — a savage and vicious attack upon civilian populations with a callous and total lack of concern for the welfare of civilian lives.

A second communist purpose appears to have been the destruction of the Armed Forces of the Republic of Vietnam, the ARVN, as a cohesive and disciplined national military instrument. If that was their purpose — they failed. Everywhere, the ARVN behaved well, and in many places they behaved with outstanding gallantry and professional competence. In the past, a number of prominent Americans have seized every opportunity to criticize the fighting capacity and will of the ARVN. In view of the ARVN performance in the past few days, and in view of the very heavy casualties which they have sustained and the much heavier casualties which they have inflicted — I suggest it is time for such criticism to stop.

Finally, the communists undoubtedly intended to shatter the government of the Republic of Vietnam by simultaneous assaults on its national and districts centers. The primary communist purpose in South Vietnam is, of course, to destroy the Government of South Vietnam, and to replace it with a communist government. Thus, throughout Vietnam the communist assault on the cities concentrated on government offices and police stations, on the Vietnam equivalent of the city hall, the county courthouse, and the State Capitol. The communists even announced the creation of a new government in the hope that people would rally to it — and if not rally to it, then at least accept it as an alternative preferable to a continuation of the fighting. This phony coalition government was treated by the Vietnamese people with the contempt which it deserved.

In these purposes, then, the communists have failed. And they have failed at the cost of 22,000 of their best men slain. The tidings in Washington and Saigon have been heavy this week. But they cannot have been light in Hanoi.

It is a fact that the attacks which began on January 30 were more ambitious in concept, broader in scope, more savage in execution, and more secure in their development than we had thought

TOP SECRET

possible.

It is certain that in the savagery of the past week, the enemy has squandered, for little gain that we can see, a major part of the human and material resources available to him. All of these will be hard for him to replace and some of them may prove impossible to replace. It may be that what we have witnessed the past week is a convulsive effort which he can hardly repeat. But we cannot, in prudence, assume that to be the case.

We know that he has many more forces which were not committed to the assault upon the cities. We believe he is capable of repeating that assault, if he is willing to pay the price.

We also know that the enemy has brought down from the north large and well-trained forces of the North Vietnamese regular Army. They have concentrated these forces in the northern part of South Vietnam — and particularly around our Marines at Khe Sanh. We expect in the very near future that the enemy will attempt to overrun the Marines at Khe Sanh. We expect that he will make a determined effort to do that. We expect that he will fail, and we expect that he will suffer appalling casualties before he discovers that there-is-not-going-to-be-any-Dien-Bien-Phu-in-this-war.

I cannot, therefore, hold out to you the prospect of quiet weeks ahead. There will be fierce fighting around Khe Sanh. There may be a recurrence of the assault on the cities of Vietnam. There will be casualties for us and for our friends to mourn.

You may ask, why is it necessary for us to bear this heavy burden, I have discussed with you many times the reasons why we are in Vietnam. This is not the time to discuss those reasons again. There is nothing new to add to the reasons. The only thing that is new is the intensity of the enemy's effort to break our will. He is waiting to see what the effect will be upon the American public — and upon the Vietnamese public — of last week's savagery.

I believe that I can tell him what the effect will be. We have known savagery before. And we have known how to deal with it. We still do. Do not look to Iowa, or New York, or Oregon or Alabama for a reward for your deeds of last week. You will not find it.

As for the Vietnamese people, I will let them speak for themselves. They have endured this kind of gangsterism for many years with a fortitude and an endurance which compliment the human race. I will say simply this: We will not let you down. Do not fear that we will cut and run when the going gets tough.

TOP SECRET

Neither this administration nor any other elected by the American people will betray you — or the American soldiers who fight with you. We will be there to the end. And in the end, it will all come out right.

Now — what is left of the hopes for peace after the events of the last week — and the events we believe will come in the next few weeks. I will tell you frankly that I do not see any prospect for an early peace. At San Antonio I set forth our minimum requirements for peace. We would stop the bombing of North Vietnam if the enemy would assure us, publicly or privately, that prompt and productive peace talks would result, and that they would not take advantage of the cessation of bombing to mount a larger war effort. We set these conditions because we have had some experience with peace talks with communists. At Panmumjon in Korea we talked for 372 days and during that period 12,700 American soldiers lost their lives and almost 49,000 were wounded. I am not interested in such peace talks as that. I have no intention of denying to the American troops in South Vietnam the advantages of American air power if the only purpose of that denial is the well-being of those who are shooting at American troops. That is the meaning of the San Antonio formula. We want peace. We will stop the bombing of the

North to get quick and serious peace talks. We will not stop it for any other reason.

I think we have clearly had our answer to our offer of peace talks. I think that the assault upon the cities of Vietnam was the answer. I think that the massive effort the enemy has made to besiege the American garrison at Khe Sanh is the answer — and incidentally, every man and every pound of material surrounding our men at Khe Sanh came down from North Vietnam. If it were not for our bombing of the North, our Marines at Khe Sanh would face more enemies and better armed and supplied enemies.

The enemy does not want peace. He wants to try to win a military victory. He expects to defeat us as he defeated France — by fighting us fiercely in the field and propagandizing us fiercely in our own homes. It was a communist who said that a coffin is better propaganda than a leaflet. They believe that principle, and they are acting upon it in Vietnam.

I repeat to you: they do not want peace at this time. They want to continue the fight. You cannot make peace with a man who is determined to fight you. It is not a question of finding the right words, the right place, the right gimmick. It would be easy to find the formula for peace — if they wanted peace. It is impossible to

TOP SECRET

find the formula for peace so long as they are determined to have war.

What are we going to do about this? We are going to give them the fight they want — and more than they want. We are going to mete out the measure they have asked for — and more than the measure. We will not do this with any joy — for we are a people who hate war. But we are also a people who are winning — and not for the first time — to do what is necessary to preserve our freedom and the freedom of our friends.

Peace is available to the communists in Vietnam — when they want it. The San Antonio terms are reasonable. Indeed, they are more than reasonable. When the enemy wants peace it is available to him. In the meantime, we do not intend to confuse him and to raise his hopes of a cheap victory with constant pleas that he talk peace. He has heard us at San Antonio. We have heard him in the mortars that he fired into the heart of the largest cities in South Vietnam. We fully expect to hear him in the fury of the attack upon our Marines. We understand the message. We do not like it — but we are prepared to accept it. As Winston Churchill put it to another enemy who specialized in savagery, "you do your worst — and we will do our best."

For that is the way to peace. In this war as in many others, the aggressor will not make peace until he has been convinced that he has no choice. He has chosen to make a supreme effort to obtain victory. That has made the last week a hard one and it is likely to make for other hard weeks to come. If we meet this challenge with fortitude and with unity, then the answer is clear to the enemy. If we meet it with dismay and panic — if we respond to the enemy attack by calling for our own forces to retreat — by questioning whether our own forces should be there at all — by criticizing our friends and our allies — then the enemy will be succeeding — and he will see that he is succeeding. He will redouble his efforts, with all that implies for the safety of the American men in Vietnam.

This is a time for steadiness — and for resolution — and for determination. I intend to do my best to show all three on your behalf. I ask your help.

INFORMATION

>Thursday, February 8, 1968
>6:10 p.m.

Mr. President:
A note from Amb. Lodge.

W. W. Rostow

TOP SECRET

DEPARTMENT OF STATE
AMBASSADOR AT LARGE
WASHINGTON

February 8, 1968

TO: The President
FROM: H. C. LODGE

1. I have heard that my views on the desirability of holding Khe Sanh were recently discussed in your presence.

2. So that there may be no misunderstanding, I wish to state that I support the decision to hold Khe Sanh. For many reasons I consider it vital that it be held.

Status reports from General William Westmoreland, in Vietnam, and from General Earle Wheeler, are forwarded through channels to the President...

INFORMATION

THE WHITE HOUSE
WASHINGTON

    Friday, February 9, 1968
    9:15 a.m.

Mr. President:
Herewith Westy's latest on Khe Sanh.

W. W. Rostow

Friday, February 9, 1968

TEXT OF CABLES FROM
    GENERAL WESTMORELAND

This is the fifth report on the Khe Sanh area and covers the 24 hour period of Thursday, February 8, 1968.

    During the period the Khe Sanh Combat Base and the surrounding area continued to receive sporadic mortar, rocket, and harassing small arms and sniper fire. A total of 21 Marines were killed and 27 were wounded and evacuated. There were 124 enemy killed, one captured, and 27 individual and 23 crew-served weapons captured as a result of the enemy mortar and

TOP SECRET

ground attack on the Marine Company yesterday morning.

Marine aircraft flew 49 sorties in support of the Khe Sanh area while the Air Force flew 101, and the Navy flew 77, for a total of 227. Ten secondary fires and one secondary explosion were reported. Three personnel carriers and a "tank-like" vehicle were destroyed, and 10 other vehicles were damaged. The latter was the action taken against the enemy tanks and vehicles sighted yesterday southwest and west of Khe Sanh.

Seven ARC LIGHT strikes (39) sorties were run in the Niagara area. Four of these strikes were in proximity to Khe Sanh. Marine units in the area fired 5543 rounds of mortar and artillery ammunition.

The Khe Sanh logistics position continues to improve. A total of 214 short tons of supplies were airlifted in during the period for an increase of 87 short tons. The bulk of the airlift was the delivery of 140 short tons of ammunition. 41.5 short tons of engineering equipment, including bunkering material, and 24 short tons of vehicles were also delivered. Airlift resupply is being accomplished with Air Force C-130 and C-123 Aircraft and Marine C-130 and Ch-53 helicopters. The 26 days of individual combat rations reported yesterday was not correct. The revised status of these ratios is 12 days. The ammunition stocks are adequate, the lowest being 11 days for the 105 MM howitzers. No COFRAM type ordnance was used during the period.

For the next period, four ARC LIGHT strikes

(27 sorties) will be flown in support of Khe Sanh. Marine tactical air plans 44 sorties (additional 16 on call), the Air Force plans 74 sorties, and the Navy 52, in support of Khe Sanh, for a total of 172 sorties. The Air Force will also have 128 tactical air sorties on call, and a potential of diverting pre-planned strikes from other areas for a total of 631 sorties (Air Force 381, Navy 250).

There is no new information on enemy identification, strengths, and capabilities.

The weather in the Khe Sanh area for the early afternoon of the 8th February was good but about 2:00 PM it became marginal. Fog formed at about 8:00 PM making the weather poor for the rest of the night and for the morning of the 9th. The forecast for the afternoon of the 9th is for marginal weather. The information of fog by 8:00 PM will make the rest of the night poor with improvement to marginal again by noon on the 12th.
[Redacted]

INFORMATION

THE WHITE HOUSE
WASHINGTON

>Saturday, February 10, 1968
>9:25 a.m.

Mr. President:
Herewith Westy's latest on Khe Sanh.

W. W. Rostow

TOP SECRET

THE JOINT CHIEFS OF STAFF
WASHINGTON, D. C. 20301

CM-3001-68
11 February 1968

MEMORANDUM FOR THE PRESIDENT
Subject: Situation in Vietnam

You have received General Westmoreland's seventh report on the situation in the Khe Sanh area for the period through 11:00 PM EST, 10 February 1968. I talked to General Westmoreland at 8:15 AM EST this morning and obtained the information on the situation in Vietnam which is contained in the succeeding paragraphs.

As General Westmoreland's report indicated, Khe Sanh airfield was shelled yesterday. A C-130 aircraft was hit by fragments of a mortar shell upon landing, damaging its hydraulic system; they may be able to repair this aircraft tomorrow. General Westmoreland plans to use C-123 and Caribou aircraft in resupplying Khe Sanh and, to meet this need, has had General Momyer convert for airlift use some C-123s used in the defoliation effort.

Sniper fire continued in Hue. The first of the three Vietnamese Marine Battalions to reinforce in Hue arrived there yesterday; in addition, elements of a US Marine Battalion were moved in. There was heavy fighting south of Danang, resulting in 195 enemy killed. There was light contact on the outskirts of Dalat.

In the IV Corps area there was light contact in

several towns.

A rallier (defector) taken at Khe Sanh gave information on the following order of enemy attack: (1) Lang Vei; (2) Con Thien; (3) Khe Sanh. He stated also that he had seen near Thanh Hoa several weeks ago about 20 missiles mounted on PT-76 Amphibious Tank chassis (the PT-76 was used at Lang Vei). General Westmoreland indicated these could be FROG missiles (see attachment) and that this could be the "big surprise" which the Soviet correspondent in Hanoi wrote about recently. Other possibilities for the "big surprise", in General Westmoreland's view, could be the use of SA-2 missiles near the DMZ, air strikes in the DMZ area by IL-28s, and MIG attacks against B-52s. General Westmoreland and his commanders are alert to all of these possibilities and taking appropriate measures.

In addition, General Westmoreland provided me the following assessment of South Korean and Australian troops in Vietnam:

"South Korean and Australian forces have aggressively and professionally fought the enemy wherever and whenever encountered. In addition to providing very capable defense of their own tactical areas of responsibility (TAOR) the presence of these allies has provided us the flexibility for redeployment of our own more mobile forces to contend with other threat areas. It is also significant that Highway 1 has remained open through the length of the Korean TAOR during the current situation. The fact that the more dramatic events of well coordinated enemy attacks have bypassed Korean and Australian

TOP SECRET

areas is attributable to an extent to the emphasis of enemy strategy."

EARLE G. WHEELER
Chairman
Joint Chiefs of Staff

Attachments
    FROG Missile
    PT-76 Amphibious Tank

THE WHITE HOUSE
WASHINGTON

    February 11, 1968
    Sunday 11:05 am

Mr. President:
Here is Gen. Westmoreland's morning report. Figures on the Khe Sanh supply situation are given on page 2.

Bromley Smith

SECRET EYES ONLY

Sunday, February 11, 1968

Following is the text of a cable sent by General Westmoreland this morning.
    This is the seventh report on the Khe Sanh area and covers a period of 24-hours ending at midnight last night.
    During the reporting period the Khe Sanh

combat base and the surrounding area continued to receive sporadic shelling and mortars, rockets and an occasional artillery round. Between 7:17 February 10 and noon February 10 units had brief exchanges of small arms fire and grenades on the western end of the perimeter and western outposts resulting in three enemy killed. At 7:15 February 10 a trip flare exposed 14 enemy just west of Khe Sanh near the wire. An exchange of fire resulted in one enemy killed. At noon February 10 lights were spotted moving between Hills 861 and 881S, and metallic noises were heard. Lights and noises were fired on with unknown results. Tactical air strike runs during the period resulted in four secondary explosions.

Several enemy encroachments toward friendly positions and increasing enemy pressure was noted during the period. Marines in the area continued to prove their defensive positions with emphasis on anti-tank defense. On February 10, 136 mines were emplaced southwest of the airfield. A review of all 106mm recoilless rifle, 3.5 rocket launchers, light-antitank weapon, and tank positions has been conducted to ensure complete coverage of all likely tank approaches.

Latest information received on the Marine C-130 crash which was reported yesterday reveals that the aircraft is believed to have received 50-caliber machine gun fire on its approach. The aircraft was loaded with POL which caught on fire and burned upon landing resulting in two killed and four wounded in critical condition and three missing. Search continues for the missing. During the period a total of 2,985 rounds of various caliber and types of mortar/artillery was fired in response to enemy efforts in the area.

Marine tactical air flew 54 sorties, and the Navy flew 102 missions for a total of 257 sorties. Aside from the tactical strikes mentioned, there were five additional secondary explosions, 14 secondary fires, 42 enemy killed, two bridges damaged, and 193 military structures destroyed.

Weather continues to hamper visual (??). There were no sightings of enemy vehicles.

Thirty-eight B-52 aircraft ran six strikes during the period delivering a total 975 tons of ordnance in the Niagara area.

The airfield at Khe Sanh is back in operation following the C-130 crash of yesterday, and received a total of 53 short tons of supplied. The resupplies represented four of the five classes, class I, rations, excepted. Unfavorable weather continues to effect air resupply in the northern highlands; however, early sorties were able to land on February 11, without the aid of the ground control facility. Requisitions received from Khe Sanh on the night of February 10 are being scheduled for air delivery or air drop on February 11.

The Khe Sanh dump or ammo supply point status reported as number of days on hand on February 11 is as follows: Class I: Rations, 10 days on hand; Class III: Aviations fuel 12 days on hand, jet fuel, 4 days on hand; motor fuel, 6 days on hand and diesel fuel, 6 days on hand; Class V: ammunitions, 50mm and high explosives, 12 days on hand; 81mm, 17 days on hand; 90mm, 94 days on hand; 4.2 inch shells, 36 days on hand; 105mm, 10 days on hand and 155mm, 25 days on hand. Class V (firecracker). 105mm, 5 days on hand; 155mm, 5 days on hand; 40mm, 5 days on hand and hand grenades, 10 days on hand. The ammo supply point status of anti-tank ordnance, not including basic loads on position is as follows: 90mm head, 478 rounds; 66mm rocket, 190 rounds; M19 mines, 100 mines and 106mm head, 316 rounds. NOTE: Firecracker ammo is COFRAM.

No COFRAM type ordnance was used during the period.

For the next 24-hour period Marine tactical air plans 44 sorties in support of Khe Sanh, while the Air Force has 76 scheduled and the Navy has 100, for a total of 220 sorties. The Marines will have 16 aircraft on call for additional runs, and the Air Force will have 120 alert sorties on call. Five Arc Light strikes (33 sorties) are scheduled in support of the Khe Sanh area.

The weather for the afternoon of February 10 was marginal and deteriorated to poor after noon EST with zero visibility in fog by 3:00 PM EST, February 10. Weather conditions continued to be poor through the morning of February 11. The forecast for the afternoon of February 11 is for marginal weather conditions. By 8:00 AM EST fog and low clouds will cause poor weather which will last until 10:00 AM EST on the 12th of February. Conditions should improve to marginal with cloud ceilings increasing to 1,200 feet by mid-night February 11.

There is no (??) in enemy identification in the area.

TOP SECRET

Lao personnel evacuated from Khe Sanh and now located at DaNang for on-shipment to Laos, total 114. Four persons remain to be evacuated on February 11, including the BV-33 battalion commander. Arrangements are underway to transport the Lao personnel to ultimate destination by Lao aircraft.

INFORMATION

THE WHITE HOUSE
WASHINGTON

> Monday, February 12, 1968
> 8:30 a.m.

Mr. President:
Herewith Westy's daily report on Khe Sanh.
We will send up shortly a table on the supply situation.

W. W. Rostow

Monday, February 12, 1968, 8:20 AM

TEXT OF CABLE FROM GENERAL WESTMORELAND

This is the eighth report on the Khe Sanh area and covers the 24-hour period of February 11, 1968.
    During the period the Khe Sanh Combat Base and the surrounding area continued to receive

heavy enemy shelling by mortars, rockets, and artillery. By 1:00 AM the shelling had subsided to sporadic incoming and terminated at 3:00 AM. Early Sunday morning a 122 MM rocket impacted 15 feet away from a Air Force C-130 in the process of off-loading troops, resulting in one killed and four wounded and evacuated. The aircraft was damaged, but repairs are underway and hopefully it can be flown out today.

A helicopter conducting medical evacuation on Hill 861 received small arms fire resulting in one wounded and evacuated.

Two Navy aircraft dropped eight tanks of tear gas on a village eight kilometers southwest of Khe Sanh and followed with air strikes. No movement was observed from the village.

For the period there were four Marines killed and eight wounded, including those mentioned above. Two thousand two hundred and five rounds of mortar and artillery were fired by friendly forces. Tactical air sorties for the period totalled 258, Marine Tactical Air flew 75 sorties, and reported one road cut, four secondary fires, and one tank destroyed. The Air Force and Navy Tactical flew 88 and 95 sorties respectively, reporting six road cuts, four military structures destroyed, one secondary explosion, eight secondary fires, and one bridge damaged. Five ARC LIGHT strikes (33 sorties) were flown in the Niagara area.

Aerial resupply of Khe Sanh increased to 83 short tons on February 11. Ammunition and engineer bunkering material accounted for 40 and 25 short tons respectively. Seventeen short tons of

TOP SECRET

replacement were delivered along with one short ton of medical supplies. C-123 Aircraft are providing air landed delivery to the Khe Sanh Airfield and air drops from C-130 Aircraft began at 11:00 hours.

No COFRAM Type Ordnance was used during the period.

For the next 24 hours Marine Air Plans 44 Tactical Air Sorties, the Air Force will run 74, while the Navy plan 100, for a total of 218 tactical air sorties in support of the Khe Sanh area. I have just instructed Momyer to increase the above with emphasis in the B-52 ring.

The Marines will have 16 aircraft on call. The Air Force will have 120 sorties on call. There will be five ARC LIGHT strikes (36 sorties) run in the Niagara area.

There is no change in enemy unit identification in the area.

The weather was poor on the afternoon of February 11. Cloud ceilings were 500 to 700 feet and visibilities were 3 to 5 miles in fog. By 6:00 PM the fog increased and visibility was reduced to 1/16 of a mile. The weather remained poor all night and through the morning hours. The weather is forecast to remain poor until about midmorning on February 13. During this period cloud ceilings will remain 600 feet or lower and visibilities will be near zero at night. Late on the morning of the 13th weather should improve to marginal.

Confidential Files on the Siege and Loss of Khe Sanh

INFORMATION

THE WHITE HOUSE
WASHINGTON

>Tuesday, Feb. 13, 1968
>9:45 a.m.

Mr. President:
Herewith Westy's Khe Sanh daily, plus the supply table.
You will note he plans to move to a daily air drop of 140 tons.

W. W. Rostow

Wednesday, February 14, 1968, 9:30 AM

TEXT OF CABLE FROM
GENERAL WESTMORELAND

This is the tenth report on the Khe Sanh - DMZ area and covers the 24-hour period of February 13, 1968.

During the reporting period Khe Sanh Combat Base and surrounding areas received over 200 rounds of mixed mortars, artillery and rocket fire. Neighboring elements at Camp Carroll received 10 rounds of mortar fire while Marines in the vicinity of A-3 (5 kilometers northeast of Con Thien) received three consecutive afternoon barrages of 30 rounds of enemy mortar and 70 rounds of artillery. Seven mortar rounds impacted within the perimeter at Con Thien. Concluding

TOP SECRET

the day's bombardment, shortly after noon, elements at Gio Linh received nine rounds of artillery.

Although damage attributed to the shelling was minimal, one Marine was killed and 12 Marines wounded, 6 of whom required medical evacuation.

In Operation Scotland in the Khe Sanh area, a 37th RVN Ranger Battalion Patrol encountered a small enemy force at mid-afternoon, killed two North Vietnamese Army and captured an 82 MM recoilless gun.

Elsewhere in northern I Corps, at 7:45 AM a Marine unit ambushed a 20 man North Vietnamese Army Patrol around Gia Linh and counted 7 North Vietnamese Army bodies and 1 detainee resulting from the engagement. One Marine was killed, and one Marine was wounded.

Other elements along the DMZ reported no significant contact for the period. Total casualties for the period in the Khe Sanh area were: friendly, killed 1, wounded 10; enemy, killed 2. Elsewhere along the DMZ one Marine was killed and three Marines were wounded; nine North Vietnamese Army were killed.

Marine aircraft flew 65 sorties in support of the Khe Sanh area, the Air Force flew 192 tactical air sorties in support of the Khe Sanh area, the Navy flew 51, for a total of 308 sorties. Bomb Damage Assessment included 4 secondary explosions (one extremely large), 6 artillery positions were destroyed, 5 artillery positions damaged, there were 2 secondary fires, and 250 meters of trench were destroyed. ARC LIGHT ran 4 strikes

(30 sorties) in the Niagara area in support of Khe Sanh.

Khe Sanh was resupplied with 83 short tons on February 13. Ammunition amounted to 50 short tons. There were 16 short tons of vehicles and 4 short tons of general supplies delivered. In addition, 175 replacements were air lifted into the Khe Sanh Airfield.

Air operations on February 14 began at 9:00 AM with air drops from C-130 aircraft. So far today, some 76 short tons have been air dropped. C-123 aircraft are enroute for air delivery to the airfield. Present weather looks favorable for air resupply operations.

For the next 24 hours Marine Tactical Air plans 44 sorties in support of Khe Sanh, the Air Force will have 150 sorties, and the Navy 100 sorties, for a total of 294 sorties planned. There will be 16 additional Marine aircraft and 120 Air Force sorties on call for Khe Sanh. There will be six B-52 strikes (27 sorties) run in the Niagara area.

During the period the weather at Khe Sanh was characterized by low clouds and heavy night time and morning fog. Until 5:00 PM on February 13 the ceiling was 500 feet and visibility 3 - 7 miles in fog. After 5:00 PM the ceiling was 100 feet and the visibility 1/4 mile in fog. Low ceilings and visibilities continued throughout the remainder of the night and early morning with an improving trend beginning after 2:00 AM on the 14th. By 9:00 AM the ceiling had improved to 2,000 foot overcast with the visibility to 7 miles. By noon the ceiling was 2,000 foot broken.

TOP SECRET

The forecast is for partly cloudy skies and visibility 6 miles by early afternoon on the 14th. The sky will continue to be partly cloudy throughout the afternoon and evening and continued through noon on the 15th. The visibility will continue to be 6 miles throughout the period except lowering to 5 miles in smoke and haze near sunrise on the 15th.

INFORMATION

THE WHITE HOUSE
WASHINGTON

     Wednesday. February 14, 1968
     11:25 a.m.

Mr. President:
Herewith Gen. Wheeler's report of his daily conversation with Gen. Westmoreland.
   As you will see, a number of offensive operations are under way.

W. W. Rostow

THE JOINT CHIEFS OF STAFF
WASHINGTON, D. C. 20301

     CM-3010-68
     14 February 1968

MEMORANDUM FOR THE PRESIDENT

Subject: Telephone Conversation with General

Confidential Files on the Siege and Loss of Khe Sanh

Westmoreland

1. I talked to General Westmoreland for some forty minutes beginning at 0800 hours this morning. In addition to his tenth report on the Khe Sanh area which you have already received, and the attachment to this memorandum setting forth combat operations throughout the country, General Westmoreland reported several interesting developments:

He spent yesterday (last night Washington time) visiting the I Corps Tactical Zone. He met with General Lam, Commander I Corps; General Cushman, and other senior US and ARVN commanders. He also visited the ARVN 51st Infantry Regiment and the American 7th Marine Regiment. He says that the ARVN troops have their tails up; they are proud of themselves because of the way they defeated the enemy.

General Lam had been marked for assassination at the outset of the attack on Danang when he was scheduled to visit a pagoda to pay his respects to his ancestors. Lam got wind of this, went to another pagoda to worship and arranged for a force to seize the assassination group.

Lam states that the young VC captured (mostly NVA) have been propagandized that the South Vietnamese wouldn't fight and that there would be an uprising; also that there would be peace in six months under a coalition government. As a matter of fact, there was no uprising and in certain instances some South Vietnamese civilians actually captured NVA soldiers and turned them over to the authorities.

TOP SECRET

The attack on Danang, according to General Lam, was poorly planned, hastily put together, and not too well executed. Regional Force and Popular Force units acquitted themselves well.
The food situation in Danang is satisfactory. The local citizens have voluntarily donated 600,000 plasters to provide assistance to the homeless.
2. In Hue, the remaining enemy is bottled up in three or four strong points; they are short of food. The weather is better today and flyable, and General Westmoreland has ordered General Cushman to use Napalm on these strong points in order to reduce them. The people in Hue have been generally cooperative with US and ARVN troops; they have voluntarily provided food and water to friendly forces. The radio station is operating and electricity is available throughout the town. There was no uprising in Hue.
3. As to ARVN combat effectiveness, General Westmoreland reports that in the First ARVN Division, which is an excellent fighting outfit, the 1st Regiment has an average strength present of 420 per battalion; the 2d Regiment an average of 320 per battalion; the 3d Regiment (which was heavily engaged) has only about 200 effective per battalion. The Ranger Battalions in I Corps are in good shape as are the 2d ARVN Division and the 51st ARVN Regiment. He Vietnamese Joint General Staff is taking extraordinary actions to provide replacements for understrength units.
4. The elements of the Americal Division, which attacked the 2d NVA Division south of Danang, is still finding additional dead enemy in the very

extensive area over which they fought. Westmoreland still does not have an accurate estimate of the very heavy losses sustained in that area by the enemy. Parenthetically, he remarked that he saw 500 POWs being held in a compound at General Lam's I Corps Headquarters. Lam states that the people are indignant at the violation of Tet by the VC and the brutality they have displayed towards civilians and their homes.

5. General Abrams has been at Headquarters MACV Forward, located in the Hue/Phu Bai area, for a couple of days. The headquarters has been operational for several days, has a strong staff, and is prepared to control all military operations north of the Ai Van Pass.

6. On his return to Saigon late yesterday, after consulting with Ambassador Bunker, he informed President Thieu, in the presence of General Vien, of the additional US reinforcements being sent. Both were very happy to learn of this fact. President Thieu has agreed to replace General Vinh Loc, Commander II CTZ, this week. Westmoreland has urged, and Thieu has agreed, that General Thang should assume command of IV CTZ at an early date.

7. Yesterday, near Quang Ngai, a refugee center was overrun and burned. Casualties and destruction are unknown at this time. Moreover, there was a contact in this area with the NVA 33rd Regiment resulting in 30 enemy KIA. General Westmoreland has instructed General Rosson, Commander II FFV, to seek out and destroy this already battered enemy unit.

TOP SECRET

8. North of Saigon, an ARVN unit searching for the enemy made a rather heavy contact in which they killed 70 enemy while losing four of their own men.

9. The Riverine Force, which, as I reported to you yesterday, had moved into the Can Tho area in the Delta, had a light contact with the enemy yesterday. However, they located and captured a cache of large quantities of ammunition to include rocket and mortar rounds.

10. The weather opened up briefly in the Mu Gia Pass area and a North Vietnamese POL convoy was seen in the open. General Momyer put 36 tactical air sorties on it. Results not yet known.

11. The Army Engineer Battalion is working to open Highway 1 through the Ai Van Pass. General Westmoreland believes he can restore the railroad part way to the north and establish a rail head from which he can shuttle supplies by truck.

12. He is moving an Armored Cavalry Battalion from the II Corps area into the northern I CTZ in order to provide additional highway security as well as an anti-tank capability in the Con Thien/Gio Linh area where he anticipates the enemy may employ PT-76 light Soviet tanks.

13. General Westmoreland discussed with Ambassador Bunker yesterday the establishment of a Tet Assistance Relief Fund (TARF) to be funded by donations from American troops in South Vietnam, to provide relief to those unfortunate South Vietnamese who were made homeless and destitute by the recent enemy attacks. General Westmoreland considers that this fund

will not only create good will between the people and the US Military Forces, but will help to establish a good image of the American soldier — that is, that he is not a cold blooded killer but is compassionate to the unfortunate. Ambassador bunker may well query State on this matter in order to receive guidance of a policy nature.

EARLE G. WHEELER
Chairman
Joint Chiefs of Staff

TOP SECRET

A memo from Walt Rostow is sent to Secretary of Defense Robert S. McNamara. Rostow, in the past, had referred to Westmoreland as "Westy."

SECRET
LITERALLY EYES ONLY

February 14, 1968

Bob —
This is the paper the President wished you to have and handle in the way he indicated.

W. W. Rostow

Honorable Robert S. McNamara
Secretary of Defense

SECRET

Memo
Subject: Khe Sanh

SECRET EYES ONLY

February 14, 1968

MEMORANDUM FOR THE PRESIDENT

Subject: Khe Sanh

I know that Khe Sanh is very much on your mind as it is on mine. It may be too late to do anything about the situation; if so, we should put all doubts behind us and prepare for the fight. On the other hand, if there is still time to exercise a useful influence, we should move quickly.

I have reviewed what General Westmoreland has said about Khe Sanh in his recent messages. To paraphrase his cables, he points out that the original occupation of the position was justified by the need to establish a forward operating base to permit operations against the key infiltration routes in Eastern Laos. More importantly, he also considers that its occupation has blocked the route of enemy advance into Quang Tri and has kept the fighting away from the populated coastal belt of I Corps. He concedes that Khe Sanh has not had much effect on infiltration from Laos and it is not clear whether he regards the role of blocking the Quang Tri approach as of current or of past importance.

Thus, General Westmoreland does not appear to argue strongly for the defense of Khe Sanh because of its present value either in relation to the infiltration routes in Laos or in the defense of major areas of the northern provinces. Although he mentioned to General Wheeler in a telephone conversation his belief that the maintenance of our position in the Khe Sanh area would offer us the opportunity at some time of dealing the enemy a severe blow, he has not amplified this point and, in his cables, he stressed rather the difficulty of getting out of Khe Sanh at the present time and the adverse psychological effects of a withdrawal upon South Viet-Nam and upon the American public.

My review of Westy's cables does not convince

me of the military importance of maintaining Khe Sanh at the present time if it is still feasible to withdraw. Whatever the past value of the position, it is a positive liability now. We are allowing the enemy to arrange at his leisure a set-piece attack on ground and in weather favorable to him and under conditions which will allow us little opportunity to punish him except by our air power. The latter can be neutralized to some degree by the favorite Communist tactic of closing tightly around our positions in areas which our air forces, particularly the B-52s, can not attack with safety to our own forces.

General Westmoreland recognizes the difficulties of air supply of Khe Sanh and indicates an intention to open Highway 9 to provide an overland line of communication. To do so will require a large number of troops to keep Highway 9 open in the face of the intermittent road-cutting operations which can be expected from the enemy.

THE WHITE HOUSE
WASHINGTON

>Thursday, February 15, 1968
>9:20 a.m.

Mr. President:
They really got some supplies into Khe Sanh yesterday — 188 tons.

Walt
W. W. Rostow

Intelligence reports to the President are becoming more intense, reflecting the continued fighting in and around Khe Sanh:

Thursday, February 15, 1968, 8:45 AM

TEXT OF CABLE FROM
GENERAL WESTMORELAND

This is the eleventh report on the Khe Sanh - DMZ area and covers the 24-hour period of February 14, 1968.

Significant activity yesterday in the First Corps continued to center in northern Quang Tri Province as renewed enemy shelling impacted at Khe Sanh Combat Base and outlying areas bordering the DMZ.

At Khe Sanh, elements of the 26th Marines received 65 rounds of mortars and 13 rounds of rocket scattered throughout the day and night. Friendly casualties for the period amounted to three Marines killed, 10 wounded (nine evacuated). The 2nd Battalion, 4th Marines in the vicinity of Camp Carroll counted 30 rounds of mortars during mid-day shellings. Friendly casualties were one killed, nine wounded (seven evacuated).

A noontime barrage of 13 rounds of mortar at Con Thien inflicted no casualties or damage on the 2nd Battalion, 1st Marines. Twenty additional mortar rounds fell at C1, seven kilometers south of Gio Linh, causing minor injuries to four ARVN soldiers.

Marine aircraft flew 106 tactical air sorties in support of the Khe Sanh area, the Air Force flew

TOP SECRET

98 sorties and the Navy flew 39, for a total of 243 tactical air sorties. Bomb Damage included 15 bunkers destroyed, six anti-aircraft positions destroyed, numerous secondary fires, 10 secondary explosions, 14 killed by air, one rocket position destroyed. Twenty-one B-52's flew over ARC LIGHT strikes delivering 525 tons of ordnance in the Niagara area.

Khe Sanh was resupplied with 188 short tons during the period, with 80 short tons being air dropped from Air Force C-130 air4craft. Nineteen C-123 and helicopters air landed the additional 107.5 short tons. A total of 141 short tons of ammunition and 31 short tons of engineering equipment were included.

For the next 24-hour period Marine Tactical Air plans 44 sorties in support of Khe Sanh, the Air Force plans 150, and the Navy 100, for a total of 294 sorties. Sixteen Marine aircraft and 120 Air Force sorties will be on call. ARC LIGHT will run 15 strikes (45 sorties) in the Niagara area, commencing the Bugle Note Program of three-aircraft strikes with time over targets' each 1 1/2hours.

Weather at Khe Sanh throughout the period was favorable for most military operations. The visibility was greater than five miles except for a short period near midnight due to ground fog. During most of the afternoon the sky condition was 2500 foot broken. By early evening cloudiness decreased and remained scattered throughout the night. Valley stratus formed after sunrise 1500 to 2000 feet producing a broken ceiling which remained in the area throughout the morning.

Forecast for Khe Sanh during the next period is for generally good visibility in daytime. After sunset, fog and stratus will gradually form lowering the ceiling to from 200 - 500 feet and the visibility to one mile or less by sunrise. Shortly thereafter, the ceiling will gradually improve to 100 broken and the visibility to five miles.

INFORMATION

THE WHITE HOUSE
WASHINGTON

>Thursday, February 15, 1968
>11:30 a.m.

Mr. President:
Herewith Westy's daily report via Bus Wheeler. Its tone and substance continue to be optimistic.

Aside from the unresolved situation in Hue today, my major concern, arising from current reports, is the enemy is exploiting the loose situation in the countryside to take back some villages where we had established security, and is probably trying to recruit men to make up their losses. Aside from the I Corps battle, I suspect getting pacification back on its feet will gradually become a number one task.

W. W. Rostow

THE JOINT CHIEFS OF STAFF
WASHINGTON, D. C. 20301

TOP SECRET

CM-3016-68
15 February 1968

MEMORANDUM FOR THE PRESIDENT
Subject: Telephone Conversation with General Westmoreland

1. In addition to General Westmoreland's eleventh report on the Khe Sanh/DMZ area, I have attached hereto a summary of the more significant actions in South Vietnam yesterday. At 0800 this morning I talked with General Westmoreland on the telephone, and he made the following comments:

a. Weather in the Khe Sanh area was generally good yesterday, permitting air operations, both tactical and logistic, to be accomplished. However, the weather was not good enough to permit him to distribute gravel* in certain areas north of Khe Sanh as he would like to do.

b. Our air had a good day yesterday. They destroyed a large ammunition cache southwest of Khe Sanh, struck a large storage area near Tchepone in Laos, with smoke rising 6,000 feet in the air. The tactical air strike reported to you yesterday near Mu Gia Pass uncovered a North Vietnamese storage area which was also attacked during the period.

c. The Vietnamese Ranger Battalion at Khe Sanh carried out an excellent small unit operation yesterday. They moved a platoon outside of the perimeter during darkness to a hilltop; as day broke, they sent out a small patrol which deliberately exposed itself. The North Vietnamese troops came out of their holes to attack the patrol, and the whole Ranger platoon attacked them, inflicting casualties, and captured an 82 mm mortar.

* small anti-personnel mines.

d. At Hue, the enemy is still dug into the south wall of the Citadel. General Westmoreland plans to use air strikes again today, employing high explosives, white phosphorous, and Napalm weapons. He now has three ARVN Marine corps Battalions (which replaced the understrength ARVN Airborne Battalions in Hue). There are also seven companies of US Marines engaged in the operation. He anticipates that the enemy can hold out for about three more days.
e. North of Saigon, armed helicopters and tactical air caught a large force of the enemy in the open, inflicting about 120 casualties on them. General Westmoreland thinks that the enemy's command and control system has broken down in the Saigon area. At any rate, the enemy seems to be confused and apparently has no orders or plans to withdraw. He considers this a satisfactory situation since it will permit him to destroy them element by element.
f. As reported to you yesterday, the Riverine Force operating near Can Tho discovered and captured a very sizeable enemy ammunition depot containing large quantities of grenades, 120 mm mortar rounds, etc.
2. General Westmoreland yesterday (last night Washington time) visited the 1st US Infantry

TOP SECRET

Division, the 25th US Infantry Division and the 199th Infantry Brigade. These units have done and are doing extremely well. He stated that the 199th Brigade, located near Bien Hoa, has been commanded during the recent heavy fighting by a negro colonel named Davidson who did a splendid job in leading and commanding his forces. General Westmoreland believes that in the first two or three days of the fighting, this brigade killed over 1,100 of the enemy.

3. I discussed the Khe Sanh situation at some length with General Westmoreland. I conveyed to him the message which you transmitted to me through Secretary McNamara. General Westmoreland told me that he understands and appreciates greatly your firm support. Pertinent to this aspect of the war, he stated that all events support the belief that the pounding from the air and from our artillery is having a good effect from our point of view on enemy capabilities in the area; i.e., his supply and command system is being constantly disrupted, and casualties are being inflicted on enemy troops in the Khe Sanh area.

4. General Westmoreland reported that except for the foregoing, the situation was quiet elsewhere.

EARLE G. WHEELER
Chairman
Joint Chiefs of Staff

INFORMATION

THE WHITE HOUSE

WASHINGTON

    Friday, February 16, 1968
    9:15 a.m.

MR. PRESIDENT:
In DMZ:

— scattered shelling;
— an incredible number of secondary explosions (p. 2);
— 19 tons delivered

We have a firm report that one enemy unit around Khe Sanh has 193 combat-ready men from an original 289. How they lost 96 is not indicated.

W. W. Rostow

Friday, February 16, 1968, 8:40 am

TEXT OF CABLE FROM
GENERAL WESTMORELAND

This is the twelfth report on the Khe Sanh - DMZ area and covers the 24-hour period of February 15, 1968.
    Enemy shelling continued throughout much of northern First Corps yesterday as Khe Sanh Combat Base and neighboring areas in proximity to the DMZ received scattered incoming rocket, artillery and mortar rounds. Latest information received indicates that the enemy fired 14 rocket

TOP SECRET

rounds and 110 rounds of mixed caliber mortar at the Khe Sanh Combat Base, resulting in two Marines killed, 28 wounded (16 evacuated). While Khe Sanh bore the heaviest barrage, moderate concentrations fell upon other friendly locations, as Marine elements at Camp Carroll received five mid-afternoon mortar rounds and 9 rounds of 152 artillery. Fifty-two additional mortar rounds impacted four kilometers southwest of Gio Linh, in the area occupied by the 3d Battalion, 3d Marines. The 1st Battalion, 3d Marines, in the vicinity of Quang Tri Airfield, received five mortar rounds and at noon, the 2d Battalion, 1st Marines, at Con Thien, received 30 rounds of mortar.

In Operation Lancaster, elements of K Company, 3d Battalion, 9th Marines engaged an unknown size enemy force 12 kilometers northeast of Khe Sanh. Relief force of I Company, 3d Battalion, 9th Marines arrived to render support. Contact broke at 3:45 PM but resulted in 12 Marines killed, 107 wounded (37 evacuated). Enemy casualties are unknown at this time.

In other action in northern Quang Tri Province, small unit contacts in Operation Kentucky accounted for three North Vietnamese Army killed; two additional North Vietnamese Army were confirmed as a result of mortar mission on an enemy location. No significant contacts were reported in either the Napoleon or Saline Operations.

Disposition of friendly forces and allied armament in the Khe Sanh area did not change during the period.

In all, there were 317 tactical air sorties flown in support of the Khe Sanh area and the adjacent Niagara area. Marine aircraft flew 111 sorties in support of Khe Sanh delivered 282 tons of ordnance. Bomb Damage Assessment included five structures damaged, (3 - 50) caliber machine gun position destroyed, and two tanks destroyed. The Air Force flew 166 sorties and the Navy flew 40, reporting the attack on two major supply areas. One supply area six nautical miles south of Tchepone had a total of 89 sorties with over 500 secondary explosions and fires. A second storage area had 23 sorties with the Forward Air Control reporting over 1000 secondary explosions. B-52's flew 15 ARC LIGHT strikes (45 sorties) on Niagara targets.

Khe Sanh was resupplied with 119 short tons during the period. A total of 19 sorties (Air Force: five C-130 air drops; 11 - C-123 airlanded) (Marines: one C-130; two CH-53 airlanded) delivered the material.

For the next 24 hours the Marine Tactical Air Sorties in support of the Khe Sanh area will total 44. The Air Force plans 202, and the Navy plans 100. ARC LIGHT planning calls for 15 strikes (45 sorties) continuing the Bugle Note Series in the Niagara area.

Regarding the weather for the period in the Khe Sanh area, the sky was mostly cloudy with ceilings near 2000 feet during the daylight hours of February 15 but lowering to 1500 feet broken after sunset, and remaining so throughout the night. For the next 24-hour period, the morning visibility will be restricted to 1 - 3 miles with

TOP SECRET

ground fog beginning about 6 AM, and will gradually improve to 7 miles by noon.; The sky will be mostly cloudy with the lower ceiling near 1000 feet, but improving to 1000 feet scattered, 2500 feet broken from 1 PM to 7 PM.

Rostow's memo to the President referring to "The most worrying thing at the moment . . ." *appears to be the paragraph beginning:* "a Forward Air Controller reported that as soon as the secondary explosions ceased, North Vietnamese troops swarmed in like ants, attempting to recover boxes of ammunition":

INFORMATION

THE WHITE HOUSE
WASHINGTON

    Friday, Feb. 16, 1968
    10:30 a.m.

MR. PRESIDENT:
Herewith Westy's morning telephone conversation.
    The most worrying thing at the moment (see pages 1 and 2 of the attached operational intelligence briefing) is the VC exploitation of the withdrawal of our forces from the countryside.

W. W. Rowstow

THE JOINT CHIEFS OF STAFF
WASHINGTON, D. C. 20301

Confidential Files on the Siege and Loss of Khe Sanh

CM-3019-68
16 February 1968

MEMORANDUM FOR THE PRESIDENT
Subject: Telephone Conversation with General Westmoreland

1. Attached hereto is a very brief biography of Colonel Davison, the negro Deputy Commander of the 199th Brigade whose performance as Acting Commander of the brigade was so highly praised by General Westmoreland yesterday. (Not included as part of this archive — Ed.)
2. In addition to General Westmoreland's twelfth report on the Khe Sanh/DMZ area, I have attached hereto an Operations/Intelligence brief which I believe you will find of interest. When I talked to General Westmoreland at 0800 hours this morning, he furnished additional information as follows:
a. Weather has been good in the Hue area, permitting air support to ground units attempting to eliminate the tenacious group of enemy ensconced in the south wall of the Citadel. The enemy has moved a considerable force, exact size still unknown, north of Hue in an apparent attempt to reinforce the enemy elements still in Hue.
b. Battalions of the US 1st Cavalry Division are in contact with them, and General Abrams is maneuvering to get more battalions deployed to defeat this force. Of interest is the fact that armed helicopters of the 1st Cavalry Division caught one company of the reinforcing enemy in

TOP SECRET

the open as they attempted to charge our forces across an open field.

c. Air operations in support of Khe Sanh continue to be heavy and successful. As mentioned to you earlier, our attack air struck with much success a POL convoy on Highway 15 near the Mu Gia Pass; additionally, strikes in the Tchepone area caused at least 1,000 secondary explosions. An ammunition depot in Laos southwest of Khe Sanh was struck heavily causing many secondary explosions;

A Forward Air Controller reported that as soon as the secondary explosions ceased, North Vietnamese troops swarmed in like ants attempting to recovery boxes of ammunition. General Momyer is continuing to bomb the area during the night, using radar control, tactical air, and, as I dictate this memorandum, a B-52 mission is ready striking this particular depot.

d. At Tay Ninh, the MACV compound and the province headquarters were attacked with mortar fire, and, apparently, enemy elements have infiltrated into the city of Tay Ninh. This force, which apparently came from Cambodia, is being dealt with by elements of the ARVN 25th Division and the US 25th Division. The strength of the enemy is at present unknown.

e. IV Corps was rather quiet yesterday although there were small contacts with enemy forces near Can Tho and My Tho.

f. Highway 4 is now open all the way from Saigon to the city of Gan Tho. The traffic on it is heavy. Dak To is still threatened by enemy elements; however, General Westmoreland considers that he has ample troops in the area. Moreover, he is scheduling B-52 strikes in the area over the next several days.

3. General Abrams is in residence at MACV Forward in the Hue/Phu Bai area in order to control combat operations in the northern portion of I Corps.

EARLE G. WHEELER
Chairman
Joint Chiefs of Staff

Saturday, February 17, 1968

TEXT OF CABLE FROM
GENERAL WESTMORELAND (MAC 02269)

This is report number thirteen on the Khe Sanh/DMZ area and covers the 24-hour period of February 16, 1968.

During the reporting period the relative hill continued in northern Quang Tri province with interruptions caused by enemy shelling. While ground contacts were minimal, the Khe Sanh combat base and neighboring areas bordering the DMZ received a total of 222 rounds of mixed mortar, artillery and rocket rounds.

Characteristic of enemy shelling, Marine elements at Khe Sanh combat base bore the heaviest concentration as 35 mortar rounds and seven rounds of rocket impacted in the area. Casualties attributed to the shelling were one killed, 10 wounded (8 evacuated).

A mid-afternoon barrage brought 40 rocket

TOP SECRET

rounds, 31 rounds of mortar and three artillery rounds to friendly elements at Camp Carroll, resulting in five wounded (two evacuated). The 2nd Battalion, 9th Marines at the rockpile counted two additional rounds of artillery in late evening. At Con Thien, the 2nd Battalion, 1st Marines was the recipient of 18 rounds of mixed caliber mortars. Eight additional rounds of mortar were received by friendly elements at C-3 causing major injuries to three Marines.

Harassment moved northeasterly as a midday artillery barrage brought 14 rounds to friendly elements positioned at Gio Linh. Fourteen additional mortar rounds were received near the Cua Viet, as positions occupied by the 1st ARMTRAC Battalion. Casualties attributed to the day's incoming were light and damage was reported minimal.

Significant contacts in northern Quang Tri centered in the DMZ with sightings of three reported enemy tanks 12 kilometers north of Con Thien. Reaction was instantaneous as friendly tanks and artillery fired several missions earmarked for their locations. Results are unknown at this time.

No COFRAM type ordnance was used during the period. There were no changes in the dispositions of friendly forces and Allied armament.

In the memo Rostow forwarded to the president, the "marked passages" included:
*Almost all of the first paragraph (except the last sentence);
*The third sentence "Bomb Damage included . . ." *and the fifth sentence:* "Bomb Damage Assessment . . .", *of the second paragraph;*
*As well as the first sentence in the following paragraph "Khe Sanh was resupplied with 191 short tons on February 16."

THE WHITE HOUSE
WASHINGTON

    Saturday, Feb. 17, 1968
    9:15 a.m.

MR. PRESIDENT:
Today's DMZ report shows (marked passages);

— light mortaring;
— 191 tons of resupply;
— Khe Sanh attack expected "within a week";
— enemy 324B division heading for Quang Tri.

W. W. Rostow

In the Khe Sanh area, the enemy still threatens with two divisions, and most evidence points to an attempted assault within a week. Friendly firepower, however, is undoubtedly hurting the enemy there and may further disrupt his timing. New instructions to the 324B Division apparently committed it to a new assault on Quang Tri and

TOP SECRET

they are moving in that direction. The 320th seems to have backed off from Camp Carroll to fill the void created by the departure of the 324B. Threat of major ground assault against Camp Carroll is apparently reduced.

Tactical Air Support for the Khe Sanh totalled 388 sorties. Marine aircraft flew 80 sorties in support of the Khe Sanh area. Bomb damage included one secondary explosion and one secondary fire. The Air Force flew 232 sorties and the Navy flew 76 (27 Navy sorties were diverted because of weather). Bomb Damage Assessment included 35 secondary explosions, eight secondary fires, and 10 mortar positions damaged. The secondary explosions and fires resulted from strikes put in against a supply area. The Forward Air Control reported yesterday that the enemy had made attempts to remove munitions and weapons from the area, however, there were still areas where supplies of weapons, munitions and rice remain. ARC LIGHT strikes for the period in the Niagara area totalled 16 strikes (44 sorties).

Khe Sanh was resupplied with 191 short tons on February 16. A total of 21 sorties were delivered, including seven air drops by C-130 aircraft. Seven Air Force C-123 aircraft landed at the airfield as did Marine helicopters.

During the next 24-hour period, the Marine Air Wing will fly 44 tactical air sorties in support of the Khe Sanh area, with 16 additional aircraft on call to run sorties as the situation indicates. The Air Force plans to run 150 sorties, and the Navy schedules 100 sorties. Total tactical air effort will be 294 sorties. The ARC LIGHT effort will total 16 strikes (48 sorties) in the Niagara area.

The weather for the period resulted in fog and stratus on both days reduced the ceiling and visibility to zero during the morning hours. The visibility improved to seven miles by noon of the 16th but was again lowered by fog after 11:00 p.m. Ceilings improved to 500-1000 feet during the afternoon and early evening hours. During the next 24-hour period, in the mornings of both days the visibility will be restricted to less than one mile by fog, but will increase to five miles or more from 12:00 Noon to 9:00 p.m. Ceilings will be 1000 feet or less except from 1:00 p.m. to 5:00 p.m.

TOP SECRET

The Westmoreland report (reference below) to General Wheeler was not a part of this archive file, but the key sentence is obvious: "the long - heralded (sic) second wave of enemy attack may start tonight; i.e., today Washington time."

THE WHITE HOUSE
WASHINGTON

Saturday, February 17, 1968 — 12:10 pm

Mr. President:
Herewith Westy's report to Bus Wheeler.

You will note that Westy now concludes that "the long-heralded second wave of enemy attack may start tonight; i.e., today Washington time."

You will note also (para 5) Westy's concern about the NEWSWEEK leak on Abrams' new headquarters. This raises the question of whether we cannot clamp down military censorship at least in I corps.

W. W. Rostow

THE WHITE HOUSE
WASHINGTON

    Monday, February 19, 1968
    10:10 a.m.

Mr. President:
In I Corps (attached):
— shelling and light ground contact;
— 160 tons delivered by air drop despite contin-

ued bad weather.

W. W. Rostow

Monday, February 19, 1968, 10:00 AM

TEXT OF CABLE FROM GENERAL WESTMORELAND

This report is number fifteen on the situation in the Khe Sanh area and covers the 24-hour period of February 18, 1968.

Activity in the northern First Corps continued to focus on enemy shelling: as 175 rounds of mixed mortar and artillery rounds were distributed among friendly elements bordering the DMZ. Forty rounds of mortar and 35 rounds of artillery impacted at Khe Sanh Combat Base in positions occupied by the 26th Marines, which resulted in one Marine wounded.

Marines positioned at Camp Carroll, received a mid-day barrage of 42 rounds of mortar with two intermediate rounds of artillery. Friendly casualties were: one killed, nine wounded (four evacuated).

Three small craters were caused at C-2 outside Con Thien, as three rounds of mortar were aimed at friendly elements. Marine elements at Con Thien and Gio Linh received 33 and8 rounds respectively, none of which inflicted casualties nor caused significant damage.

Ground contacts in northern Quang Tri were limited to two light skirmishes, both inflicting moderate enemy losses while causing only minor

TOP SECRET

injuries to friendly elements. Five North Vietnamese Army were killed at the hands of a 37th ARVN Ranger Patrol east of Khe Sanh, in an early morning contact which inflicted no friendly casualties.

There were a total of 358 tactical air sorties flown in the Khe Sanh area during the period. Marine tactical air flew 78 sorties, reporting four secondary explosions and one secondary fire. The Air Force flew 215 sorties, and the Navy flew 65. The weather was workable only for combat sky spot strikes, with a few isolated attempts to put in visual strikes. Bomb Damage Assessment was correspondingly bad. There were 12 ARC Light strikes (35 sorties) flown in the Niagara area. For the next period, 19 - 20 February, 354 tactical air sorties will be flown in the Khe Sanh and surrounding areas. The Marines will fly 44, the Air Force 210, and the Navy 150. There will be 15 ARC LIGHT strikes (45 sorties) flown in the Niagara area. Air resupply for the reporting period amounted to 160 short tons of which 133 short tons was ammunition.

No COFRAM type ordnance was used during the period.

Weather at Khe Sanh during the period was bad. Low clouds and dense fog reduced the ceiling and visibility to less than 500 feet and one mile throughout the period. Most of the time the ceiling and visibility were near zero. Little change is expected on 19 - 20 February. The sky will be obscured by low stratus clouds and fog. Ceilings and visibilities will be near zero except for a slight improvement to a ceiling of 400 feet and visibility of 1/2 mile from 2 PM to 6 PM on 20 February.

THE JOINT CHIEFS OF STAFF
WASHINGTON, D. C. 20301

CM-2980-68
19 Feb 1968

MEMORANDUM FOR THE PRESIDENT
SUBJ: TELEPHONE CONVERSATION WITH GENERAL WESTMORELAND

1. You will have received General Westmoreland's 15th report on the situation in the Khe Sanh/DMZ area. Attached hereto is an operations/intelligence summary of events of the past two days. I have also attached a copy of the trip report of General Bruce C. Clarke, U.S. Army (Retired) giving his impressions during his recent trip to South Vietnam. General Clarke was accompanied by Mr. Frank W. Mayborn of Temple, Texas whom I am sure you know.

2. Due to communications difficulties between Washington and Hawaii my telephone conversation with General Westmoreland was not possible until 0830 hours. He provided the following information:

a. Yesterday an OP-2E aircraft with a crew of 9 was shot down in the MUSCLE SHOALS area while laying sensors.

b. The ground control approach equipment was knocked out at Khe Sanh yesterday; there is a backup set available and it is being installed.

TOP SECRET

c. Light contact continues with the enemy in the vicinity of Dalat.

d. The stickiest situation at present is at Phan Thiet. The enemy force which penetrated the town, seized the jail and the hospital, still occupies about one-third of the town. It continues to hold the hospital area and occupied bunkers outside of town. Despite the fact the force has lost 103 men killed, the going to clear the town is tough and proceeding slowly.

e. There continue to be contacts with the enemy north of Saigon and south of Saigon. In a heavy contact south of Saigon Vietnamese Marine Corps units killed 144 enemy:

f. North of Tay Ninh City an enemy force apparently preparing rocket positions was discovered and attacked, resulting in 60 enemy KIA.

g. Certain new units of the enemy have been identified near Song Be. These appear to be groups of replacement which have been formed into combat units to continue enemy pressure in the Song Be area.

h. The enemy has been driven out of Vinh Long. There was some damage to the Cathedral in the town and 58 enemy were killed.

i. The Riverine force had a contact with the enemy south of Can Tho. Results are not yet known.

3. He anticipates that there may be additional enemy activity in the Khe Sanh area tonight; however, this is not positive information.

4. The additional battalion of the First Cavalry Division which I reported yesterday as moving to the Quang Tri area began closing into Quang

Tri today.

5. As a general observation, General Westmoreland stated that the enemy continues to hang in close to the cities. The enemy is apparently attempting to resupply his forces and bring up replacements and reinforcements.

EARLE G. WHEELER
Chairman
Joint Chiefs of Staff

TOP SECRET

The NMCC (National Military Command Center) report referred to in the next memo from Rostow to Lyndon Johnson is also not a part of this archive file...

THE WHITE HOUSE
WASHINGTON

>Tuesday, February 20, 1968
>10:55 a.m.

Mr. President:
   The first two pages are Bus Wheeler's report of his morning conversation with Westmoreland. I have marked the key elements.
   Attached is a full length NMCC (National Military Command Center) report which you saw early this morning in summary form.

W. W. Rostow

THE JOINT CHIEFS OF STAFF
WASHINGTON, D. C. 20301

>CM-3031-68
>20 Feb 1968

MEMORANDUM FOR THE PRESIDENT
SUBJECT: TELEPHONE CONVERSATION WITH GENERAL WESTMORELAND

1. You have already received General Westmoreland's 16th report on the situation in the Khe Sanh/DMZ area. In addition, I am attach-

ing hereto the Presidential operational/intelligence brief (you may have already seen this but I wish to make sure that it comes to your personal attention). Moreover, I am attaching a sheet setting forth two or three late items of interest.

2. I talked to General Westmoreland at 0810 hours this morning. He made the following comments:

a. After talking to General Vien and analyzing information from intelligence reports, he has called a full alert tonight in the Saigon area, and he is particularly arranging to defend the Tan Son Nhut airbase. There is a reported increased threat north of Saigon with fresh elements of the NVA and 9th VC Divisions moving into the area. It is also reported that villagers are fleeing to get out of the way of their advance. Among other precautionary measures, General Westmoreland has organized a provisional defense battalion from the MACV Staff.

b. A few rocket rounds were fired in the direction of Tan Son Nhut today; one fell on the runway; one landed in an open field, and one apparently went into the city. He now has complete aerial photographic reconnaissance of the rocket site area and the photo interpreters have picked up several suspected rocket sites for attack by air.

c. A new rocket round was found north of Saigon today; it is a 170 mm round in diameter and has a range of about 9,000 meters.

d. In general, the enemy is hanging in close to Saigon and gives no indication of withdrawal.

e. The Song Be situation has cleared up; the

TOP SECRET

enemy has been driven out of the town.

f. The city of Phan Thiet has been cleared of the enemy after a hard fight.

g. The enemy has been cleared out of Vinh Long, but there seems to be a buildup commencing south of Can Tho by a new enemy battalion of picked-up troops.

3. He conferred with General Vien today. The latter is concerned about the fatigue factor on the ARVN. They have been fighting continuously now for over two weeks. He has been trying to push the ARVN out into the country, but this is difficult to do when the enemy continues to stay in close to the populated areas.

4. Enemy KIA now stands at over 38,000. General Westmoreland recognizes that some of them are undoubtedly porters and other support elements. He has charged his J-2 with trying to get a break out of the enemy casualties so that he will be able to estimate the effect of enemy losses on his combat elements.

5. As a general observation, after visiting all of the Corps Areas and senior commanders, if General Westmoreland had to make an estimate now as to further troop reinforcements he will need, he will probably require the remainder of the 82d Airborne Division. He is not asking for it at this time because he believes that he will have a better feel for the problems facing him when I visit whim within the next couple of days.

EARLE G. WHEELER
Chairman
Joint Chiefs of Staff

Confidential Files on the Siege and Loss of Khe Sanh

THE WHITE HOUSE
WASHINGTON

   Wednesday, February 21, 1968
   8:55 a.m.

Mr. President:
Another quiet day at Khe Sanh/DMZ;
— mortar fire less;
— 143 tons delivered;
—weather continues poor.

W. W. Rostow

Wednesday, February 21, 1969

TEXT OF CABLE FROM
   GENERAL WESTMORELAND

This is report number seventeen on the situation in the Khe Sanh/DMZ area and covers the 24-hour period of February 20, 1968.

A small unit encounter and intermittent enemy shelling constituted the principal activity in northern First Corps yesterday. The pace of enemy incoming fire slackened somewhat during the period. Incoming to friendly forces bordering the DMZ totaled 124 rounds of mixed caliber mortar and artillery.

A marked decline in enemy efforts were evident yesterday as only 69 rounds of mortar fell at Khe Sanh. Five kilometers east of Ca Lu, the Marines received six rounds of mortar and an equal amount of artillery rounds. The ramp at

TOP SECRET

Dong Ha received six mid-afternoon rounds of artillery, causing minor injuries to two Marines. Elements of the Marines at Camp Carroll bore 13 enemy rounds of mortar; and finally Marines, at Con Thien received 28 rounds of mortar in an early morning barrage. Casualties attributed to the shelling: 10 Marines wounded (five evacuated).

In ground contact during the day, a contact at Thon Le Xuyen confirmed nine North Vietnamese Army killed and captured seven POW's, two recoilless guns, one mortar and nine individual weapons. Casualties to friendly forces were: three killed, eight wounded (evacuated).

There were a total of 296 tactical air sorties flown. The Marine aircraft wing flew 64 sorties in support of the Khe Sanh area. Bomb Damage Assessment included three secondary explosions, two secondary fires. The Air Force flew 146 and the Navy flew 86. The weather was still unsuitable for any but combat sky spot missions.

Thirty-nine B-52's flew 13 strikes in the Niagara area.

Aerial resupply for the reporting period amounted to 143 short tons. In addition, 90 passengers were flown into the airfield in three C-123 aircraft. Eleven C-130 completed 11 airdrops.

There was one COFRAM mission of 15 rounds fired on the basis of a sensor report of enemy troop movement. Results were observed.

For the next 24-hour period, the Marines will fly 44 tactical air sorties in support of Khe Sanh, the Air Force will fly 148, and the Navy plans 100, for a total of 292 sorties. There will be nine

ARC LIGHT strikes (27 sorties) flown in the Niagara area.

Weather at Khe Sanh during the period produced low clouds and dense fog and reduced the ceiling and visibility to near zero except from 2:00 PM to 4:00 AM when the ceiling improved to 100 - 500 foot overcast and the visibility from 1/4 to five miles in fog. The forecast for Khe Sanh for the next 24 hours is for little change.

THE WHITE HOUSE
WASHINGTON

>Wednesday, February 21, 1968
>10:55 a.m.

Mr. President:
Herewith Bus Wheeler's report on today's call to Westy.
Main item: firepower now allocated to try to clean up Hue by the end of this week.
Gen. Johnson will report the daily phone call in Bus' absence.

W. W. Rostow

THE JOINT CHIEFS OF STAFF
WASHINGTON, D. C. 20301

>CM-3032-68
>21 Feb 1968

MEMORANDUM FOR THE PRESIDENT

TOP SECRET

SUBJECT: TELEPHONE CONVERSATION WITH GENERAL WESTMORELAND

1. You will have already received General Westmoreland's 17th report on the situation in the Khe Sanh/DMZ area. Additionally, I am attaching hereto a copy of the Presidential operations/intelligence brief of salient activities over the past twenty-four hours, together with a sheet of recent items which you will find of interest.

2. General Westmoreland reported that the situation was generally quiet and that he had little of significance to add to what is in the operational/intelligence brief. He made really only two points:

a. General Abrams, located at Headquarters MACV Forward in the Hue/Phu Bai area, conferred today with General Cushman, over-all Marine Commander; General Lam, the Vietnamese I Corps Tactical Zone Commander; and General Tolson, Commander of the U. S. First Cavalry Division. The subject of their conference was the situation in Hue and how best to deal with it. General Westmoreland has agreed to send one troop of U.S. armored cavalry (units such as this are equipped with medium tanks) to Hue tomorrow to provide additional armored firepower to friendly forces operating against a heavily dug-in enemy. Moreover, he is providing an additional ten 106mm recoilless rifles to the Vietnamese Marine Corps battalions which are fighting in the Citadel in order to give them more mobile destructive power against enemy bunkers. He thinks that with the added firepower Hue can be cleaned out by the end of this week.

b. Another new weapon, a 107 mm rocket made by the CHICOMS has been picked up in-country. He describes the projectile as being about 42 inches long and weighing 40 odd pounds; no launcher has yet been captured. The technical intelligence people estimate that this weapon would have a range of between 8,000 to 9,000 meters. Samples of this weapon will be provided to technical intelligence agencies in the United States for further evaluation.

3. General Westmoreland has arranged for me to see President Thieu, Vice President Ky, and General Vien during my stay in Vietnam. Ambassador Bunker has also made arrangements for me to confer with him and key members of the mission staff.

4. During my absence General Johnson, Chief of Staff, U.S. Army, will talk by telephone to General Westmoreland each morning to provide you with the updates of the situation. I shall, of course, communicate with you and the secretary of Defense promptly any significant items which cannot await my return next week.

EARL G. WHEELER
Chairman
Joint Chiefs of Staff

FROM WHITE HOUSE SITUATION ROOM
   (MCCAFFERTY)
TO THE PRESIDENT
CITE CAP50474

TOP SECRET

SECRET EYES ONLY

TEXT OF CABLE FROM
GENERAL WESTMORELAND

This is report number eighteen on the situation in Khe Sanh area and covers the 24-hour period February 21, 1968.

Enemy efforts intensified in northern Quang Tri Province yesterday as 690 enemy rounds of mixed mortar, artillery and rocket fell on friendly positions. Enemy concentrations centered at Khe Sanh as friendly elements received 250 mortar rounds, 50 rounds of artillery and 70 rocket rounds, causing minor injuries to 22 Marines. One rocket round impacted on the airstrip temporarily closing the facility to C-130 traffic. The airstrip is now open to all normal traffic.

At Camp Carroll, elements of the 4th and 9th Marines, from 3:00PM to 5:50PM, were recipients of 15 rounds of rocket, 33 rounds of mortar, 38 rounds of artillery, with one rocket round landing on the 3d battalion, 4th Marines, five kilometers east of Ca Lu. Casualties were recorded as 13 wounded in action (nine evacuated).

Five noontime rounds of artillery fell at Dong Ha combat base, with three additional mortar rounds falling at dusk. Heavy mid-day barrages fell on Con Thien as enemy launching positions delivered 55 rounds of artillery and 48 rounds of mortar. Three Marines were wounded from the shelling with one evacuated. In neighboring Gio Linh, 17 additional artillery rounds impacted on friendly positions. Finally, a 24 hour lull in enemy shelling at the Cua Viet was ended as positions occupied by 1st Amtrac battalion bore 64 rounds of rockets and 45 rounds of artillery, with casualties attributed to the day's bombardment included four killed in action, eight wounded in action (two evacuated).

Ground activity in northern Quang Trio Province was limited to an estimated company size probe at Khe Sanh. By dark activity had ceased. Results are undetermined.

A total of 284 tactical air sorties were flown in support of the Khe Sanh area. The Marine aircraft wing flew 82 sorties. Bomb damage assessment included four secondary explosions, one secondary fire. The Air Force flew 138 sorties, and the Navy flew 64 sorties. Weather difficulties required use of combat sky spot. B-52's flew five strikes (15 sorties) in the Niagara area.

Aerial resupply for the reporting period amounted to 172 short tons. In addition, 71 passengers were landed at the Khe Sanh airfield. A total of 17 sorties were flown by resupply aircraft. Fourteen C-130 aircraft made ten air drops. A single C-123 and two helicopters landed.

Seven rounds of COFRAM ordnance was expended resulting in four enemy killed.

Sixteen B-52 strikes (48 sorties) will be flown in the Niagara area for the next 24-hour period. There will be 292 tactical air sorties flown during the same period.

The weather at Khe Sanh during the period again consisted of low clouds and dense ground fog reducing the cloud ceiling and surface visibility to near zero. During the early afternoon

TOP SECRET

hours the ceiling improved slightly to 400 - 1000 feet broken and the visibility to three miles in fog. The forecast for Khe Sanh for tomorrow is more encouraging. The cloud ceiling and surface visibility will gradually improve from near zero conditions to a 2000 foot ceiling and six miles visibility by 2:00PM. After 5:00PM the ceiling and visibility will gradually lower to near zero and remain so throughout the remainder of the period.

SECRET EYES ONLY

Confidential Files on the Siege and Loss of Khe Sanh

The following reports speak for themselves . . . .

FROM WALT ROWSTOW
TO THE PRESIDENT
CITE CAP50481

TOP SECRET

Herewith General Johnson's report on his morning conversation with Westy.

General Westmoreland had just completed a call to General Abrams at MACV Forward located at Hue/Phu Bai. General Abrams stated to General Westmoreland that for the first time he, General Abrams, was permitting himself to be somewhat encouraged. We had visited the Americal division and the 2D ARVN division on 22 February as well as the elements of the 3d Brigade, 82 Airborne Division, that have arrived at Chu Lai. The brigade has not yet completed its move. Both the Americal and the 2D ARVN Division are performing effectively and are stepping up operations away from the populated areas once again. General Abrams also reported that the experience level in the 3D Brigade, 82D Airborne Division was very high; that their attitude was excellent; and they were encouraged by the reception given them by General Koster of the Americal division. It is General Westmoreland's intention to ease the brigade into combat operations slowly so that teamwork training within the brigade can be refreshed fully.

The three Vietnamese Marine battalions in Hue have made slow progress because of a lack

TOP SECRET

of direct-fire high velocity weapons. Ten 106 mm recoilless rifles arrived in Hue/Phu Bai on 22 February and will be delivered to the Vietnamese Marines on 23 February to correct this deficiency. In addition, Brigadier General Oscar Davis, assistant division commander of the First Cavalry Division, is located at the First Division command post with General Truong, the first ARVN division commander. General Davis is acting as fire coordinator for General Truong, and General Westmoreland indicated that this arrangement is working well.

The First Cavalry Division has encountered four enemy battalions north and east of Hue and is in heavy contact with these units. The division commander reported some success but has not reported any details. Further, two 8 inch howitzers have arrived near Quang Tri to reinforce the First Cavalry Division and an additional two are expected to be in position tomorrow (23 February) at the same location. The First Cavalry Division captured 12 prisoners. Initial reports indicate that three different enemy regiments are represented by the 12 prisoners. General Westmoreland does not know what this means, but he expects to obtain significant information from interrogation that will be exploitable in terms of identifying some indication of enemy intention.

General Westmoreland expressed the view that Hue may have been the enemy's primary objective from the outset of the Tet offensive. Reports indicate an enemy effort to reinforce Hue through the A Shau Valley and he is watching the

A Shau Valley very carefully.

There was little activity in the II Corps area.

There was contact early 22 February about 3 kilometers west of Saigon with the enemy repulsed and dispersed. North of Saigon in southern Binh Duong Province the reconnaissance company of the 5th ARVN division engaged an enemy force killing 20 enemy while losing only one killed. Southeast of Saigon in the Rung Sat special zone an enemy force overran a local police station killing 7 and seizing a small number of weapons, the exact number not specified.

On the afternoon of 22 February at Cat Lai, anti-tank rockets were used by the enemy to strike several ammunition barges. Two barges exploded and two barges were beached. Demolition experts are in control in the area and are assessing damage. Small enemy detachments are interdicting roads around Saigon using the RPG-2 or B-40 rocket and RPG-7 or B-41 rocket with some effectiveness against vehicles. As we were talking General Westmoreland reported ARVN contact with two enemy battalions east of Tan Son Nhut with the Spooky gun ship with mini-guns firing on this force. Initial reports indicate 1 VC main force battalion and 1 VC local force battalion. The size of the enemy force is tentative and specific unit identifications have not been made.

General Westmoreland reports that since the Tet offensive began on 29 January, 39,417 enemy have been reported killed in action and 6,590 individuals have been detained.

TOP SECRET

TOP SECRET

THE JOINT CHIEFS OF STAFF
WASHINGTON, D. C. 20301

MEMORANDUM FOR THE PRESIDENT
SUBJECT: TELEPHONE CONVERSATION WITH GENERAL WESTMORELAND

1. General Westmoreland reported quite a bit of shelling at Khe Sanh and in the DMZ area. Other intelligence reports cover the scale. The helicopter reported hit by mortar fire at Khe Sanh may have been hit by a rocket according to information that General Abrams passed to General Westmoreland. An attack on Khe Sanh is expected during the night of 23-24 February, Saigon time. The Vietnamese Ranger Battalion holding a part of the perimeter at Khe Sanh was probed by a force estimated to be a possible enemy battalion. The probing force used fire crackers, but initial reports indicate the probe was not successful.
2. U.S. Marines continued to clear the area of the Citadel in Hue for which they are responsible. The Vietnamese Marines have been less active than desirable. Recoilless rifles discussed in yesterday's telephone call were delivered to Vietnamese Marines on 23 February. More aggressive attacks by this force are expected on 24 February. Security forces on Highway 1, between Da Nang and Hue-Phu Bai continued to be thickened. One battalion of the 82d Airborne Division Task Force moved from Chu Lai and closed at Hue-Phu Bai just southeast of Hue.

3. Throughout the rest of South Vietnam the tempo of activity decreased. There were no reports of activity in II Corps. Contact continues with enemy forces west, north and east of Saigon. General Weyand reported to General Wheeler that forces in III Corps are killing about 300 enemy a day. There is some indication that enemy forces have been directed to break up into smaller units in the Saigon area and to focus their efforts on disrupting normal activity to the maximum extent of their capability. This indication has not been confirmed.

4. In IV Corps there is a mixed picture. General Eckhardt reported to General Wheeler that the main road from Saigon to the south should be opened to Cau Mau in the southernmost province of the Delta by the night of 24 February. He expects interruptions to occur during hours of darkness but expects to be able to restore traffic during daylight hours.

TOP SECRET

5. The damage to regional and popular forces appears to be small in III Corps. Reports are not yet complete. There is a mixed picture in IV Corps. Some regional forces have been hard hit. Reports indicate that approximately 500 popular forces are still missing, although General Westmoreland does not believe that this is an alarming number because it is a relatively small proportion of the total popular forces in IV Corps.

6. Special B-52 strikes were directed at a reported location of the Headquarters, 7th NVA

TOP SECRET

Division, approximately 10 kilometers south of Phuoc Vinh. Initial assessment indicated some underground complexes have been opened up, and there were numerous secondary explosions. Additional bomb damage assessment will be made. General Westmoreland had intended to direct an intensive bombing by the B-52s of enemy concentrations in the A Shau Valley. He has delayed these strikes in favor of shifting the B-52 effort to the Khe Sanh area because of the reported imminence of enemy attack on Khe Sanh.

7. General Westmoreland reported the latest casualty figures accrued since 29 January 1968: KIA 40,199; detained 6,671; individual weapons captured 9,853; and crew-served weapons captured 1,482. General Westmoreland went on to explain that he believes the casualty count is a reasonable one, although it probably includes porters and laborers assisting enemy forces. Any inflation of reported casualties caused by the inclusion of porters and laborers is offset by casualties resulting from artillery and air strikes that are not included in the reports of enemy casualties.

8. I also talked briefly to General Palmer who believes that the situation throughout southern Vietnam is stabilizing somewhat, although obviously not yet back to normal.

HAROLD K. JOHNSON
ACTING CHAIRMAN
JOINT CHIEFS OF STAFF

SECRET

    Received Washington CommCen
    9:59 A.M. EST Friday 23 Feb 68

    Received LBJ Ranch CommCen
    10:05 A.M. CST Friday 23 Feb 68

FROM WHITE HOUSE SITUATION ROOM
   (MCCAFFERTY)
TO THE PRESIDENT
CITE CAP80511

SECRET

TEXT OF CABLE FROM
   GENERAL WESTMORELAND.

This is report number nineteen on the situation in the Khe Sanh area and covers the 24 hour period February 22, 1968.
   Significant activity in northern Quang Tri Province yesterday paralleled the previous day, as heavy enemy shelling pounded positions occupied by friendly troops. The day's total climbed to 935 rounds of enemy artillery, mortar and rocket fire. Repetitious of recent weeks, the Khe Sanh combat base received the brunt of the incoming as the 26th Marines bore 170 rounds of mortar, 155 rounds of artillery and 52 rocket rounds casualties attributed to the shelling were seven killed, 22 wounded: (18 evacuated).
   While Camp Carroll received only 29 rounds of mixed mortar and artillery, friendly elements

TOP SECRET

at Dong Ha counted 81 rounds of heavy artillery. At the DMZ, four mid-afternoon barrages brought 193 rounds of mixed mortar and artillery to Con Thien. Two Marines required medical evacuation due to wounds sustained from the barrage. At neighboring Gio Linh, the receipt of 125 artillery rounds has linked with eight late morning rocket rounds. Incoming rounds at Cua Viet ceased at 10:00 A.M. but only after 86 artillery rounds had been received by 1st Amtrack battalion positions. Casualties from the shelling were: one killed, 12 wounded (nine evacuated).

In ground activity, only one contact was reported. Marines in operation Kentucky, ambushed a small enemy force and killed five NVA. One Marine was killed and nine wounded in the encounter.

At 4:45 P.M. a helicopter, while attempting to lift off at Khe Sanh, was hit by a mortar round causing the aircraft to crash. Resulting casualties were two killed, one wounded (evacuated).

241 tactical air sorties were flown in the Khe Sanh area. The Marine aircraft wing flew 87 sorties. Bomb damage assessment included one secondary fire, one mortar position destroyed and three killed. The air force flew 132 sorties, the Navy flew 22, using combat sky spot. ARC LIGHT B-52's flew 14 strikes (40 sorties) in the Niagara area.

Aerial resupply for the reporting period amounted to 183.5 short tons. There were 82 short tons of Class V, ammunition. Nineteen short tons of vehicles, consisting of forklifts. Mail and medical supplies amounted to 1.5 and 4 short tons respectively. In addition, 76 replacement passengers were landed at the airfield. Sorties increased to a total of 26. Eleven C-130 aircraft completed 11 air drops. Two C-130's and one USAF C-123 aircraft landed on the airfield. In addition, resupply sorties by Marine helicopters were flown.

There were two missions fired during the period using firecracker. Twelve rounds were fired on enemy troops in the open with undetermined results. Another six rounds were expended in close defensive fires.

For the next 24 hours a total of 288 tactical air sorties will be flown in support of the Khe Sanh. There will be eight ARC LIGHT strikes (24 sortie) flown in the Niagara area.

The weather at Khe Sanh during the period remained bad. Low clouds and dense ground fog reduced the ceiling and visibility to near zero during most of the period. Conditions improved somewhat during the afternoon when the cloud ceiling and visibility became 1500 foot broken and seven miles. The forecast for today calls for gradual improvement from near zero conditions to a 1200 foot ceiling and six miles visibility by 1:00 P.M. after 6:00 P.M. The cloud ceiling and visibility will both lower to near-zero and remain so throughout the remainder of the period.

DTG 231459Z FEB 68
SECRET

TOP SECRET

TOP SECRET

Received Washington CommCen
11:21 A.M. EST Friday 23 Feb 68

Received LBJ Ranch CommCen
11:40 A.M. CST Friday 23 Feb 68

FROM WALT ROSTOW
TO THE PRESIDENT
CITE CAP50513

TOP SECRET

Herewith General Johnson's telephone conversation with General Westmoreland.
1. General Westmoreland reported quite a bit of shelling at Khe Sanh and in the DMZ area. Other intelligence reports over the scale, the helicopter reported hit by mortar fire at Khe Sanh may have been hit by a rocket according to information that General Abrams passed to General Westmoreland. An attack on Khe Sanh is expected during the night of 23-24 February, Saigon time. The Vietnamese Ranger battalion holding a part of the perimeter at Khe Sanh was probed by a force estimated to be a possible enemy battalion. The probing force used fire crackers, but initial reports indicate the probe was not successful.
2. U.S. Marines continued to clear the area of the Citadel in Hue for which they are responsible. The Vietnamese Marines have been less active than desirable. Recoilless rifles discussed in yesterday's telephone call were delivered to Vietnamese Marines on 23 February. More aggressive attacks by this force are expected on 24 February.

Security forces on Highway 1, between Da Nang and Hue-Phu Bai continued to be thickened. One battalion of the 82d Airborne Division task force moved from Chu Lai and closed at Hue-Phu Bai just south east of Hue.

3. Throughout the rest of South Vietnam the tempo of activity decreased. There were no reports of activity in II Corps. Contact continues with enemy forces west, north and east of Saigon. General Weyand reported to General wheeler that forces in III Corps are killing about 300 enemy a day. There is some indication that enemy forces have been directed to break up into smaller units in the Saigon area and to focus their efforts on disrupting normal activity to the maximum extent of their capability. This indication has not been confirmed.

4. In IV Corps there is a mixed picture. General Eckhardt reported to General Wheeler that the main road from Saigon to the south should be opened to Cau Mau in the southernmost province of the Delta by the night of 24 February. He expects interruptions to occur during hours of darkness but expects to be able to restore traffic during daylight hours.

5. The damage to regional and popular forces appears to be small in III Corps. Reports are not yet complete. There is a mixed picture in IV Corps. Some regional forces have been hard hit. Reports indicate that approximately 500 popular forces are still missing, although General Westmoreland does not believe that this is an alarming number because it is a relatively small proportion of the total popular forces in IV Corps.

TOP SECRET

6. Special B-52 strikes were directed at a reported location of the headquarters, 7th NVA Division, approximately 10 kilometers south of Phuoc Vinh. Initial assessment indicated some underground complexes have been opened up, and there were numerous secondary explosions. Additional bomb damage assessment will be made. General Westmoreland had intended to direct an intensive bombing by the B-52s of enemy concentrations in the A Shau Valley. He has delayed these strikes in favor of shifting the B-52 effort to the Khe Sanh area because of the reported imminence of enemy attack on Khe Sanh.

7. General Westmoreland reported the latest casualty figures accrued since 29 January 1968: KIA 40,199; detained 6,671; individual weapons captured 9,853; and crew-served weapons captured 1,482. General Westmoreland went on to explain that he believes the casualty count is a reasonable one, although it probably includes porters and laborers assisting enemy forces. Any inflation of reported casualties caused by the inclusion of porters and laborers is offset by casualties resulting from artillery and air strikes that are not included in the reports of enemy casualties.

8. I also talked briefly to General Palmer who believes that the situation throughout southern Vietnam is stabilizing somewhat, although obviously not yet back to normal.

DTG: 231621Z FEB 68

TOP SECRET

Confidential Files on the Siege and Loss of Khe Sanh

TOP SECRET

THE JOINT CHIEFS OF STAFF
WASHINGTON, D. C. 30301

CM-3051-68
24 FEB 1968

Subject: Telephone Conversation with General Westmoreland and General Abrams

1. General Westmoreland's daily cable reports on activity at Khe Sanh and in the DMZ area. Following heavy artillery, mortar and rocket fire at Khe Sanh on the afternoon and evening of 23 February, reports for 24 February indicate only light and sporadic fire at Khe Sanh.
2. Vietnamese forces have captured the Palace inside the Citadel and the VC flag that was flying over the Palace is now in the First ARVN Division Command Post. Friendly forces hold all of Hue except a quarter circle 500 meters in radius at the southwest corner of the Citadel wall. General Westmoreland commented that it appeared that enemy resistance was crumbling. President Thieu plans to visit Hue on 25 February, although General Westmoreland indicated that the weather forecast is such that President Thieu may not be able to land. General Abrams reports a number of gallant actions by the First ARVN Division starting with attack on Citadel west wall at 0200 hours on 24 February and culminating in seizure of the Palace after daylight. The responsible company commander was promoted to Captain on the

TOP SECRET

spot by the Vietnamese Division Commander. The remaining enemy-held area is tightly encircled. Enemy withdrawal is expected.

3. There was little activity in the II Corps Area.

4. In III Corps Area the major activity was the rocket attack on Tan Son Nhut and the area around Tan Son Nhut. One round landed not far from the house where General Wheeler was spending the night. General Wheeler and General Westmoreland are spending the night of 24-25 February in General Westmoreland's Headquarters.

5. In IV Corps Area 19 separate operations throughout the Corps Area resulted in 109 enemy killed at a cost of 30 Vietnamese killed. Two battalions of the U.S. Riverine Force swept an island in the river immediately north of Can Tho and Binh Tuy airfield and picked up a number of Viet Cong suspects. This island has been a source of fire against river patrol craft and has constituted a long-time nuisance. Highway 4 was open from Saigon to Bac Lieu on 24 February.

6. I questioned General Westmoreland concerning intelligence reports that indicate an early attack on Da Nang. General Westmoreland indicated that he and General Wheeler visited Da Nang on 24 February and that the threat of ground attack on Da Nang does not appear to be significant. I also questioned him about the movement of substantial enemy forces from the north into the Saigon area. He believes that the three divisions reported in the area have suffered substantial casualties in earlier contacts and that the forces guarding Saigon can handle the situation. General

Westmoreland has the capability to reinforce Saigon promptly.

7. Following the visit to Da Nang, General Wheeler and General Westmoreland met with President Thieu, Vice President Ky and General Vien. Topics discussed were not reviewed by General Westmoreland, but he indicated a wide-ranging, useful and realistic exchange of views.

8. General Westmoreland is endeavoring to divert some B-52 strikes into the A Shau Valley where he reports that 30 ground targets exist that constitute what he considers to be an alternate logistics complex built up to support the attack on Hue. Diversions of B-52 strikes will not be at the expense of a continued pounding around Khe Sanh. In addition, intelligence teams will be inserted in and near A Shau Valley as weather permits; unfavorable weather has prevented attempts made during this past week.

HAROLD K. JOHNSON
ACTING CHAIRMAN
JOINT CHIEFS OF STAFF

TOP SECRET

Virtually every paragraph in this February 24, 1968 report to President Lyndon Johnson is crucial . . .

SECRET

>Received Washington CommCen
>9:10 A.M. EST Saturday 24 Feb 68
>
>Received LBJ Ranch CommCen
>10:00 A.M. CST Saturday 24 Feb 68

FROM WALT ROSTOW
TO THE PRESIDENT
CITE CAP80537

SECRET

FEBRUARY 24, 1968

Today's Khe Sanh report:
— 1500 rounds of mortar and artillery fire;
— small probing ground contacts;
— 165 tons delivered;
— bad weather continues;
— nevertheless, considerable air support and some secondary explosions.
Additional late item: intelligence indicates the enemy's major artillery regiment has moved up close to the base near Khe Sanh town.

Text of cable from General Westmoreland
    This is report number twenty on the situation in the Khe Sanh/DMZ area and covers the 24-

hour period February 23, 1968.

Friendly elements bordering in the DMZ experienced an accelerated enemy thrust yesterday as enemy firing was in excess of 1500 rounds of mixed mortar and artillery, earmarked for friendly held installations. Khe Sanh combat base, the preferred enemy target, bore over 85 percent of these enemy explosives as 1000 rounds of artillery, and 300 rounds of mortar impacted in the vicinity. Casualties were: 10 killed in action, 51 wounded in action (21 evacuated). Incident to the bombardment was a fire in an ammunition supply dump, as 1000 high explosive rounds, 120 canister rounds both 90MM and 500 beehive rounds 106MM were destroyed. Resupply is scheduled for tomorrow. Counter battery was fired on suspected enemy firing positions resulting in one large secondary explosion.

Few areas went untouched in northern Quant Tri Province during the reporting period. Camp Carroll received 23 rounds of mortar; 26 artillery rounds impacted at Dong Ha. Four Marines required evacuation at Camp Carroll; two Marines were slightly wounded at Dong Ha. At Con Thien, four afternoon enemy barrages brought 65 rounds of heavy artillery atop positions held by the Marines. An artillery bombardment fell in the saline (one line garbled) area as elements from the 1st Marines counted 61 rounds, which inflicted minor wounds on one Marine. Finally, enemy attention continued to focus at Cua Viet as the 1st Amtrac received 18 rounds of artillery.

In Ground action yesterday, an ARVN Ranger

TOP SECRET

battalion made contact with an estimated enemy battalion at Khe Sanh, 200-400 meters from the perimeter. Friendly artillery was fired in support. Casualties are unreported. Also, in a small contact against a small enemy force, a Marine company succeeded in killing 7 NVA, while sustaining one friendly fatality.

Thirty rounds of 105MM COFRAM ordnance were employed in one mission in support of the ARVN Ranger battalion in the vicinity of the Khe Sanh combat base on a suspected NVA battalion, with undetermined results.

A total 351 tactical sorties were flown during the period in support of Khe Sanh. Marine aircraft flew 68 sorties. Bomb damage assessment included three secondary explosions, two secondary fires, and six bunkers destroyed. The Air Force flew 199 sorties and the Navy flew 84 sorties. Weather again necessitated the majority of missions being combat sky spot. Bomb damage assessment from visual strikes included six secondary explosions, seven secondary fires, nine road outs, two rocket positions destroyed, and five trucks and four bunkers destroyed. There were 14 B-52 strikes (45 sorties) flown in the Niagara area.

Aerial resupply to the Khe Sanh for the period amounted to 165 short tons. Medical supplies amounted to one short tone. In addition 17 replacement passengers were landed at the air field. Resupply sorties totaled 15 on 23 Feb. Ten C130 aircraft completed 10 airdrops. Three C123 aircraft landed at the airfield as did 2 Marine helicopters.

For the next period 288 tactical air sorties will be flown in support of Khe Sanh. There will be seven ARC LIGHT strikes (42 sorties) flown in the Niagara area.

Throughout the period, the weather at Khe Sanh was poor, with low stratus clouds reducing the ceiling to 100 to 1000 foot broken and dense ground for lowering surface visibility to 1/16 to 5 miles.

The forecast for today is for cloud ceilings and surface visibilities near zero except from 1000 AM to 6:00 PM when the ceiling will raise to 500 foot broken and the visibility to 1 mile in ground fog and drizzle.

DTG 241410Z FEB 68

SECRET

TOP SECRET

There is almost a lyrical or literary quality to the first paragraph "IN THE PAST TWENTY-FOUR HOURS . . ." of the following report to President Johnson . . . .

TOP SECRET

>Received Washington CommCen
>11:17 A.M. EST Saturday 24 Feb 68

>Received LBJ Ranch CommCen
>11:22 A.M. CST Saturday 24 Feb 68

FROM WALT ROSTOW
TO THE PRESIDENT
CITE CAP80543

TOP SECRET

FEBRUARY 24, 1968

Herewith Gen. Johnson's report of telephone conversation with Westy and Abrams.
    In the past twenty-four hours a tone of somewhat increased confidence is emerging from our military in Saigon — as if the scale and limits of the task ahead had become more measurable and manageable. But much obscurity still beclouds the countryside where most of the people are.
1. General Westmoreland's daily cable reports on activity at Khe Sanh and in the DMZ area. Following the heavy artillery, mortar and rocket fire at Khe Sanh on the afternoon and evening of 23 February, reports for 24 February indicate

only light and sporadic fire at Khe Sanh.

2. Vietnamese forces have captured the palace inside the Citadel and the VC flag that was flying over the palace is now in the First ARVN Division command post. Friendly forces hold all of Hue except a quarter circle 500 meters in radius at the southwest corner of the Citadel wall. General Westmoreland commented that it appeared that enemy resistance was crumbling. President Thieu plans to visit Hue on 25 February, although General Westmoreland indicated that the weather forecast is such that President Thieu may not be able to land. General Abrams reports a number of gallant actions by the First ARVN division starting with attack on Citadel west wall at 0200 hours on 24 February and culminating in seizure of the palace after daylight. The responsible company commander was promoted to Captain on the spot by the Vietnamese Division commander. The remaining enemy-held area is tightly circled. Enemy withdrawal is expected.

3. There was little activity in the II Corps area.

4. In III Corps area the major activity was the rocket attack on Tan Son Nhut and the area around Tan Son Nhut. One round landed not far from the house where General Wheeler was spending the night. General Wheeler and General Westmoreland are spending the night of 24-25 February in General Westmoreland's headquarters.

5. In IV Corps area 19 separate operations throughout the corps area resulted in 109 enemy killed at a cost of 30 Vietnamese killed. Two battalions of the U.S. Riverine force swept an island in the river immediately north of Can Tho and

TOP SECRET

Binh Tuy airfield and picked up a number of Viet Cong suspects. This island has been a source of fire against river patrol craft and has constituted a long-time nuisance. Highway 4 was open from Saigon to Bac Lieu on 24 February.

6. I questioned General Westmoreland concerning intelligence reports that indicate an early attack on Da Nang. General Westmoreland indicated that he and General Wheeler visited Da Nang on 24 February and that the threat of ground attack on Da Nang does not appear to be significant. I also questioned him about the movement of substantial enemy forces from the north into the Saigon area. He believes that the three divisions reports in the area have suffered substantial casualties in earlier contacts and that the forces guarding Saigon can handle the situation. General Westmoreland has the capability to reinforce Saigon promptly.

7. Following the visit to Da Nang, General Wheeler and General Westmoreland met with President Thieu, Vice President Ky and General Vien. Topics discussed were not reviewed by General Westmoreland, but he indicated a wide-ranging, useful and realistic exchange of views.

8. General Westmoreland is endeavoring to divert some B-52 strikes into the A Shau Valley where he reports that 30 ground targets exist that constitute what he considers to be an alternate logistics complex built up to support the attack on Hue. Diversions of B-52 strikes will not be at the expense of A continues pounding around Khe San. In addition, intelligence teams will be inserted in and near A Shau Valley as weather permits:

unfavorable weather has prevented attempts made during this past week.

SECRET

HEADQUARTERS
UNITED STATES MILITARY ASSISTANCE COMMAND. VIETNAM
APO SAN FRANCISCO 96222
Combat Operations Center

MACCOC
24 February 1968

MEMORANDUM FOR RECORD
SUBJECT: Commander's Guidance

1. On 24 February 1968 at III MAF Headquarters, General Westmoreland accompanied by General Wheeler, received briefings on current operational situation from MGen Peers, DCG, II FFORCEV and from General Abrams and LTGen Cushman on I CTZ matters.
2. At the conclusion of the III MAF briefing, General Westmoreland issued the following guidance:
a. In order to contend with the multiple threat posed by the enemy in I Corps North, III MAF has been heavily reinforced. In providing these reinforcements, COMUSMACV has utilized all of his reserves. II Corps is an economy of force area, and III and IV Corps have been reduced to a point where further reinforcements cannot be obtained, under present conditions. Therefore, CG

TOP SECRET

III MAF and DEPCOMUSMACV will develop a contingency plan for the application of strict economy of force measures in 1 CTZ South of AI VAN PASS in order to have additional forces ear marked for operations in I Corps North, if required. In developing such plans, the enemy threat in the North should be considered not only in KHE SANH, DMZ and CAMP CARROLL areas, but also along ASHAU Valley and on approaches to Hue from the west. HUE must be considered as a primary target.
b. A comprehensive reconnaissance plan will be developed to ascertain the dimensions of enemy movement in ASHAU Valley and on the road leading out of the valley near TABAT. If weather precludes air insert of reconnaissance elements, ground reconnaissance and exploitation forces (possibly from 1/102st Bde) will be employed.
c. Arc Light targets for ASHAU area will be developed to include the road network.

J. R. CHAISSON

SECRET

SECRET

    Received Washington CommCen
    8:35 A.M. EST Sunday 25 Feb 68

    Received LBJ Ranch CommCen
    8:24 A.M. CST Sunday 25 Feb 68

FROM WALT ROSTOW
TO THE PRESIDENT
CITE CAP80564

SECRET

Mr. Rostow will be in later this morning and will have a comment on this report for you.
Text of cable from General Westmoreland.
This is report number twenty-one on the situation in the Khe Sanh/DMZ area and covers the 24-hour period February 24, 1968.

Enemy action slackened considerably in northern Quang Tri Province yesterday as compared to the previous day's activities. Enemy shelling decreased greatly. The Khe Sanh combat base was again the primary target of the enemy shelling as the friendly forces received over half of the 532 rounds of artillery, rocket, and mortar rounds directed against our areas yesterday. Friendly casualties at Khe Sanh as the result of the enemy shelling amounted to seven killed and 20 wounded, with 11 wounded evacuated.

Enemy efforts relaxed in the Lancaster area as only one mortar round impacted at Camp Carroll. Four rounds of mortar fell at Dong Ha with four additional rounds falling at C-2. Five Marines required evacuation at C-2. Enemy shelling intensified at Con Thien, however, as that base received 237 early afternoon rounds of mortar and artillery, resulting in two Marines killed, and five wounded and evacuated. At Cua Viet, the 1st Amtrac battalion received 18 rounds of 100MM artillery in the afternoon, with three

TOP SECRET

Marines requiring evacuation. Other than shelling, activities in the area consisted of three sporadic contacts involving the 3D battalion, 3D Marines and the 1st battalion, 4th Marines in operation Kentucky. They engaged and killed 11 NVA while sustaining no friendly casualties. In an observed fire mission yesterday, five NVA were killed in the open about seven kilometers southeast of Camp Carroll. At CUA Viet a Navy convoy with three utility landing crafts, one mechanized landing craft, and patrol craft, received anti-tank rocket, automatic weapons fire and mortar fire, resulting in two USN wounded and evacuated.

There were five rounds of COFRAM type ordnance fired during this period, mixed with high explosives, on troops in the open, with undetermined results due to observer-to-target range.

A total 294 tactical air sorties were flown during the period in support of Khe Sanh. Marine aircraft flew 92 sorties, with bomb damage including three secondary explosions, four secondary fires, and two bunkers destroyed. The air force flew 162 sorties, the Navy flew 40, with 106 sorties on combat sky spot. Visual bomb damage included two secondary explosions, seven secondary fires, five military structures destroyed, and 30 military structures damaged. Seven B-52 strikes (36 sorties) were flown in the Niagara area.

Aerial resupply to Khe Sanh for the period amounted to 152 short tons. Sixty-nine passengers were landed at the airfield. Resupply sorties totalled 24 on 24 February. Nine C-130 aircraft completed nine air-drops. Five C-123 aircraft landed at the airfield as did ten Marine helicopters.

For the next 24 hours 288 tactical air sorties will be flown in support of Khe Sanh. There will be seven Arc Light strikes (39 sorties) flown in the Niagara area.

Weather at Khe Sanh during the period remained about the same. Clouds reduced the ceiling to less than 600 feet and dense fog lowered the surface visibility to less than three miles, from 11:00AM - 5:00PM there was some improvement as the ceiling lifted to 1700 feet and the visibility to seven miles. The forecast for 25 - 26 February does not indicate any significant change.

I am very pleased to report that Hue Citadel was cleared of enemy and secured at 7:30Am. I have just sent my congratulations to Gen Truong.

DTG 25/1335Z FEB 67

TOP SECRET

The following report, from General Westmoreland via Walt Rostow to the President shows great skepticism about the effectiveness of the Army of the Republic of Vietnam (ARVN) — the South Vietnamese Army.

TOP SECRET

>Received Washington CommCen
>10:32 EST Sunday 25 FEB 68
>
>Received LBJ RANCH CommCen
>10:28 CST Sunday 25 FEB 68

FROM WALT ROSTOW
TO THE PRESIDENT
CITE CAP805 65

TOP SECRET
FEBRUARY 25, 1968

Herewith Gen. Johnson's report of telephone conversation with General Westmoreland.
1. General Westmoreland indicated that his daily cable and operations reports covered the situation in South Vietnam comprehensively. He added the following comments as of the time of my conversation with him.
    The recovery of Hue was a significant morale booster to the Vietnamese in the area. President Thieu visited Hue and extended his congratulations to the forces there. The Vietnamese intend to retain three Vietnamese Marine battalions in and around the city. The 3D ARVN regiment of

the first ARVN division will return to its operational area northwest of the city where it will receive replacements and have its combat capability restored.

2. During the day some enemy 130MM artillery shells landed at Dong Ha. In the Rung Sat special zone southeast of Saigon one tug one merchant ship were taken under fire by what are presumed to be recoilless rifles and possibly RPG-2 and RPG-7 rockets. All damage was above the water line and the tug and the ship proceeded to Saigon under their own power.

3. The pattern of enemy actions indicates an enemy effort to isolate and strangle major population centers with a special effort directed toward Saigon.

4. The general tempo of activity throughout South Vietnam appears to be slowing down somewhat. The enemy is harder to find and he appears to be breaking down into smaller units.

5. General Westmoreland continues to be concerned about the detail contained in news stories filed form South Vietnam. He expects to have a review of his procedures completed by the evening of 26 February and is prepared to withdraw the credentials of certain reporters if ground rules have, in fact, been violated by them.

6. The staying power of the ARVN continues to be under intensive study. Vietnamese units have now been engaged actively for about 26 days. They have suffered more than a normal number of casualties. South Vietnamese military authorities have taken the following actions:

A. Separations (discharges) from the military

TOP SECRET

forces have been discontinued for those individuals who have performed less than 5 years of active service.

B. Individuals who have been separated in the past with less than 5 years of active service are being recalled to active service. General Westmoreland does not believe any substantial number have yet returned to duty because this program has just been started.

C. Individuals charged with military offenses and serving in labor units or confined in military confinement facilities have been granted amnesty and are being returned to their military units.

D. Some individuals are in training to meet requirements of the expanded Vietnamese military structure. General Westmoreland did not know whether these individuals will be diverted to replace the higher than expected casualties in the existing military structure. (My comment: Diversion to replace casualties will be at the expense of forming the additional ARVN military units.)

7. General Westmoreland received a letter day before yesterday from General Vien, Chief of the South Vietnamese Joint General Staff, pointing out the unfavorable impact on Vietnamese morale of the large number of modern weapons in the hands of enemy units, including individual guerrillas. General Westmoreland indicated the Vietnamese have no confidence in the carbine and described it as a "pop gun."

8. General Wheeler departed Saigon at approximately 4 P.M., Sunday, Saigon time for Bangkok.

DTG: 25 1532Z FEB 68

Rostow's reports to the President continue to be tactful: "And to get the ARVN back on their feet and moving, which will have Gen. Abram's full attention . . . ."

TOP SECRET

 Received Washington CommCen
 12:00 P.M. EST Monday 26 Feb 68

 Received LBJ Ranch CommCen
 12:00 P.M. CST Monday 26 Feb 68

FROM: WALT ROSTOW
TO: THE PRESIDENT
CITE: CAP80582

TOP SECRET

FEBRUARY 26, 1968

Herewith Westy reports his new dispositions:
— To deal with a probable attack (Feb. 27 or 28) in the western highlands (Dak To-Kontum-Pleiku);
— And to get the ARVN back on their feet and moving, which will have Gen. Abrams' full attention, with Gen. Cushman taking over the I Corps.

Subject: General Johnson's telephone conversation with General Westmoreland
1. General Westmoreland's daily report number 22 covers the significant activity in South Vietnam. General Westmoreland is now turning

TOP SECRET

his attention to both the near-term and longer-term future. In the I Corps area he intends to convert MACV forward to a provisional corps headquarters to command operations north of AI Van Pass. When this conversion takes place, the provisional corps, the First Marine Division in the Da Nang-Ai Van Pass area and the Americal Division will be subordinate to III Maf headquarters, commanded by General Cushman. It is the intention to concentrate now in conjunction with the first ARVN division in clearing the enemy from the coastal areas and as the monsoon shifts, to work against the enemy and his base areas to the west away from the coastal areas. In the meantime, B-52 strikes will be employed against enemy troop concentrations in the A Shau Valley. Intelligence teams are standing by waiting for a weather break to be inserted in the vicinity of the A Shau Valley, to get better intelligence of enemy activities in that area.

2. Some troop adjustments are taking place in the II Corps area. Two battalions of the 173rd brigade have been moved to this area from Ban Me Thuot within the next 48 hours. The enemy who have threatened Ban Me Thuot (the 33D NVA regiment) appears to have withdrawn to the west. General Westmoreland estimates that they have one or two combat effective battalions; that they are now engaged in restoring their combat strength; and he expects contact will be gained again with this unit three or four weeks from now. General Westmoreland has discussed the friendly tactical posture in II Corps with General Rosson, and the two of them believe that forces

are well disposed to meet any attack in the western highlands, if such attack takes place.

3. General Westmoreland met today with General Weyand and General Khang in the III Corps area. Friendly forces are disposed to meet attacks on province and district towns in the Corps area, although neither General Weyand nor General Khang are optimistic about preventing future rocket attacks. They both believe that the forces can react rapidly but cannot prevent the early rocket rounds from being launched.

4. General Westmoreland is planning to assign General Rosson to replace General Abrams when MACV forward is converted to a provisional corps headquarters under General Cushman's command. General Abrams will then resume his full-time deputy responsibilities and renew his focus on ARVN and popular and regional forces. General Westmoreland is particularly anxious to return General Abrams to the primary task of restoring full combat effectiveness in the ARVN.

DTG: 261700Z FEB 68

TOP SECRET

The first page from this resupply report may be missing from the archives . . . .

A total of 229 tactical air sorties were flown in support of Khe Sanh. Marine aircraft flew 85 sorties. Bomb damage included two secondary explosions, one secondary fire and one rocket position destroyed. The Air Force flew 110 sorties, and the Navy flew 34 sorties. Bomb damage assessment included 30 secondary explosions, one rocket position destroyed, seven secondary fires, two trucks destroyed. Five Arc Light strikes (30 sorties) were flown in the Niagara area.
Air resupply for the Khe Sanh during the period amounted to 162 short tons. In addition, 27 passengers were air landed. Resupply sorties totalled 15 on 25 February. Nine C-130 aircraft completed nine air drops. One C-123 landed at the airfield, while two C-123 aircraft air-dropped material at the drop zone. Three Marine helicopters landed at the airfield.

For the next 24 hours, a total of 286 tactical air sorties are planned in support of the Khe Sanh area. Five Arc Light strikes (21 sorties) will be flown in the Niagara area.

Khe Sanh weather during the morning of February 25, was marked by low clouds and fog until 10:00 A.M. at that time the fog dissipated and the cloud ceilings improved to 1600 feet. Visibility then remained good. The forecast for 26 - 27 February is for good visibility until about 9:00 P.M. 26 February when fog will form and cause low visibility again. The cloud ceilings during daylight of 27 February are expected to be up near 2500 feet but lowering at night to 300 feet or less with fog formation.

The Khe Sanh dump and ammunition supply point (USP) status as of 8:00 P.M. Feb. 25 is as follows:

	Previous Status Days Supply 8:00 P.M. 24 Feb	Est On Hand (9:00 A.M. 25 Feb SVN)
Class I (Rations)		
Meal, Combat, Individual	12	4 Days
B Rations	9	9 Days
Class III (Fuel)		
Aviation Gas (AVGAS)	7.2	7.2 Days
JP-4 Fuel (Jet Fuel)	1	1 Day
Motor Gasoline (Mogas)	8.7	7.2 Days
Diesel	6.8	5 Days
Class V (Ammunition)		
A. High Explosive		
60-MM Mortar	23	23 Days
81-MM Mortar	13	14 Days
90-MM (Tank)	30	30 Days
4.2" Mortar	21	22 Days
105-MM Howitzer	18	19 Days
155-MM Howitzer	19	16 Days

B. Anti-Tank	Rounds on Hand
90-MM Heat	89
66-MM Rocket (Law)	1,386
Unit-Tank Mines (M-15)	234
Anti-Tank Mines (M-19)	334

TOP SECRET

Anti-Tank Mines (M-21) 100
106-MM Heat 144
106-MM Recoilless Rifle (Hep-T) 866
3.5" Rocket 950

     Previous Status
   Days Supply 8:00 P.M. 24 Feb
EST
   On Hand (9:00 A.M. 25 Feb SVN)

Class V (COFRAM)
  105-MM Howitzer 5 5 Days
  155-MM Howitzer 5 5 Days
  40-MM Grenade Launcher 5 5 Days
  Hand Grenades 10 10 Days

2. On 25 February Khe Sanh was resupplied with 162 tons as follows:
  Class I 30.5 Tons
  Class III 22 Tons
  Class IV 17.25 Tons
  Class V 90 Tons
  Class VII 2.25 Tons

DTG: 261538Z FEB 68

Confidential Files on the Siege and Loss of Khe Sanh

The 23rd and 24th reports on the status of Khe Sanh are delivered to the President via Walt Rostow . . . .

TOP SECRET

>Received Washington CommCen
>8:00 A.M. EST Tuesday 27 Feb 68

>Received LBJ Ranch CommCen
>9:45 A.M. CST Tuesday 27 Feb 68

FROM WALT ROSTOW
TO THE PRESIDENT
CITE CAP80602

SECRET EYES ONLY

Text of report from General Westmoreland. This is report number twenty-three on the situation in the Khe Sanh/DMZ area and covers the 24 hour period February 26, 1968.

The Khe Sanh combat base continued to receive moderate shelling during the period as 150 rounds of artillery, 50 rounds of rocket, and 50 rounds of mortar fell within the perimeter. The shelling resulted in one killed and 23 wounded, nine of whom were evacuated. No materiel damage was reported.

Although there were no significant ground contacts made at Khe Sanh, several significant sightings were made resulting from or resulting in friendly actions. At 10:50 AM, a company of Marines spotted an enemy mortar firing from a

TOP SECRET

position one kilometer north of Hill 881. Counter mortar registered and suppressed the enemy mortar fire. At 5:00 PM, an air observer, adjusting fire on five artillery positions 17 kilometers southwest of Khe Sanh, in Laos, observed one secondary explosion and one secondary fire. At 6:30 PM, a Marine company sighted what appeared to be a tracked vehicle about four kilometers west of the Khe Sanh base, but fog made it impossible to adjust a fire mission. At 7:25 PM, the 37th ARVN Ranger battalion reported that personnel manning a listening post saw a squad size NVA unit moving toward their perimeter. Small arms fire was exchanged resulting in three NVA killed. At 8:30 PM, Marines observed three large secondary explosions resulting from an Arc Light strike.

Elsewhere along the DMZ heavy incoming fire was reported at Dong Ha and Con Thien. A total of 300 rounds fell on Dong Ha during the period. Results were one killed and 22 wounded. Materiel destruction was heavy and included 20,000 gallons of diesel fuel, two light observation planes, four generators, one armored personnel carrier, and one jeep and trailer. Major damage was reported to two AHIG's, two generators, two personnel carriers two five tons trucks, one wrecker, two dump trucks, one asphalt distributer and one water trailer. Con Thien received 181 rounds of artillery and 35 rounds of mortar. There was no report of casualties or damage.

Wednesday, February 28, 1968, 9:50 AM

TEXT OF CABLE FROM GENERAL WESTMORELAND

This is report number twenty-four on the situation in the Khe Sanh/DMZ area and covers the 24-hour period of February 27, 1968.

Enemy incoming lessened somewhat yesterday at Khe Sanh compared with previous days as enemy shelling totaled 115 rounds of mortar, 15 rounds of artillery and 10 rounds of rocket. Casualties attributed to the shelling were one killed, 20 wounded (11 evacuated). There were no significant ground contacts reported, however, several significant sightings of enemy activities were made.

At 10:00 AM a resupply helicopter received small arms fire from enemy positioned 1000 meters east of Khe Sanh. At 10:25 AM an air strike was executed southwest of Khe Sanh in Laos, and destroyed one vehicle believed to be an enemy tank. At 11:10 AM Marines sighted eight enemy troops moving towards the Khe Sanh area with a 50 caliber weapon 2 1/2 kilometers east of Hill 881; air strikes were called with undetermined results. At 11:15 AM, an administrative officer directing air strikes 20 kilometers southwest of Khe Sanh reported three large fires around the Co Roc area. A vehicle convoy was spotted at the same location and air strikes were called in with undetermined results.

Throughout the afternoon incoming continued but of a sporadic nature. An artillery mission was fired on a known mortar site three kilometers southwest of Hill 881 resulting in several sec-

TOP SECRET

ondary explosions. An air strike run four kilometers southwest of Hill 881 resulted in nine secondary explosions. At 8:25 PM Marine Listening Post heard movement to the left of its position and received one grenade injuring two Marines. Fire was returned with unknown results. Three additional large secondary explosions were observed four kilometers north of Khe Sanh as a result of a tactical air run. Damages attributed to the day's incoming at Khe Sanh consisted of a helicopter destroyed by an enemy artillery round. Aircraft personnel were not injured.

SECRET

SECRET

Elsewhere at friendly installations bordering the DMZ, enemy incoming artillery, rocket and mortar rounds were significant. Camp Carroll received five rounds of mortar. At Dong Ha Combat Base, 11 rounds of artillery fell. No damages or casualties were recorded in either instance. Con Thien and Gio Linh received five mortar rounds and 38 artillery rounds respectively, with negative damage and casualties reported. Friendly casualties of two killed, seven wounded (six evacuated) were caused by 115 rounds of artillery and 25 mortar rounds falling at positions held by Marines in the Cua Viet area. The 1st AMTRAC received nine rounds of mixed artillery and mortar causing minor injuries to one individual.

In ground contacts yesterday in Operation

Saline, search and destroy operations conducted by elements from the 3rd Battalion, 1st Marines, in Mai Xa Thi Village, accounted for six North Vietnamese Army killed. In the contact one Marine was killed and three injured. On the Cua Viet, three landing craft convoys were fired upon with automatic weapons fire and mortars. In each instance negative casualties were reported.

There were five COFRAM missions fired expending 27 rounds of 155 MM and one round of 8" ordnance, resulting in 26 North Vietnamese Army killed.

The high total of 415 tactical air sorties were flown in support of Khe Sanh during the period. Marine aircraft flew 157 sorties, with Bomb Damage including 10 secondary explosions, six secondary fires, one mortar position destroyed. Three bunkers destroyed, 20 structures destroyed, 20 structures destroyed, and 22 enemy killed. The Air Force flew 153 sorties and the Navy flew 105 sorties. Bomb Damage Assessment included 11 large fires (numerous small fires), 39 secondary explosions, 39 road cuts, eight confirmed enemy killed (15 probable). One automatic weapons position destroyed, and two 37 MM guns destroyed. Six ARC LIGHT strikes (33 sorties) were flown in the Niagara area.

Air resupply for the period amounted to 237 short tons. Fifteen short tons of vehicles, six short tons of mail and three short tons of medical supplies completed the largest resupply tonnage delivery in many weeks. In addition, 68 passengers were landed at Khe Sanh. Resupply sor-

TOP SECRET

ties totaled 46 on February 27. Fourteen C-130 aircraft completed ten air drops, and three air landed at the airfield. Twenty-eight Marine helicopters delivered passengers and cargo.

SECRET

SECRET

For the next 24 hours, a total of 282 tactical air sorties are scheduled in support of Khe Sanh. Eight ARC LIGHT strikes (48 sorties) will be flown in the Niagara area.

Except for a brief period of fog at 9:00 AM on February 27 the weather was good the remainder of the morning and afternoon with partly cloudy skies and good visibilities. The weather remained generally good through the night until 4:00 AM on February 28 when fog formed, reducing visibilities to two miles by 8:00 AM. The forecast for the period next 24-hour period is for cloudy skies with continued visibility restrictions because of fog.

TOP SECRET

THE JOINT CHIEFS OF STAFF
WASHINGTON, D. C. 20301

    CM-3055-68
    28 Feb 1968

MEMORANDUM FOR THE PRESIDENT
SUBJECT: Telephone Conversation with General

Kerwin, CS, MACV

1. General Westmoreland was out of the office and I talked to General Kerwin, General Westmoreland's Chief of Staff. There is little to report concerning activities in SVN except for some updating of information reported in the Presidential operational/intelligence brief and in General Westmoreland's report #24 on the situation in the Khe Sanh/DMZ area.
2. In the action reported west of Tam Ky, a sweep of the areas increased enemy casualties to 239 KIA from the 148 reported earlier while U.S. losses increased from two to three KIA. No change in U.S. wounded. There is no further information on the reported movement of major communist elements to the coastal area between Da Nang and Tam Ky.
3. Action is underway to secure Highway 1 from Ai Van Rass to Phu Loc and it is estimated that the road should be secure to permit engineer work within the next 72 hours. Concurrently, security operations are underway on Highway 1 between Phu Loc and Hue/Phu Bai; it is estimated that several more days will be required to secure the latter segment fully.
4. In II Corps at Dak To there is no change to reports already received here. A friendly long-range patrol ambushed enemy forces 5 kilometers west of Konfim City resulting in 20 enemy killed and no friendly casualties.
5. Activities in III Corps consisted of indirect fire attacks already reported. Some of the casualties at Bien Hoa resulted from a direct rocket hit on

TOP SECRET

a friendly bunker. I raised a question concerning any changes in location of the 5th and 9th VC Divisions and the 7th NVA Division and their subordinates in the Saigon area. General Kerwin reports no evidence of significant change in location of these units.

6. In IV Corps Area no information was provided beyond that contained in the Presidential operational/intelligence brief.

>HAROLD K. JOHNSON
>ACTING CHAIRMAN
>JOINT CHIEFS OF STAFF

SECRET

Wednesday, February 28, 1968, 9:50 AM

TEXT OF CABLE FROM
>GENERAL WESTMORELAND

This is report number twenty-four on the situation in the Khe Sanh/DMZ area and covers the 24-hour period of February 27, 1968.

Enemy incoming lessened somewhat yesterday at Khe Sanh compared with previous days as enemy shelling totaled 115 rounds of mortar, 15 rounds of artillery and 10 rounds of rocket. Casualties attributed to the shelling were one killed, 20 wounded (11 evacuated). There were no significant ground contacts reported, however, several significant sightings of enemy activities were made.

At 10:00 AM a resupply helicopter received

small arms fire from enemy positioned 1000 meters east of Khe Sanh. At 10:25 AM an air strike was executed southwest of Khe Sanh in Laos, and destroyed one vehicle believed to be an enemy tank. At 11:10 AM Marines sighted eight enemy troops moving towards the Khe Sanh area with a 50 caliber weapon 2 1/2 kilometers east of Hill 881; air strikes were called with undetermined results. At 11:15 AM, an administrative officer directing air strikes 20 kilometers southwest of Khe Sanh reported three large fires around the Co Roc area. A vehicle convoy was spotted at the same location and air strikes were called in with undetermined results.

Throughout the afternoon incoming continued but of a sporadic nature. An artillery mission was fired on a known mortar site three kilometers southwest of Hill 881 resulting in several secondary explosions. An air strike run four kilometers southwest of Hill 881 resulted in nine secondary explosions. At 8:25 PM Marine Listening Post heard movement to the left of its position and received one grenade injuring two Marines. Fire3 was returned with unknown results. Three additional large secondary explosions were observed four kilometers north of Khe Sanh as a result of a tactical air run. Damages attributed to the day's incoming at Khe Sanh consisted of a helicopter destroyed by an enemy artillery round. Aircraft personnel were not injured.

SECRET

Elsewhere at friendly installations bordering the

TOP SECRET

DMZ, enemy incoming artillery, rocket and mortar rounds were significant. Camp Carroll received five rounds of mortar. At Dong Ha Combat Base, 11 rounds of artillery fell. No damages or casualties were recorded in either instance. Con Thien and Gio Linh received five mortar rounds and 38 artillery rounds respectively, with negative damage and casualties reported. Friendly casualties of two killed, seven wounded (six evacuated) were caused by 115 rounds of artillery and 25 mortar rounds falling at positions held by Marines in the Cua Viet area. The 1st AMTRAC received nine rounds of mixed artillery and mortar causing minor injuries to one individual.

In ground contacts yesterday in Operations Saline, search and destroy operations conducted by elements from the 3rd Battalion, 1st Marines, in Mai Xa Thi Village, accounted for six North Vietnamese Army killed. In the contact one Marine was killed and three injured. On the Cua Viet, three landing craft convoys were fired upon with automatic weapons fire and mortars. In each instance negative casualties were reported. There were five COFRAM missions fired expending 27 rounds of 155 MM and one round of 8" ordnance, resulting in 26 North Vietnamese Army killed.

The high total of 415 tactical air sorties were flown in support of Khe Sanh during the period. Marine aircraft flew 157 sorties, with Bomb Damage including 10 secondary explosions, six secondary fires, one mortar position destroyed. Three bunkers destroyed, 20 structures destroyed, 20 structures destroyed, and 22 enemy killed. The Air Force flew 153 sorties and the Navy flew 105 sorties. Bomb Damage Assessment included 11 large fires (numerous small fires), 39 secondary explosions, 39 road cuts, eight confirmed enemy killed (15 probable). One automatic weapons position destroyed, and two 37 MM guns destroyed. Six ARC LIGHT strikes (33 sorties) were flown in the Niagara area.

Air resupply for the period amounted to 237short tons. Fifteen short tons of vehicles, six short tons of mail and three short tons of medical supplies completed the largest resupply tonnage delivery in many weeks. In addition, 68 passengers were landed at Khe Sanh. Resupply sorties totaled 46 on February 27. Fourteen C-130 aircraft completed ten air drops, and three air landed at the airfield. Twenty-eight Marine helicopters delivered passengers and cargo.

SECRET

SECRET

For the next 24 hours, a total of 282 tactical air sorties are scheduled in support of Khe Sanh. Eight ARC LIGHT strikes (48 sorties) will be flown in the Niagara area.

Except for a brief period of fog at 9:00 AM on February 27 the weather was good the remainder of the morning and afternoon with partly cloudy skies and good visibilities. The weather remained generally good through the night until 4:00 AM on

TOP SECRET

February 28 when fog formed, reducing visibilities to two miles by 8:00 AM. The forecast for the period next 24-hour period is for cloudy skies with continued visibility restrictions because of fog.

INFORMATION
THE WHITE HOUSE
WASHINGTON

>Thursday, February 29, 1968
>1:45 p.m.

Mr. President:
Herewith Westy's telephone conversation of today. The best news is that Highway 1 should be open by March 1.
    Gen. Johnson suggests a weekly rather than a daily call from Gen. Westmoreland. Given the quality of the reporting we have now organized with the Pentagon, this seems acceptable.

W. W. Rostow

TOP SECRET

THE JOINT CHIEFS OF STAFF
WASHINGTON, D. C. 20301

>CM-3065-68
>29 Feb 1968

MEMORANDUM FOR THE PRESIDENT
SUBJECT: Telephone Conversation with General Westmoreland

1. General Westmoreland had little to report beyond the items contained in his report #25 on the situation in the Khe Sanh-DMZ area. Weather was good in the Khe Sanh-DMZ-Coastal area and effective air strikes were made. He made special mention of the B-52 strikes conducted inside the normal three kilometers restraining or safety line from friendly force locations. He expects to continue to target some strikes within this normally restricted area.

2. The logistic situation in I Corps is improving. Scabees have opened the road from the coast to Highway 1 south of the DMZ that can carry one-way traffic and are continuing to make improvements so that the road will handle two-way traffic. Highway 1 is open for one-way traffic from Hue/Phu Bai to Dong Ha. Engineers are working on the road between Ai Van Pass and Hue/Phu Bai so that it is expected to be open for one-way traffic on 1 March. This will make Highway 1 open from Da Nang to Dong Ha for one-way traffic.

3. The 3d Brigade, 82d Airborne Division will complete its move from Chu Lai to Hue/Phu Bai during the next seven days. One battalion is already at Hue/Phu Bai.

4. General Rosson will relinquish command of I Field Force Victor (II Corps Area) to General Peers on 1 March. General Rosson will then overlap with General Abrams at MACV FORWARD for a period of 10 days to 2 weeks preparatory to redesignation as a Provisional Corps Headquarters which will control operations north of Ai Van Pass. General Westmoreland has not yet

TOP SECRET

established a specific date for redesignation to a Provisional Corps Headquarters.

5. General Westmoreland reviewed with General Rosson and General Peers rainy season plans for operations in the II Corps Area, on the assumption that no additional troops will be provided in this geographic area.

6. South of Saigon a Vietnamese Ranger battalion seized an enemy ammunition cache. Quantities have not yet been reported. Some indiscriminate mortar fire was received at Can Tho resulting in 20 civilians killed.

7. Three Popular Force outposts on a canal south of Saigon were attacked. It is General Westmoreland's view that enemy attacks are now shifting to Popular Force outposts in view of enemy failures to seize major population centers.

8. One intelligence team was inserted in the A Shau Valley on 27 February and made immediate contact with the enemy. An effort was made on 29 February to reinforce this team, but General Westmoreland did not have any reports of results.

9. The 3d Brigade, 4th Infantry Division, less one battalion, has relocated from the area south and southwest of Da Nang to Binh Dinh Province to replace the remaining brigade of the First Cavalry Division, which will join its parent unit in the Hue area.

10. General Westmoreland stated that activity was <u>comparatively</u> quiet throughout South Vietnam.

11. I recommend that the daily telephone call to General Westmoreland be discontinued.

Information obtained in the daily call is not of sufficient importance or urgency to warrant an additional commitment on the overburdened commander in Vietnam. As an alternative, I suggest a weekly call on Saturday morning to obtain a general assessment and an indication of short-term plans for the 7 to 10 days following the call.

    HOWARD K. JOHNSON
    CHIEF OF STAFF, U.S. ARMY
    ACTING FOR CHAIRMAN, JCS

INFORMATION
THE WHITE HOUSE
WASHINGTON

    Thursday, February 29, 1968 - 2:30 p.m.

Mr. President:
Herewith Westy's Khe Sanh report:
— weather pretty good;
— some effective bombing;
— resupply 252 tons (excellent);
— enemy digging trenches closer and trying to get on out of the B-52 bomb line, which Westy has moved closer to the base.

W. W. Rostow

    Thursday, February 29, 1968, 10:30 AM

TEXT OF CABLE FROM
    GENERAL WESTMORELAND
This is report number twenty-five on the situa-

TOP SECRET

tion in the Khe Sanh/DMZ area and covers the 24-hour period of February 28, 1968.

Favorable weather conditions continued yesterday at Khe Sanh with visibility recorded up to five miles. Light winds and scattered clouds provided optimum flying conditions for fixed and rotary wing aircraft. Logistic resupply of Khe Sanh was executed without difficulty.

For the most part, enemy activity against Khe Sanh again consisted of shelling. A total of 186 rounds of mixed artillery, rockets and mortars were received in the area. Incident to the shelling, artillery rounds struck an ammo bunker, destroying 36 - 106 MM high explosive and 30 - 106 MM armor piercing rounds. Injuries resulting from incoming rounds were nine wounded (minor).

Ground contacts during the reporting period were limited to small unit contacts. At 9:30 AM two rounds of recoilless rifle were received at positions held by the 1st Battalion. 26th Marines, injuring one Marine. At 11:10 AM Marines fired a 106 MM mission at an North Vietnamese Army bunker located 800 meters southeast of Khe Sanh resulting in the destruction of the bunker. At 2:00 PM, Marines observed one secondary fire and heard small arms ammo exploding as a controlled air strike destroyed an enemy 50 caliber position one kilometer south of Hill 881. A bridge located three kilometers southeast of Khe Sanh was damaged as a result of an air strike. An air observer controlled air strike on an enemy automatic weapons position about three kilometers southeast of Lang Vei and destroyed the weapon.

Another air strike was run on an enemy bunker located about the same location; it was destroyed, one secondary explosion was observed, and one North Vietnamese Army killed. At 4:00 PM an air observer spotting a group of North Vietnamese Army gathered at one kilometer southeast of Khe Sanh, ran an air strike and killed one. An artillery mission fired on three North Vietnamese Army manning an anti-aircraft position, two kilometers northeast of Khe Sanh village, destroying the position and confirming three enemy killed. All available arms were employed to suppress enemy fire and to destroy their positions as 2074 rounds of mixed artillery and mortar were expended during the period in support of the Khe Sanh area.

Small unit contacts and enemy incoming comprised the bulk of significant activity reported in areas neighboring Khe Sanh. Elements at Camp Carroll received 10 rounds of mortar during the period. Gio Linh and A-3 shared 15 and 32 rounds of artillery respectively. No casualties or damages were reported in either instance. The 3rd Battalion, 1st Marines in Operation Saline received 32 rounds of enemy artillery with three additional artillery rounds of enemy artillery falling on the 1st AMATRAC Battalion positions. One Marine received minor injuries resulting from nine artillery rounds falling at Dong Ha. Twelve rounds of enemy artillery fell one kilometer west of C-4 inflicting negative casualties and damage.

Significant ground activity in northern Quant Tri Province included activity in Operation

TOP SECRET

Napoleon as a combat patrol from K Company, 3rd Battalion, first Marines engaged an enemy force in a fortified position six kilometers west from the mouth of the Cua Viet. Utilizing available air, naval gunfire and artillery support, they succeeded in destroying five bunkers while killing an equal number of North Vietnamese Army. In the contact one Marine was killed and 16 wounded; activity ended at 5:00 PM. In Operation Kentucky, a small unit from a company, 1st Battalion, 4th Marines engaged three North Vietnamese Army manning a machine gun position. When action closed, three North Vietnamese Army were killed and three crew served weapons were captured. No friendly casualties were recorded.

Enemy attacks on convoys continued yesterday as two convoys were fired upon north of Dong Ha, resulting in two sailors killed and 16 wounded. At 12:30 PM yesterday, four kilometers southwest of the rock pile, a helicopter received heavy ground fire and exploded upon contact with the ground. Latest reports indicate that of 23 passengers abroad, there was only one survivor.

There were two COFRAM missions fired as follows: three rounds resulting in five killed. Thirteen rounds were fired on North Vietnamese Army massing in Operation Scotland, good target coverage but with undetermined results.

A total of 329 tactical air sorties were flown in support of Khe Sanh. The Marine aircraft wing flew 129 sorties. Bomb Damage Assessment included one secondary explosion, three secondary fires, one automatic weapons position destroyed and one damaged, and six North Vietnamese Army killed. The Air Force flew 143 sorties and the Navy flew 57, with damage listed as 17 secondary explosions, 20 road cuts, three trucks destroyed, two guns silenced, 16 secondary fires, one automatic weapons position destroyed, 41 military structures destroyed, and two North Vietnamese Army killed (15 probable). B-52, ARC LIGHT, flew eight strikes (48 sorties) in the Niagara area. Headquarters 3rd Marines reports that strikes on one target produced three large secondary explosions. Another target produced continuous secondary explosions for two hours after the strike. Four the ARC LIGHT strikes scheduled for February 29 are emergency targets and are less than the normal three kilometers from friendly forces. The close-in strikes are proving to be most profitable as the enemy has concentrated forces within the three kilometer sanctuary. Headquarters 3rd Marines reports that the shock waves created by the close-in strikes do not damage structures in friendly areas. On the basis of four close-in drops so far, the risk to personnel is negligible.

Air resupply during the period amounted to 252 short tons. Medical supplies amounted to three short tons. In addition, 112 passengers were landed at Khe Sanh. Air delivery sorties totaled 39 on February 28, sixteen C-130 aircraft completed 10 air drops, and six air-landed at the airfield. One C-123 aircraft landed at the field. Twenty-two Marine helicopters delivered passengers and cargo.

For the next period there are 282 tactical air

TOP SECRET

sorties scheduled in support of the Khe Sanh area. There will be seven ARC LIGHT strikes (42 sorties) flown in the Niagara area.

Shortly after noon on February 28, cloud ceilings raised to 2500 feet and visibilities improved. Clouds became scattered after 2:00 PM and visibility increased to 10miles. Low clouds and fog again formed after midnight producing ceilings at 1000 feet or less and visibilities of from zero to four miles. These persisted through 9:00 AM February 29. The forecast is for continued cloudy conditions with fog during the morning hours of February 29 with cloudiness decreasing rapidly and visibility improving after noon. Low clouds and fog will form after 10:00 PM and persist into the early morning hours of March 1.

SECRET

FROM: WALT ROSTOW
TO: THE PRESIDENT
CITE: CAP80629

SECRET

MARCH 2, 1968

Herewith Khe Sanh — I Corps report:

— poor weather;
— only 99 tons delivered;
— considerable but not major ground contacts.
Text follows:
    This is report number twenty-seven on the sit-

uation in the Khe Sanh/DMZ area and covers the 24 hour period March 1, 1968.

Weather conditions yesterday at Khe Sanh were less than optimum as prohibitively low ceiling and fog occurred through much of the day. Although visual fixed wing support was not possible, effective radar control and combat sky spot sorties were flown. Resupply aircraft offloaded only 99 short tons of supplies and equipment.

Although fixed wing strikes were affected by the weather, artillery batteries expended a total of 1562 rounds on known and suspected enemy targets with good target coverage. Enemy activity throughout the period was generally light with scattered enemy night-time movements detected by activated trip flares. Specifically, during the period, enemy activities consisted of small probes and harassing fires. At 3:00 AM yesterday, D Company, 1st Battalion, 9th Marines, heard movement outside its wire; illumination was fired revealing four North Vietnamese running away. One was killed as a result of small arms fire. In a late report, as a result of the enemy probe at positions occupied by the 37th ARVN Rangers, in addition to seven enemy killed by Ranger elements, 60 North Vietnamese bodies were found at first light attributed to artillery missions. At 8:05PM yesterday, the Marines observed troops with lights moving five kilometers northwest of Khe Sanh. Artillery and mortar missions fired with good target coverage.

The place of enemy incoming slackened yesterday, paralleling enemy ground activity, as a comparative low 157 rounds of mixed artillery,

TOP SECRET

rocket and mortar rounds fell during the period. Incident to the day's shelling, two fatalities were recorded, with injuries sustained by an additional 23 Marines. A C-123 aircraft was destroyed when struck by incoming mortar rounds.

At bordering installations along the DMZ, enemy incoming followed its normal distribution. Twelve rounds of mortar fell at Camp Carroll inflicting injuries to one Marine. Six mortar rounds fell at Ca Lu. A reconnaissance team operating 10 kilometers southeast of Camp Carroll received five rounds of mortar. Six rounds of artillery fell at Dong Ha. At A-3 and Gio Linh, six and 34 rounds of artillery were received respectively. Three Marines were injured from the 3D Battalion, 3D Marines, positioned at A-3. ARVN units at A-1 received 57 rounds of artillery. Finally, the 3D Battalion, 1st Marines in operation Napoleon/Saline, received 35 rounds of mixed mortar and artillery rounds. Damages attributed to the day's shelling were minimal.

Ground contacts in northeastern Quang Tri Province accelerated as 3D Battalion, 1st Marines, while sweeping through Mai Xa Thi Village in contact throughout the day, utilized tanks, naval gunfire and air strikes; and killed 36 North Vietnamese while capturing four individual and three crew served weapons. Friendly casualties were listed as 22 killed, 87 wounded with seven missing. In Lam Son 187, an ARVN battalion (1st Battalion, 1st Regiment) engaged a large enemy force seven kilometers northeast of Dong Ha. When contact broke, 189 enemy bodies were counted with 32 individual and 14 crew served weapons captured. ARVN losses amounted to seven killed and 24 wounded.

At 1159AM yesterday, six NVA were killed eight kilometers north of Gio Linh in the DMZ by an artillery mission which also caused six secondary explosions. At 1228PM yesterday, a forward observer working with the 2D Battalion, 1st Marines, conducted a fire mission on 50 North Vietnamese assembled in the open 1000 meters south of A-3 resulting in 20 North Vietnamese killed. Even additional North Vietnamese were killed yesterday as a result of a fire mission on North Vietnamese in the open three kilometers south of A-3. At 4:45PM, A Company, 3D Battalion, 3D Marines came in contact with an unknown size enemy force two kilometers west of Gio Linh. Initial reports indicate one Marine was killed with enemy casualties unknown.

The following equipment was recovered from the enemy junk captured at the mouth of the Cua Viet: 44 individual weapons, 3600 rounds of small arms, 210 kilos of TNT, 120 grenades, and 126 rounds of mixed mortar and ammunition. At 11:00AM a sampan was discovered beached at Cua Viet containing the following supplies: 112 - 82 MM mortar rounds, four 75MM RR rounds, 102 - 82MM mortar fuses, 13 individual weapons, 630 kilos of TNT, 14 RPG-2 rounds, and 2880 rounds of small arms ammunition. Off the DMZ coast yesterday, the USS Hull received 12 rounds of artillery. The closest round landed 12 meters off the starboard bow. There was no damage to the ship. Fire was returned at the enemy position silencing the enemy fire.

TOP SECRET

There were four COFRAM missions fired during the period, expending 54 rounds, and resulting in 20 North Vietnamese killed.

Tactical air sorties in support of Khe Sanh totalled 219 for the period. Marine aircraft flew 83 sorties, producing three secondary explosions and three secondary fires. The Air Force flew 77 sorties and the Navy flew 59, reporting one bridge destroyed, three secondary explosions, 17 secondary fires, four bunkers destroyed, and 13 road cuts. Six ARC LIGHT strikes (35 sorties) were flown in the Niagara area. Preliminary bomb damage reports indicate favorable results. Three of the strikes flown were the closest to date to friendly forces (1.2 kilometers).

Air resupply for the reporting period amounted to 99 short tons. However, the fuel drop landed outside of the drop zone and was destroyed by U.S. forces. There was one short ton of vehicles. Thirty-one replacements were air-landed. Resupply sorties totalled 14 on 1 March, six C-130 aircraft completed five air drops and one landed at the airfield. Eight C-123 aircraft also landed at the field. Helicopter operations were prevented by unfavorable weather. The ground commander requested that air drops be curtailed so material received during preceding days could be handled.

For the next period, 279 tactical air sorties are scheduled in support of Khe Sanh. A total seven ARC LIGHT strikes (42 sorties) are scheduled for the Niagara area.

As indicated, the weather worsened in the Khe Sanh area. Low clouds and fog persisted throughout most of the day at Khe Sanh on 1 March as ceilings lowered until noon yesterday with visibilities restricted from one-half to two miles. The best conditions of the day were reported between noon and 3:00 PM when ceilings ranged from 600 to 2000 feet and visibilities ranged from two to six miles. Conditions began dropping rapidly after 3:00 PM producing low ceilings and visibilities during the night and early on 2 March of 200 to 500 feet and one-quarter to one-half mile. The forecast for the period 2 - 3 March is for continued poor to marginal conditions with the best weather occurring after 10:00 AM when ceilings and visibility are expected to reach 1000 feet and four miles. Deteriorating conditions will again occur after 10:00 PM when low clouds and fog will form and persist into the morning of 3 March.

1. The Khe Sanh Dump and Ammunition Supply Point (ASP) status as of 8:00 P.M. March 1 is as follows:

	Previous Status	
	Days Supply	8:00 PM 29 Feb
EST		
	On Hand	(9:00 AM 1 Mar SVN)

Class I   (Rations)
    Meal, Combat,
        Individual   15   13 Days
        B Rations   10   10 Days

Class III (Fuel)
        Aviation Gas (AV Gas)   3   3 Days
        JP-4 Fuel (Jet Fuel)   8.3   7.5 Days

TOP SECRET

    Motor Gasoline (Mogas) 9.3   8.7 Days
    Diesel 10   8.4 Days

Class V   (Ammunition)
High Explosive

60-MM Mortar	44	44 Days
81-MM Mortar	24	19 Days
90-MM (Tank)	92	92 Days
4.2" Mortar	15	31 Days
105-MM Howitzer	16	16 Days
155-MM Howitzer	15	15 Days

Anti-Tank
Rounds on Hand

90-MM Heat	1,059
66-MM Rocket (Law)	2,343
Anti-Tank Mines (M-15)	168
Anti-Tank Mines (M-19)	668
Anti-Tank Mines (M-21)	0
106-MM Heat	154
106-MM Recoilless Rifle (Hep-T)	706
106-MM Beehive	909
3.5" Rocket	946
90-MM AP-T	329

                Previous Status
        Days Supply   8:00 PM 29 Feb
EST
        On Hand   (9:00 AM 1 Mar SVN)

Class V   (COFRAM)
    105-MM Howitzer 5   5 Days
    155-MM Howitzer 5   5 Days

40-MM Grenade Launcher	5	5 Days
Hand Grenades	10	10 Days

2. On 1 March Khe Sanh was resupplied with 99 tons as follows:

Class I	29 Tons
Class II	2 Tons
Class III	16 Tons
Class IV	8 Tons
Class V	43 Tons
Class VII	1 Ton

FROM: WHITE HOUSE SITUATION ROOM
    (HAYDEN)
TO: THE PRESIDENT
CITE: CAP80639

SECRET

TEXT OF GENERAL WESTMORELAND'S REPORT. This is report number twenty-eight on the situation in the Khe Sanh/DMZ area and covers the 24 hour period 2 March 1968.

For the second successive day, enemy activity at Khe Sanh was limited to small probes and comparatively light incoming. Cloudy skies with low ceiling limited fixed wing support throughout most of the morning and evening. An afternoon break in the weather permitted limited support. While fixed wing support was affected by the weather, fire support elements expended 3099 rounds of mixed artillery and mortar earmarked

TOP SECRET

for known and suspected enemy positions. Of the missions fired, 32 percent were observed. Resupply aircraft were able to land, offload 192.5 short tons of supplies and equipment and take off without enemy interference. Generally, the pace of the action yesterday was slow with no material enemy effect on friendly activities. Enemy ground activity was light. A few scattered NVA were spotted in the open during the day. 81 MM mortar missions were fired with undetermined results. An operation of the 2nd Battalion, 26th Marines observed 13 secondary explosions caused by air strikes five kilometers northwest of Khe Sanh. An air observer sighted 648 rocket positions four kilometers south of Khe Sanh; he also spotted trail, bunker and living area 10 kilometers south of Khe Sanh. Supporting arms were fired with undetermined results. An operation from the 20 Battalion, 25th Marines observed 18 secondary explosions resulting from an air strike five kilometers northwest of Khe Sanh. Two Marines were wounded from the 1st AMTRAC battalion when 13 rounds of 100MM artillery fell at Cua Viet. Ground contacts were limited throughout the period. In one significant encounter, a "kill team" of the 1st Battalion 4th Marines engaged a small enemy force, four kilometers southeast of Con Thien, and killed 10 NVA while sustaining o friendly casualties, in the vicinity of Mai Xa Thi Villar, final sweeping operations by the 3D Battalion, 1st Marines uncovered 45 NVA bodies yesterday which had not been previously reported. This contact now totals 81 NVA killed with three POW's and eight individual weapons captured. Another Cua Viet To Dong Ha convoy was fired upon yesterday in the vicinity of its destination. Minor damage was caused from the four or five recoilless rifle rounds received. Gun ships in the area rendered support.

One COFRAM mission of 15 rounds was fired as part of night defense fires for the 37th ARVN Ranger Battalion at Khe Sanh, with undetermined results.

A total of 296 tactical air sorties were flown during the period in support of the Khe Sanh area. Marine aircraft flew 89 sorties; the USAF flew 127 sorties; the Navy flew 80 sorties, bomb damage included 24 secondary explosions, six secondary fires, 20 road cuts, 11 ford cuts, two bunkers destroyed, and 12 enemy killed. Seven ARC LIGHT strikes (42 sorties) were scheduled and flown in the Niagara area.

For the next period a total of 284 tactical air sorties will be flown in the Khe Sanh area. The Marines plan 44 sorties; the USAF will fly 140 sorties; the Navy plans 100 sorties. The Marines will have 16 aircraft on call, and the USAF will reserve 120 sorties for Khe Sanh. Seven ARC LIGHT strikes (42 sorties) are scheduled for the Niagara area.

The morning of 2 March at Khe Sanh was cloudy with light drizzle and fog. During the afternoon the weather conditions improved with the cloud ceiling at 2500 feet and good visibility. By 6:00 AM the fog formed and visibility was reduced to one-quarter mile by 11:00 AM. The remainder of the early morning hours remained

TOP SECRET

cloudy with occasional drizzle and fog restricting visibility to one-half mile or less. The forecast for the next 24 hours is for little change with fog persisting until 1:00 AM 3 March. From 1:00 AM to 8:00 AM visibility will remain good and the cloud ceiling is forecast to be 2000 feet. After 8:00 AM fog will form and remain through the early morning reducing visibilities to about one-quarter mile after 1:00 AM.

The Khe Sanh Dump and Ammunition Supply Point (ASP) status as of the above time is as follows:

```
                    Previous Status
              Days Supply       8:00 PM 1 Mar
EST
              On Hand      (9:00 AM 2 Mar SVN)
```

Class I   (Rations)
    Meal, combat,
    Individual   15   15 Days
    B Rations   9   10 Days

Class III   (Fuel)
    Aviation Gas (AVGas)   3   3 Days
    JP-4 Fuel (Jet Fuel)   8.3   8.3 Days
    Motor Gasoline (MOGas) 9.3   9.3 Days
    Diesel 10   10 Days

Class V   (Ammunition)
A. High Explosive

60-MM Mortar   44   44 Days
81-MM Mortar   4   24 Days

Confidential Files on the Siege and Loss of Khe Sanh

90-MM (Tank)	92	92 Days
4.2" Mortar	47	15 Days
105-MM Howitzer	14	16 Days
155-MM Howitzer	16	15 Days

B. Anti-Tank

	Rounds on Hand
90-MM Heat	1,059
66-MM Rocket (Law)	3,313
Anti-Tank Mines (M-15)	158
Anti-Tank Mines (M-19)	668
Anti-Tank Mines (M-21)	0
106-MM Heat	154
106-MM Recoilless Rifle (Hep-T)	706
106-MM Beehive	909
3.5" Rocket	1,306
90-MM AP-I	329

Class V   (COFRAM)
    105-MM Howitzer 5   5 Days
    155-MM Howitzer TS   5   5; $-6
    40-MM Grenade Launcher   5   5 Days
    Hand Grenades   10   10 Days

On 2 March Khe Sanh was resupplied with 192.5 tons as follows:

    Class I   39 Tons
    Class IV   64.5 Tons
    Class V   87.5 Tons
    Class VIII   1.5 Tons

DTG: 03/1416Z MAR 68

TOP SECRET

In the following report, note paragraph seven "buying time": "the enemy must have been hurt. These were only the visible signs." And ". . . we must buy additional time to get ARVN back on its feet . . . ."

SECRET

HEADQUARTERS
UNITED STATES MILITARY ASSISTANCE COMMAND, VIETNAM
APO SAN FRANCISCO 96222

Combat Operations Center

MACCOC   3 March 1968

MEMORANDUM FOR RECORD
SUBJECT: COMUSMACV Visit to I CTZ

1. On 3 March COMUSMACV visited I CTZ. First stop was at CHU LAI where he was briefed by MGen Koster. Gen Cushman was present.
2. The status of the move of the 2/35 to DUC PHO was discussed. Gen Koster indicated that he needed it in WHEELER/WALLOWA AO for about ten days, the might be able to move it south to DUC PHO, relieving a battalion of the 11th Bde. Gen Koster stated that his first additional battalion would close by 31 March; it is the 5/46 of the 198th Bde. By 17 April the remaining two additional battalions will have closed. He estimated that by 10 April, he could deploy 2/35th to BINH DINH. COMUSMACV stated that he would try to

leave it in Americal Division until 10 April, but it might have to deploy sooner, if situation worsened in II CTZ. He further stated that he would leave it up to Gen. Koster as to whether he moved 2/36 to DUC PHO, or, made one move directly to BINH DINH.

3. Gen. Koster stated that 2D ARVN Division was in good shape and was conducting offensive operations. Most of these were daylight operations, with the units returning around the cities at night.

4. Highway 1 is open throughout zone, although there is an average of one mining incident per day. A convoy of 3d Bde, 82d Abn was moving today from CHU LAI to DANANG.

5. At 1400, COMUSMACV arrived at HUE - PHU BAI for briefing by DEPCOMUSMACV. Present were LT Gens Cushman and Rosson and Mgens Van Ryzin, Anderson and Pearson.

6. Gen Abrams gave a rundown on enemy and friendly situation and on the logistical situation. Gen Abrams stated that requirement of 2000 S/T for I CTZ North per day was not being met, but that by 10 march with opening of LOTS it was anticipated that 3350 short tons per day could be moved into I CTZ North. The daily requirement on that date would be 2650 short tons (this excludes KHE SANH requirements and POL, both of which are handled separately). Gen Abrams set forth his airlift priorities as follows:

a. Continue airlift into KHE SANH
b. Immediate lift of DELTA Force from NHA TRANG

TOP SECRET

c. Continue 400 S/T per day to I CTZ North
d. 38 sorties to lift Hq 101st Abn
e. Lift remainder of 2d Bde, 1st Cav

7. COMUSMACV discussed current situation and pointed out that we had been buying time (to get our forces positioned and logistically organized) by pounding the enemy with heavy air attacks at KHE SANH. He pointed out that with over 2000 secondaries, 200 fires, and two battalion equivalents KBA, the enemy must have been hurt. These were only the visible signs. COMUSMACV further indicated that we must buy additional time to get ARVN back on its feet, especially the 3d Regt. We must be prepared for enemy to attempt to cross BEN HAI with tanks. We have anticipated this by reallocating Anti-Tank weapons and increasing our AT posture. When weather improves, we must expect more observed enemy fire on KHE SANH. This can be met by air attacks.
8. COMUSMACV outlined his plan to shift Arc Light strikes, if weather permits tactical air to support KHE SANH. He indicated that ASHAU, especially, had to be hit hard, as well as route 547.
9. COMUSMACV advised DEPCOMUS that he was planning to send elements of a River Assault Division to I CTZ. He directed Gen Chaisson to inform Adm Veth to discuss with COMUSMACV the question of RAG (VN) capabilities and assets in I CTZ.
10. The question of helicopter support for the 101st Division was raised by Gen Abrams.

COMUSMACV requested Gen Abrams to send him a message addressing the question of bed down and support of additional helicopters, with a recommended time phasing.

11. Gen Westmoreland, Gen Abrams, LT Gen Cushman and LT Gen Rosson met in executive session after the opening meeting.

J. R. CHAISSON

FROM WALT ROSTOW
TO THE PRESIDENT
CITE: CAP80652

SECRET
March 4, 1968

Herewith the daily Khe Sanh-DMZ report:
— 160 tons delivered;
— COCZINUED Probing;
— Considerable casualties inflicted on the enemy; 30th on the ground and with artillery fire.

This is report number twenty-nine on the situation in the Khe Sanh/DMZ area and covers the 24 hour period March 3, 1968.

Limited visibility with low ceilings continued at Khe Sanh throughout most of the reporting period. Despite disagreeable weather conditions, several air observer controlled fixed wing air strikes were effectively executed. During the day artillery batteries from the 13th Marines fired 133 missions expending 1353 rounds of ammunition with excellent target coverage reported.

TOP SECRET

Supplies and equipment amounting to 160 short tons were offloaded during the period as resupply aircraft landed and took off without interference. Generally, enemy activity at Khe Sanh during the day was confined sporadic incoming artillery and mortar rounds and harassing probes.

Of particular note during the period, was a sighting made by an air observer at 11:45 AM, nine kilometers (??) of Hill 881. An estimated enemy battalion was (??) in a column moving east. Air strikes and artillery missions resulted in a report that 15 North Vietnamese were killed. Elsewhere during the day, the Marines found two directional mines on the left flank of their "D" company. Although one was disarmed, the other detonated and blew open a section of their defensive wire. This morning the company rescued small arms fire from a location southeast of their position. Artillery missions were called, silencing the fires, at 1:25 AM the 37th ARVN Ranger Battalion reported a probe of their lines. Mortar rounds and artillery defensive fires were employed.

Enemy incoming at Khe Sanh was comparatively light yesterday (??) only 130 rounds of mixed artillery, rocket and mortar struck in the area. Although no materiel damage was reported, 16 Marines were wounded. At adjacent installations bordering the DME, enemy shelling continued during the period, but a slackened pace of 34 rounds of mortar and 20 artillery rounds fell at Camp Carroll with only minor injuries sustained by one Marine. At Dong Ha combat base 16 rounds of artillery mixed with two mortar rounds were received between noon and 4:00 PM. There were no injuries recorded. The 3D Battalion, 3D Marines at A-3 received a total of 11 afternoon rounds of artillery with no damage reported. Offshore, six artillery rounds were fired at the USS Newport News with the nearest round impacting 200 yards away, causing no damage to the vessel.

In an all day contact A Company of Marines spotted 330 well equipped North Vietnamese 1500 meters west of A-3. Air strikes and artillery were employed. When contact closed, 136 North Vietnamese bodies were counted. Friendly casualties were one killed, three wounded (evacuated). At positions 1500 meter east of A-3, Marines engaged a dug-in enemy force. With artillery preparatory fires in support, friendly units accounted for 21 North Vietnamese killed with eight individual and one crew served weapon captured. Friendly casualties were one killed and five wounded. While sweeping in the vicinity of Mai Xa Thi Village yesterday, the 3D Battalion, 1st Marines found 32 more North Vietnamese bodies and three additional individual weapons. A landing craft struck a mine 300 meters southeast of Mai Xa Thi Village injuring three Marines and damaging the vehicle.

Three COFRAM missions were fired expending 50 rounds, and killing 9 enemy.

There were a total of 216 tactical air sorties flown in support of Khe Sanh area. The Marines flew 101 sorties, with bomb damage reported as one secondary explosion, two secondary fires, one automatic weapon position destroyed, and 15

TOP SECRET

enemy killed. The Air Force flew 96 sorties and the Navy 79, reporting 19 road cuts, one tank destroyed, four gun positions destroyed, eight enemy killed, one armored vehicle damaged, seven secondary explosions, ten secondary fires, nine military structures and two trucks destroyed, five ARC Light strikes (30 sorties) were flown in the Niagara area.

Air resupply for Khe Sanh for the period amounted to 160 short tons. Resupply sorties totalled 23 for 3 March, ten C-130 aircraft completed ten air drops. Three C-123's completed the air drops and one landed. Ten helicopters delivered passengers and cargo.

Tactical air support for the next period will total 270 sorties. There will be eight B-52 strikes (48 sorties) flown in the Niagara area.

The morning of 3 march 1968 at Khe Sanh was cloudy with fog and occasional light drizzle. Conditions improved during the early afternoon with ceilings of 1500 feet and visibility which ranged from 3 - 5 miles in fog. After 3:00 PM the weather again began to deteriorate reducing ceilings and visibility to 500 feet and 2 1/2 miles by 9:00 PM. Conditions were further restricted after midnight and until the early morning hours of 4 March as heavy fog reduced visibility to 1/15 mile. Little change is forecast through 9:00 AM of 5 March. The best conditions are expected between 11:00 PM - 7:00 PM when ceilings and visibility are forecast to be 1300 feet and six miles. After 9:00 PM heavy fog will again reduce visibilities to below one mile.

Confidential Files on the Siege and Loss of Khe Sanh

The Khe Sanh dump and ammunition supply point status as of 5:00 P.M. March 3 is as follows:

Previous Status
          Days Supply   8:00 PM 2 Mar Est
          On Hand   (9:00 AM 3 Mar SVN)

Class I   (Rations)
    Meal, Combat,
    Individual 18   15 Days
    B Rations   10   9 Days

Class III   (Fuel)
    Aviation Gas (AVGas)   3   3 Days
    JP-4 Fuel (Jet Fuel)   8.3   9.3 Days
    Motor Gasoline (MOGas) 9   9.3 Days
    Diesel 8.7   10 Days

Class V   (Ammunition)
    A. High Explosive
    60-MM Mortar   44   44 Days
    81-MM Mortar   24   24 Days
    90-MM (Tank)   92   92 Days
    4.2" Mortar 47   47 Days
    103-MM Howitzer 13   14 Days
    155-MM Howitzer 15   16 Days

    B. Anti-Tank   Rounds on Hand
    90-MM Heat   1,259
    66-MM Rocket (Law)   3,531
    Anti-Tank Mines (M-15) 158
    Anti-tank Mines (M-19) 668
    Anti-Tank Mines (M-21) 0

TOP SECRET

    106-MM Heat   154
    106-MM Recoilless Rifle (REP-T)   726
    106-MM Beehive 909
    3.5" Rocket 1,632
    32-MM AP-T   323

81

THE WHITE HOUSE
WASHINGTON

    Tuesday, March 5, 1968
    8:25 P.M.

Mr. President:
Mr. Rostow has been informed of the attached and instructed it be sent to you.

    White House
    Situation Room

The offensive of the North Vietnamese is likened to "the Battle of the Bulge; namely, a maximum effort by the enemy which he could not sustain":

THE JOINT CHIEFS OF STAFF
WASHINGTON, D. C. 20301

CM-3088-68
5 March 1968

MEMORANDUM FOR THE PRESIDENT:
SUBJECT: Telephone conversation with General Westmoreland

1. I talked to General Westmoreland on the secure telephone at 1840 hours this date. He had no specific items to report other than those appearing in your operational/intelligence daily summary. However, he made several comments which I think you will find of interest:
a. He and General Vien, Chief of the South Vietnamese Joint General Staff, have been traveling around the countryside, looking at the situation and conferring with ARVN and U.S. commanders. He stated that morale is good and everyone is behaving in a steady and confident manner.
b. As he did when I visited him in Saigon, he likened the present situation to the Battle of the Bulge; namely, a maximum effort by the enemy which he could not sustain. General Westmoreland told me that the enemy appears to have lost momentum in many areas; they tend to utilize standoff fire against friendly forces and

installations rather than attacking them as they did in early and mid-February.

c. General Westmoreland's logistical situation in northern I Corps is improving steadily. He is thinking of establishing the Provisional Corps in that area under Lieutenant General Rosson in the very near future.

2. Without implying any derogation of General Westmoreland's analogy to the Battle of the Bulge, I believe it is still too early to forecast with any great precision the extent to which the enemy can and will resume a heightened ground effort. Intelligence indicators strongly support the thesis that the enemy is preparing for a major effort in the Hue/Phu Bai area. Moreover, the enemy has the capability to renew attacks against Da Nang and in the central highlands. In other words, despite very heavy losses, I think the enemy still has unexpended resources which he can throw at us. This is not to say that I am not delighted at the slackening in enemy activity; it indicates, I think, that he is having logistical and personnel problems and his plans are being disrupted by our air and ground attacks.

EARLE G. WHEELER
Chairman
Joint Chiefs of Staff

THE WHITE HOUSE
WASHINGTON

Tuesday, March 7, 1968 — 9:30 a.m.

Confidential Files on the Siege and Loss of Khe Sanh

Mr. President:
At Khe Sanh yesterday:
— good weather;
— 217 tons delivered;
— 2367 rounds fired;
— antiaircraft fire heavier, bringing down the C-123;
— 343 tactical air sorties to good effect;
— 42 B-52 sorties.

W. W. Rostow

SECRET

Thursday, March 7, 1968, 9:50 AM

TEXT OF CABLE FROM
GENERAL WESTMORELAND

This is report number thirty-two on the situation in the Khe Sanh/DMZ area for the 24-hour period of March 6, 1968.

Clear skies at Khe Sanh throughout most of the period provided optimum flying conditions for fixed and rotary wing aircraft. Logistical and supporting arms efforts were improved throughout the area of operation. A total of 217 short tons of supplies and equipment were offloaded during the period. Fire support elements expanded a total of 2367 rounds of mixed mortar and artillery.

Enemy anti-air resistance was heavy yesterday as 13 Marine aircraft were fired on with three receiving hits. At 2:00 PM, a C-123 with 47

TOP SECRET

passengers and crew members aboard, received fire on let-down for Khe Sanh, attempted to leave the area, and crashed eight miles east of Khe Sanh. Search parties report no signs of life at the scene.

Enemy artillery, rocket and mortar rounds totaled 115 throughout the period. Eighteen Marines were wounded. An incoming rocket struck a parked C-123 aircraft. No injuries were caused, the plane sustained limited damage. Two other aircraft were reported down yesterday. A helicopter was downed by hostile fire while hovering over a position in Ashau Valley. Five of the 11 people aboard have been rescued so far. An Air Force F-105 crashed in Laos yesterday. The pilot ejected safely, and was recovered.

Along the demilitarized zone, enemy activity centered on Operation Kentucky. Elements positioned at C-2 and C-3 received five and 39 rounds of artillery respectively. Five Marines were injured at C-2, no materiel damage was reported. Con Thien received 15 artillery rounds and eight rounds of mortar, with no casualties or damage reported. At A-3, elements of the 3rd Marines received nine artillery rounds. Other 3rd Marine elements northwest of Dong Ha received 30 rounds of rocket and 15 mortar rounds with no casualties or damage reported. Dong Ha combat base in late afternoon received 10 rounds of artillery resulting in two wounded. Near Camp Carroll, elements of the 9th Marines received 12 mortar rounds, injuring five Marines.

Ground activity in northern Quang Tri Province was significant. In a sharp contact five kilometers northeast of Con Thien, two companies of the 3rd Marines engaged an unknown size enemy force. Eighty-one North Vietnamese Army were killed. Friendly casualties were 14 killed, 29 wounded. South of the Cua Viet river, a battalion of the 4th Marines in night defensive positions fired on 15 North Vietnamese Army in the open. A search at first light revealed 11 enemy bodies and seven individual weapons. South of the Cua Viet, an artillery mission fired on troops in the open killed four enemy.

Marine aircraft flew 142 tactical air sorties in support of Khe Sanh, the Air Force flew 122, and the Navy 79, for a total of 343 sorties. Bomb damage included 87 secondary explosions, 27 secondary fires, 30 bunkers destroyed, 17 enemy killed, one rocket position damaged, 29 road cuts, three trucks destroyed, and 100 meters of trench destroyed. Seven AIR LIGHT strikes (42 sorties) were flown. Twenty secondary explosions were reported from three of the seven strikes. The B-52 effort was concentrated on targets beyond three kilometers from the Khe Sanh perimeter. Only one strike was flown on a close-in target.

During the period 217 short tons of supplies and 85 passengers were flown into Khe Sanh. Twenty-nine resupply sorties were flown on March 6. Nine C-130's and three C-123's completed air drops, three C-123's landed, and 24 helicopters delivered passengers and cargo.

For the next period, 270 sorties are scheduled to support Khe Sanh. Seven ARC LIGHT strikes (42 sorties) are scheduled.

TOP SECRET

THE WHITE HOUSE
WASHINGTON

Friday, March 8, 1968 — 9:05 a.m.

Mr. President:
At Khe Sanh:
— a second consecutive good weather day;
— 3204 rounds friendly artillery; 95 enemy;
— 321 sorties; 42 B-52's;
— 221 tons delivered;
— 5 U.S. wounded.

W. W. Rostow

Friday, March 8, 1968, 8:45 AM

TEXT OF CABLE FROM
GENERAL WESTMORELAND

This is report number thirty-three on the situation in the Khe Sanh/DMZ area for the 24-hour period of March 7, 1968.

Excellent flying conditions continued at Khe Sanh for the second consecutive day, with seven mile visibility. High ceilings and broken clouds favored fixed and rotary wing aircraft support. Fire support elements, suppressing enemy firing positions and firing on targets of opportunity, expended a total of 3204 rounds of mixed artillery and mortar with excellent target coverage reported. Enemy anti-air incidents continued yesterday with eight aircraft fired on and two receiving hits.

Enemy activity was comparatively light at Khe Sanh. Enemy incoming artillery, rocket and mortar rounds comprised most of the enemy activity. A total of 95 rounds of mixed incoming fell during the 24-hour period, causing injuries to five Marines, four of whom required evacuation. As a result of a rocket round impacting on the airstrip, the runway was temporarily closed to fixed wing aircraft. Repairs were completed by 9:00 AM. At 1:45 PM, an air observer spotted several North Vietnamese Army in bunkers and trenches 17 kilometers north of Khe Sanh. A controlled air strike succeeded in killing five North Vietnamese Army.

Elsewhere within northern Quang Tri Province enemy incoming slackened somewhat, but ground activity increased. A total of 10 rounds of mortar fell near Camp Carroll during the period, causing injuries to five. At 11:00 AM yesterday, the Marines in Napoleon/Saline received 12 rounds of artillery, resulting in two killed and six wounded and evacuated. At 8:30 AM this morning, the Dong Ha combat base received 80 rounds of mixed rocket and artillery resulting in 13 killed and 26 wounded.

Significant ground contacts were recorded yesterday in northern I Corps as the Marines, working in conjunction with ARVN elements, made contact with an estimated three company size enemy force, 4 1/2 kilometers north of Dong Ha. Contact continued until 7:00 PM with artillery and air strikes being employed. Initial casualty amounted to 115 killed. Initial friendly casualty figures are two killed and 76 wounded.

TOP SECRET

In a similar all day contact, the Marines engaged an unknown size enemy force on the south bank of the Cua Viet river. Preliminary friendly casualties are 13 killed and 48 wounded. Enemy casualties are unknown. Fifteen North Vietnamese Army bodies were discovered in what appears to have been an enemy first aid shelter just north of the Cua Viet river.

At 10:10 AM yesterday, the Marines fired 23 rounds of mortar on a known enemy firing position 1500 meters north of Con Thien, and observed three secondary explosions. An air observer spotted an enemy active mortar position with North Vietnamese Army occupying trenches and bunkers, 1 1/2 kilometers northeast of Con Thien. A controlled air strike on the position resulted in 13 North Vietnamese Army killed. The mortar position was destroyed along with 200 meters of trench line. Another air observer controlled air strike four kilometers north of Camp Carroll destroyed two mortars and killed three North Vietnamese Army. At 3:10 PM, an air observer adjusted a fire mission on enemy mortar positions, at approximately the same location, resulting in the complete destruction of the mortar positions and the killing of four North Vietnamese Army.

One COFRAM mission was fired expending ten rounds with undetermined results.

Marine aircraft flew 134 sorties in support of Khe Sanh, the Air Force flew 117, and the Navy 70 for a total of 321 sorties. Bomb damage included four gun positions destroyed, 13 secondary explosions, 28 secondary fires, 35 bunkers destroyed, 21 structures destroyed, one mortar position destroyed, six road cuts, and one armored vehicle damaged. Seven ARC LIGHT strikes comprising 42 sorties were flown. Two of the strikes were against close-in targets. From the previous period additional bomb damage includes 14 secondary explosions, 100 foxholes destroyed, and several trench lines destroyed.

During the period 221.5 short tons of supplies and 21 passengers were flown into Khe Sanh. Fifty-three resupply sorties were flown on March 7. C-130's flew 11 air drops, 42 helicopters air-landed.

For the next 24 hours 268 tactical air sorties are scheduled to support Khe Sanh. Three ARAC LIGHT strikes, 18 sorties, are scheduled. The remainder of the force will hit targets in Thua Thien against suspected enemy concentrations. However, the scheduled Thua Thien strikes can be diverted to the Khe Sanh area on two hours notice.

The weather forecast for Khe Sanh is for continued good visibility from late morning on March 8 with skies clear to scattered.

SECRET

Sunday, March 10, 1968

MEMORANDUM FOR THE PRESIDENT
Herewith, General Westmoreland's report number thirty-five on the situation in the Khe Sanh/DMZ area for the 24-hour period ending 8:00 PM, March 9.

TOP SECRET

Favorable weather conditions prevailed at Khe Sanh during most of the period. Low ceilings lifted by noon, providing improved conditions for air support. Fire support elements expended 2,277 rounds of mixed artillery and mortar with excellent target coverage reported. There were only three anti-air incidents reported.

During the period, enemy action consisted mostly of shelling the Khe Sanh positions. Ground activity was light. During the day 250 rounds of mixed mortar, rocket and artillery fell at Khe Sanh and surrounding areas. Injuries attributed to the shelling were two killed and 15 wounded (four evacuated). A helicopter parked at Khe Sanh received 50 shrapnel holes causing substantial damage to the aircraft and minor injuries to two crew members.

At noon an air observer controlled air strikes on 14 North Vietnamese soldiers in the open southeast of Khe Sanh, resulted in seven enemy killed. About two-hours later an enemy bunker complex was detected 300 meters south of Khe Sanh. An air observer controlled air strike accounted for five enemy killed and the destruction of one bunker. At 6:00 PM elements from the 26th Marines spotted four enemy digging a trench four miles northeast of Hill 881. An 81mm mortar mission, followed by a fixed wing napalm strike accounted for four killed and five secondary explosions. One ARVN Ranger was killed and one wounded yesterday by sniper fire. Fire was returned with undetermined results.

At installations bordering the DMZ, enemy activity was confined mostly to incoming artillery, rocket and mortar rounds. Six Marines were wounded at Camp Carroll as 13 mortar rounds fell during the period. Yesterday evening twelve 140mm rocket rounds struck at Dong Ha injuring nine, one of whom required evacuation.

Ground contacts in northern Quang Tri Province during the reporting period were comparatively light. Yesterday afternoon elements from the 9th Marines spotted seven enemy running east from a position three miles southwest of Camp Carroll. In trying to overtake the seven, the friendly unit came under fire by 60-70 enemy. Artillery and fixed wing strikes were called. Two enemy were confirmed killed. Enemy was observed departing the area carrying

[Page missing]

THE WHITE HOUSE
WASHINGTON

SECRET

Monday, March 11, 1968 — 9:45 a.m.

Mr. President:
Khe Sanh-DMZ:
— weather less good;
— enemy fired 250 rounds;
— 178 tons delivered;
— 328 sorties plus 36 B-52's;
— our supply base at Cua Viet, at eastern end of DMZ hit quite badly by lucky enemy round;
— major successful further ARVN fire fight at

TOP SECRET

Dong Ha, 102 enemy killed, 7 captured.

W. W. Rostow

SECRET

Monday, March 11, 1968, 8:45 AM

TEXT OF CABLE FROM
GENERAL WESTMORELAND

This is report number thirty-six on the situation in the Khe Sanh/DMZ area for the 24-hour period of March 10, 1968.

Low ceilings and drizzle prevailed at Khe Sanh through most of the reporting period, with a consequent decline in the number of air strikes flown. Light enemy anti-air incidents were recorded as only two aircraft were fired on with minor damage reported to one. Enemy activity was confined to incoming mortar, artillery and rocket rounds with 250 rounds of mixed ordnance falling during the day. Two Marines were killed and 15 wounded, four of whom required medical evacuation.

No significant ground contacts were reported. Enemy activities at other installations in northern Quang Tri paralleled activity at Khe Sanh. No ground contacts were reported by Marine units. However, enemy shelling was damaging. The day's incoming included 10 rounds of artillery falling at A-3. Camp Carroll received 10 mortar rounds. No casualties or damage was reported in either instance. Several artillery rounds fell at positions occupied by the 4th Marines at C-3, with no damage or casualties reported.

Beginning at 7:30 AM on March 10, the Dong Ha combat base received 70 rounds of rocket and 82 rounds of mixed mortar and artillery resulting in three killed and 14 wounded, with seven evacuees. At 9:00 AM, one incoming ground landed at the landing ship tank ramp on the Cua Viet. The round struck a drum of fuel, spread into the fuel farm causing secondary fires. The fires subsequently set off several rounds of ammunition. Eighty-five percent of the ramp was reported destroyed. Damages included destruction of five trucks, several buildings, two fuel tanks, one artillery weapon, three communications vans, one crane, three fork lifts and a guard tower. The bladder farm was reported 33 percent destroyed. Initial casualties were recorded as one killed and 28 wounded.

ARVN operations in northern Quang Tri Province included a large contact north of Dong Ha. In Operation Lamson 193, elements of the 2nd ARVN Regiment engaged a large size enemy force. Fighting continued throughout the day. Friendly casualty figures were recorded as three killed, 37 wounded. A total of 102 enemy were killed with 20 individual and five crew served weapons captured. Seven North Vietnamese Army prisoners were captured.

Marine aircraft flew 80 tactical air sorties in support of Khe Sanh, the Air Force flew 141, and the Navy 107 for a total of 328 sorties. Bomb damage includes two trucks destroyed, 42 road cuts, 14 secondary explosions. 43 secondary fires, three bunkers and 140 meters of trench

TOP SECRET

destroyed 13 enemy killed, seven gun positions destroyed, and 14 structures destroyed. There were six ARC LIGHT strikes (36 sorties) scheduled into the Niagara area however, four aircraft went to secondary targets due to targeting equipment and aircraft malfunctions. Three strikes in the Niagara area were classified as close-in targets, ranging from 1300 - 1800 meters from friendly forces.

During the period, 178.5 short tons of supplies were airlifted into Khe Sanh. In addition, 92 passengers were flown in. In all, a total of 18 sorties were flown. Twelve C-130's conducted eleven air drops. Five C-123's conducted three air drops and two landed at the field. One helicopter landed at the field.

For the next period, 307 tactical sorties are scheduled. Six ARC LIGHT strikes (36 sorties) are scheduled.

The morning of March 10 at Khe Sanh was foggy with visibility as low as 1/8 mile at midmorning. Low clouds remained through the afternoon. After dark, fog formed again restricting visibilities to 1/16 mile by the morning of March 11. The forecast is for continued cloudy weather, with fog during the morning hours and after 8:00 PM at night, lowering visibilities to 1/2 mile after midnight.

Khe Sanh continues to be resupplied with massive tons of materiel; the following report specifies that in one day March 10, 1968, Khe Sanh received 178.5 tons of rations, fuel, ammunition and land mines (COFRAM).

THE NATIONAL MILITARY COMMAND CENTER
WASHINGTON, D. C. 20301

    11 Mach 1968
    0300 EST

MEMORANDUM FOR THE WHITE HOUSE
    SITUATION ROOM
Subject: Supply Status at Khe Sanh as of 8:00 PM EST 10 Mar (9:00 AM 11 Mar, SVN time)

1. The Khe Sahn Dump and Ammunition Supply Point (ASP) status as of the above time is as follows:

	Previous Status Days Supply On Hand	8:00 PM 9 Mar EST (9:00 AM 10 Mar SVN)	
Class I (Rations)			
Meal, Combat, Individual	18	1	7 days
B Rations	9	8 days	
Class III (Fuel)			
Aviation Gas (AVGas)	3	3 days	
JP-4 Fuel (Jet Fuel)	10.6	10.6 days	
Motor Gasoline (MOGas)	6.1	7.1 days	

TOP SECRET

    Diesel 3.3   4.3 days
Class V (Ammunition)
High explosive
    60-mm mortar   43   42 days
    82-mm mortar   20   22 days
    90-mm (Tank)   108   108 days
    4.2 mortar   40   40 days
    105-mm howitzer 25   24 days
    155-mm howitzer 14   14 days
b. Antitank Rounds on Hand
    90-mm HEAT   1,202
    66-mm rocket (LAW)   3,381
    Antitank mines (M-15)   198
    Antitank mines (M-19)   668
    Antitank mines (M-21)   0
    106-mm HEAT   872
    106-mm recoilless rifle
        (HEP-T)   2,264
    3.5" rocket   2,189
    90-mm AP-T   329

                Previous Status
        Days Supply   8:00 PM 9 Mar
EST
        On Hand   (9:00 AM 10 Mar SVN)

c. Antipersonnel   Rounds on Hand
106-mm BEEHIVE   1,027

Class V (COFRAM)
    105-mm howitzer 5   5 days
    155-mm howitzer 5   5 days
    40-mm grenade launcher 5   5 days
    Hand grenades   10   10 days

On 10 March, Khe Sanh was resupplied with 178.5 tons as follows:

Class I   13.0 tons
Class II   2.0 tons
Class III   30.5 tons
Class IV   12.5 tons
Class V   118.0 tons
Miscellaneous 2.5 tons

    JAMES A. SHANNON
    Brigadier General, USAF
    Deputy Director for
    Operations (NMCC)

THE WHITE HOUSE
WASHINGTON

    Tuesday, March 12, 1968
    10:15 a.m.

MR. PRESIDENT:
At Khe Sanh:
— poor weather;
— 150 rounds enemy fire;
— 343 sorties plus 36 B-52's;
— 207 tons delivered.

W. W. Rostow

SECRET
    Tuesday, March 12, 1968, 9:30 AM

TEXT OF CABLE FROM
    GENERAL WESTMORELAND

TOP SECRET

This is report number thirty-seven on the situation in the Khe Sanh/DMZ area for the 24-hour period of March 11, 1968.

Unfavorable weather conditions continued at Khe Sanh during the reporting period, as fog with intermittent drizzle persisted throughout most of the morning and evening hours. Low ceilings lifted somewhat during the afternoon hours, permitting limited fixed wing support. Enemy anti-air incidents were light as only two aircraft were fired on and one was hit with minor damage.

During the period enemy activity was confined to incoming artillery, rocket and mortar rounds. There were no ground contacts reported. A total of 150 rounds of mixed caliber fell on the Khe Sanh area during the day. Casualties attributed to the shelling were three killed and 23 wounded (eight evacuated).

In the DMZ area, enemy shelling comprised the majority of enemy activity with no significant casualties or damage reported. In the vicinity of the Cua Viet river, elements of the 3rd and 4th Marines received 15 mortar rounds and 12 artillery rounds. One Marine was wounded. In ARVN operations, elements of the 2nd Regiment were in heavy contact throughout most of the day, north of Dong Ha. Initial friendly casualties are recorded as 22 killed and 65 wounded. Enemy casualties are unknown. Sweep operations continue.

There was one COFRAM mission of six rounds fired with undetermined results.

Marine aircraft flew 123 sorties, the Air Force 134, the Navy 86, for a total of 343 sorties.

Bomb damage assessment included 14 road cuts, three automatic weapons positions destroyed, one rocket position destroyed, one bridge destroyed, two bunkers destroyed, eight secondary explosions, 19 secondary fires, and 15 enemy killed by air. There were six ARC LIGHT strikes (36 sorties) scheduled, however, three aircraft went to secondary targets due to beacon malfunction. Three strikes were within 1300 - 2800 meters of friendly troops.

A total of 207 short tons of supplies were airlifted into the Khe Sanh area during the period. In addition, one short ton of mail and 93 passengers were lifted into the base. A total of 28 resupply sorties were flown, eleven air drops by C-130 and two by C-123, and 15 sorties by Marine helicopters.

For the next period, 308 tactical air sorties are scheduled. In addition, the Air Force will have 120 alert sorties, and the Marines will have 16 aircraft on call. Five ARC LIGHT strikes (30 sorties) are scheduled.

The weather forecast for March 12 is for improving conditions to 800 foot ceilings and two mile visibility by mid-morning, and to 2500 to 500 foot ceilings and 7 - 10 miles visibility by early afternoon. Conditions will again deteriorate after sunset, reducing ceilings and visibility to less than 500 feet and one mile by midnight.

THE WHITE HOUSE
WASHINGTON

      Saturday, March 16, 1968 — 9:00 am

TOP SECRET

Mr. President:
Weather luck holds at Khe Sanh:
— 234 incoming rounds;
— 351 friendly sorties plus 36 B-52's;
— recce and small attacks on A Shau Valley, of which we shall have more;
— 227 tons delivered.

W. W. Rostow

SECRET

Saturday, March 16, 1968, 8:30 AM

MEMORANDUM FOR THE PRESIDENT
Herewith, General Westmoreland's report number forty-one on the situation in the Khe Sanh/DMZ area for the 24-hour period ending 8:00 PM, 15 March.

Khe Sanh had clear weather after early morning haze lifted after 11:00 am. Prior to that time, Air Force resupply operations had been hampered.

During the period, Khe Sanh received 30 rounds of artillery, 14 rounds of rocket and 190 rounds of mortar fire, for a total of 234 rounds. The incoming fire resulted in one Marine killed and 13 wounded (three evacuated). Enemy indirect fire attacks marked the only activity at the base, as no ground contacts were reported. There was no change in either the disposition of Marines in defense at Khe Sanh, or in the enemy situation.

Elsewhere along the DMZ, contact was light

with one exception. Dong Ha received twenty-five 140mm rocket rounds which wounded 13 personnel. Two required medical evacuation. Total casualty figures for the 3rd Marine Division area for the period were, two Marines killed, 39 wounded (16 evacuated), 14 enemy killed.

In tactical air operations, 351 sorties were flown. Marines flew 130, US Air Force 133, and the Navy 88. Bomb damage assessment included 53 secondary fires, 19 road cuts, 45 bunkers destroyed, three trucks destroyed, 18 secondary explosions, 25 enemy killed by air and one mortar position destroyed.

In the A Shau Valley, US Air Force flew four reconnaissance sorties and seven tactical strike sorties. Bomb damage assessment included three secondary explosions and 10 bunkers destroyed.

Six Arc Light strikes (36 sorties) were scheduled into the Niagara Area, One strike, within 1,200 meters of friendly troops, with fifteen secondary explosions reported.

Aerial resupply for the period totaled 227 short tons. One hundred and forty-two passenger replacements were landed at the field. Throughout the day, 49 sorties were flown. Fixed wing aircraft conducted 16 airdrops. Marine helicopters flew the remaining 33 sorties, delivering passengers and cargo.

Three hundred and sixteen tactical air sorties were scheduled for the next 24-hour period, with the Marines planning 88, Air Force 128 and the Navy 100. Marines will maintain their 16 aircraft on call and the Air Force will have 120 alert sorties available on call. Six Arc Light strikes (36

TOP SECRET

sorties) are also scheduled.

The forecast for 16 March is for scattered clouds and good visibility by 11:00 am. Ceilings and visibility will again lower by mid-night and fog will reduce conditions to marginal by early morning on the seventeenth.

FM GENERAL WESTMORELAND COMUSMACV
TO GENERAL WHEELER CJCS
ADMIRAL SHARP CINCPAC
INFO AMBASSADOR BUNKER
ZEM
SECRET MAC 03659 EYES ONLY
SUBJ: KHE SANH REPORT (U)

1. (U) This is report number forty-one on the situation in the Khe Sanh/DMZ area for the period 150900H to 160900H March 1968.

(S) Khe Sanh had clear weather after early morning haze lifted after 1100 hours. Prior to that time, Air force resupply operations had been hampered. During the period, Khe Sanh received 30 rounds of artillery, 14 rounds of rocket and 190 rounds of mortar fire, for a total of 234 rounds. The incoming fire resulted in one Marine killed and 13 wounded (three evacuated). Enemy indirect fire attacks marked the only activity at the base, as no ground contacts were reported. There was no change in either the disposition of Marines in defense at Khe Sanh, or in the enemy situation. Elsewhere along the DMZ, contact was light with one exception. Dong Ha received twenty-five 140MM rocket rounds which wounded 13 personnel. Two required medical evacuation. Total casualty figures for the 3D Marine division area for the period were, two Marines killed, 39 wounded (16 evacuated), 14 enemy killed.

(S) In tactical air operations, 351 sorties were flown, Marines flew 130, USAF 133, and USN 86. Bomb damage assessment included 53 secondary fires 19 road cuts, 45 bunkers destroyed, three trucks destroyed, 18 secondary explosions, 25 enemy killed by air and one mortar position destroyed. In the S Shau Valley, USAF flew four recce sorties and seven tactical strike sorties. Bomb damage assessment included three secondary explosions and 10 bunkers destroyed. Six ARC LIGHT strikes (36 sorties) were scheduled into the Niagara area. Three sorties were diverted to a secondary target due to Beacon malfunction. One strike, within 1200 meters of friendly troops, with fifteen secondary explosions were reported.

(S) Aerial resupply for the period totaled 227 short tons. Class I amounted to 45 short tons. Class II was six short tons, Class III nine short tons, Class IV four short tons, Class V 155.5 short tons. In addition, three short tons of medical supplies and 4.5 short tons of mail were delivered. 142 passenger replacements were landed at the field. Throughout the day, 49 sorties were flown, fixed wing aircraft conducted 15 airdrops. Marine helicopters flew the remaining 33 sorties, delivering passengers and cargo.

(S) 315 tactical air sorties are scheduled for the next 24 hour period, with the Marines planning 85, USAF 123 and USN 100. Marines will maintain their 16 aircraft on call and the USAF will have 120 alert sorties available on call. Six ARC

TOP SECRET

LIGHT strikes (35 sorties) are scheduled.
(U) The forecast for 16 March is for scattered clouds and good visibility by 1100H. Ceilings and visibility will again lower by midnight and fog will reduce conditions to marginal by early morning on the seventeenth.

The following report in the archives is very faint — an accurate transcription is not guaranteed.

FROM WALT ROSTOW
TO THE PRESIDENT
CITE CAP62723

Herewith Westy's Khe Sanh report.
— weather and forecast remain good;
— (??) incoming;
— probing attack repulsed: no friendly casualties;
— 312 friendly sorties plus 42 B-52's
— 258 tons delivered.

Sub: (U) This is report number forty-three on the situation in the Khe Sanh/DMZ area for the 24 hour period 18 March.

Yesterday and last night the enemy intensified his efforts (??) the Khe Sanh base with increased incoming fire and a (??) ground attack. The incoming fire for the period (??) as compared to the previous days total of (??), nineteen men were wounded as a result of the incoming (??) medical evacuation.

The ground attack by an estimated enemy battalion occurred at (??) 15 March, against the 37th ARVN Ranger position at the eastern perimeter. The ARVN fought determinedly and the attack was (??) at 3:00 PM. The wire was not penetrated. There was no friendly casualties: 2 enemy were reported killed.

As forecast, the weather remained favorable through much of the day, allowing unrestricted air activity. Three hundred ten tactical air sorties

TOP SECRET

were flown. Although this is a decrease from the previous period: bomb damage assessment disclosed over 43 secondary explosions, 24 secondary fires and numerous structures (??) weapons positions destroyed. Seven ARC LIGHT missions (42 sorties) struck the Niagara area. Seven aircraft were diverted (??) to (??), three of the strikes reported a (??) of 13 secondary explosions, seven ARC LIGHT strikes and 315 tactical air sorties are scheduled for the next 24 hours. There is no change in the number of alert sorties or aircraft on call.

Other air activity: 45 resupply sorties, (??) 215.6 (??) of supplies and mail into Khe Sanh. Ninety-five replacements were landed at the field.

Activity in the rest of Quang Tri Province was very light compared to the previous period. A total of 35 rounds of mixed (??) was received compared to 658 rounds yesterday. Total (??) casualties in the 3D Marine division area were one killed, (??) wounded (four evacuated). Enemy: seven killed.

The weather forecast is for favorable weather to continue during the daylight hours with somewhat reduced visibility and ceilings in the early morning.

The Khe Sanh Dump and Ammunition Supply Point (ASP) status as of 8:00 PM March 17 is as follows:

Previous Status
Days Supply   3:30 PM 16 Mar
EST

Confidential Files on the Siege and Loss of Khe Sanh

On Hand   (9:00 AM 17 Mar SVN)

Class I (Rations)
    Meal, combat, individual 21   22 days
    B Rations   8   8 Days

Class III (Fuel)
    Aviation gas (AVGas)   3   3 days
    JP-4 Fuel (Jet Fuel)   12.5   12.5 days
    Motor Gasoline (Mogas) 11.5   12.5 days
    Diesel 4.4   4.4 days

Class V   (Ammunition)
High Explosive
60-MM Mortar   54   55 days
81-MM Mortar   30   23 days
90-MM (Tank)   131   134 days
4.2" Mortar 31   31 days
105-MM Howitzer 22   22 days
155-MM Howitzer 13   23 days

B.   Anti-Tank   Rounds on Hand
    90-MM AP-T   329
90-MM HEAT   1,232
66-MM Rocket (Law)   3,475
Anti-Tank Mines (M-15) 336
Antitank Mines (M-19)   463
Anti-Tank Mines (M-21) 2
106-MM Heat   1,123
106-MM Recoilless Rifle (HEP-T) JS 2,165
3.5" Rocket SS   2,222

Antipersonnel
12MM Beehive   1,517

Class V (COFRAM)
    105-MM Howitzer 5   5 days

TOP SECRET

155-MM Howitzer 5   5 days
40-MM Grenade Launcher   5   5 days
    Hand Grenades   12   12 days

On 17 March, Khe San was resupplied with 255.3 tons as follows:
Class I   37 Tons
Class III   44 Tons
Class IV   18.5 Tons
Class V   159 Tons
Miscellaneous   11 Tons

THE WHITE HOUSE
WASHINGTON

    Thursday, March 21, 1968 — 10:45 a.m.

Mr. President:
At Khe Sanh:
— weather good;
— 177 enemy rounds;
— 87 friendly artillery missions;
— 203 tactical sorties plus 6 B-52's;
— 265 tons delivered;
— from other information, indications some enemy forces pulling back from Khe Sanh, others, perhaps, moving east to Quant Tri-Hue area.

W. W. Rostow

Reports from Gen. William Westmoreland continue; caves and tunnels used by the Vietcong would be paradoxical for the U.S. and South Vietnamese forces throughout the war.

SECRET

Thursday, March 21, 1968, 8:50 a.m.

TEXT OF CABLE FROM
GENERAL WESTMORELAND

This is report number forty-six on the situation in the Khe Sanh/DMZ/A Shau Valley area for the 24-hour period of March 20, 1968.

The level and character of activity at Khe Sanh has not changed over the past three days. The enemy continues to limit his efforts to indirect fire attacks. During this period, 177 incoming rounds were recorded. The majority of these were from enemy mortars (150 rounds) and twenty-one Marines were wounded. Five men required medical evacuation. Eighty-seven artillery missions were fired in support of the base; thirty-three were observed missions. Five enemy were reported killed by artillery or tactical air.

Clear weather prevailed for most of the day and 203 tactical air sorties were flown. Bomb damage assessment in the Niagara area included two secondary explosions, nine bunkers and one gun position destroyed, two road cuts and sixteen secondary fires. Unseasonably good weather in

TOP SECRET

the north uncovered lucrative targets and some Niagara sorties were diverted to the northern route packages.

There were six ARC LIGHT strikes in the Khe Sanh area during the period, four strikes within 1000 - 1500 meters of friendly troops. One mission reported eleven secondary explosions. Forty-three fixed wing and helicopter sorties lifted 265.5 short tons of supplies, and 130 replacements into the base.

During the next 24 hours, 298 tactical air sorties and six ARC LIGHT strikes are scheduled in support of Khe Sanh. Weather predictions are fair to good, with marginal conditions early in the morning, clearing up during the day. Rain may reduce conditions to 2,000 feet and three miles visibility after 2:00 p.m.

Along the DMZ, 55 incoming rounds were received with no significant casualties or damage reported. Elsewhere in Quant Tri Province, contact was light. He total casualties in the 3rd Marine Division area for the period were twenty-six Marines wounded (six evacuated), thirteen enemy killed and two individual weapons captured.

A Shau aerial surveillance on the twentieth consisted of one early morning and one photo recon mission. The good weather prediction was wrong. One ground reconnaissance team was extracted and one team failed to insert due to enemy fire. A team report from a mission near the A Luoi Airstrip contains locations of suspected caves and tunnels in the vicinity, a possible truck park and bivouac area and sightings of truck traffic on Route 548.

FM GEN WHEELER CJCS WASH DC
INFO MR ROSTOW WHITE HOUSE WASH DC
MR RUSK STATE DEPT WASH DC
MR KELIS CIA
GEN JOHNSON CSA WASH DC
GEN MCCONNELL CSAF WASH DC
ADM HOORER CNO WASH DC
ZEN/GEN CHAPHAN CHC WASH DC
Z 221135Z ZYH ZFF-3
FM GENERAL ABRAMS DEPCOMUSMACV
TO GENERAL WHEELER CJCS
ADMIRAL SHARP CINCPAC
INFO AMBASSADOR BUNKER
GENERAL WESTMORELAND COMUSMACV
ZEM
SECRET MAC 3957 EYES ONLY
SUBJ: Khe Sanh Report (U)
(U) This is report number forty-seven on the situation in the Khe Sanh/DMZ/A Shau area for the period 210900H to 220900H March 1968.
(S) The amount of incoming fire decreased from yesterday as 111 rounds of mixed fire fell on the combat base. Seventy-one rounds were artillery, a change from yesterday, when the bulk of the fire was from mortars. Twenty-seven marines were wounded; 18 required evacuation. U.S. artillery fired 2830 rounds in 105 missions; thirty-six observed. No COFRAM ammunition was expended.
(S) Clear weather prevailed throughout the Niagara AO for the fourth consecutive day, and 279 tactical air sorties were flown. Bomb damage assessment included 35 enemy killed by AO

directed strikes, one automatic weapon position destroyed, one probably destroyed, and six secondary explosions.

(S) Six B-52 strikes were scheduled into the Khe San area. One strike was scheduled as an emergency target, 2500 meters from friendly troops. ARC LIGHT damage assessment reported 10 secondary explosions.

(S) During the next 24 hours, 289 tactical air sorties and six ARC LIGHT strikes are scheduled. An additional 422 pre-planned tac air sorties can be diverted into the Khe Sanh area if required.

(S) unhampered by weather and enemy anti-aircraft area, Air Force fixed nine and Marine helicopters moved 214 short tons of supplies and 49 replacements into Khe Sanh. During the same period six tons of air delivered equipment was backloaded.

(S) The weather is expected to remain the same over the next 24 hours, with thundershower activity reducing visibility in the late afternoon.

(S) Along the DMZ, light activity was reported near Camp Carroll. Elements of the 9th Marines engaged small enemy units in sporadic action. Six enemy were killed, without friendly loss. Total casualties in the 3D Marine division area for the period were U.S. 32 wounded (20 evacuated); 43 enemy killed, one detained, one individual weapon captured. Elsewhere in Quang Tri Province, no major ground actions took place, some light casualties occurred from sporadic incoming mortar and artillery fire.

(S) Two reconnaissance teams went into the A Shau Valley this morning, the 22D. One at

YD3703 will move north. One south of the Rao Lao River at YC3691 will recon to north and east. An early morning run by 131st AVN Co and one tacair photo mission covered 80 percent of the target area. Six AAAW sites were found to be occupied.
GP-4

SSO NOTE: DELIVER DURING DUTY HOURS
520

  March 24, 1968
  8:55A.M.

MEMORANDUM FOR THE PRESIDENT
SUBJECT: Khe Sanh report

This is report number forty-nine on the Khe Sanh/DMZ/A Shau Valley area, for the period 23 March.

 Enemy indirect fire at Khe Sanh was greater than originally reported yesterday. An update report indicates that an additional 500 rounds of mixed artillery, mortar and rocket fire fell between midnight and 6:00 A.M. on 23 March. Thus the enemy surge during the night of 22-23 March was in excess of 1100 rounds. After daylight, incoming fire slackened and fell into the previous pattern; approximately 130 rounds struck Khe Sanh during this period. Thirty-nine Marines were wounded, seventeen required evacuation. Friendly artillery fired 2056 rounds in 155 fire missions. No COFRAM ammunition was expended at Khe Sanh.

TOP SECRET

Visibility remained good throughout the reporting period, except during a thundershower between 9:00 and 10:00 P.M. Scattered rain showers are forecast for the afternoon of 24 March. Early morning fog is predicted for 25 March reducing ceiling to less than 1000 feet and visibility to less than two miles.

Ten Arc Light strikes, with 60 aircraft, were flown in the NIAGARA area. Four were scheduled as emergency strikes, the nearest being 1100 meters from friendly positions. Tactical air support totaled 408 sorties during the period. Tactical air bomb damage assessment included six enemy killed and seven probably killed, eight secondary explosions, 13 secondary fires, 28 road cuts and three trucks destroyed.

Tomorrow, nine Arc Light strikes, totaling 54 sorties, and 327 tactical air sorties are planned.

Resupply of the base amounted to 224 short tons of all classes. Twenty-two passenger replacements were landed. Seventeen US Air Force aircraft and 24 Marine corps helicopters flew 41 resupply sorties.

Although there were no significant ground contacts during the period, several attacks by fire were reported. The 3rd Battalion, 3rd Marines received 26 rounds of 85mm artillery six kilometers west of Gio Linh. Four Marines were wounded. The enemy launched 11 rounds of 122mm rocket fire against the 2nd Battalion, 9th Marines at the Rockpile, killing one Marine and wounding seven. Near Cam Lo, 3rd Battalion, 4th Marines had five men wounded by ten rounds of incoming artillery. Three kilometers east of Camp

Carroll, friendly artillery engaged approximately enemy in the open. Twenty-seven rounds of 105 mm COFRAM were fired with good target coverage. Third Marine Division casualties for the period were two Marines killed, 60 wounded with 32 evacuated. There were fourteen confirmed enemy casualties.

Aerial surveillance of the A Shau continued with one infrared, three side-looking airborne radar and one morning photo mission flown. Eighty percent of the target area was covered. No vehicular activity was noted but numerous anti-aircraft positions continue to be occupied.

THE WHITE HOUSE
WASHINGTON

    Tuesday, March 6, 1968
    12:45 p.m.

Mr. President:
At Khe Sanh-DMZ-A Shau:
— 25 rounds enemy incoming;
— 252 tactical support sorties plus 47 B-52's;
— 150.5 tons resupply, hampered by low ceilings and high winds;
— heavy contact east of Quang Tri City;
— weather poor.

W. W. Rostow

SECRET

TOP SECRET

Tuesday, March 26, 1968, 9:15 a.m.

TEXT OF CABLE FROM
GENERAL WESTMORELAND

This is report number fifty-one on the situation in the Khe Sanh/DMZ/A Shau Valley area for the 24-hour period of March 25, 1968.

Resupply was hampered by low ceilings and high winds, which prevented aircraft from landing. Input consisted of ten air drops by C-130 aircraft totaling 150.5 short tons. Supplies remain at a satisfactory level with 28 days of rations and 21 or more days of large caliber ammunition on hand.

Low clouds and poor visibility are predicted for the remainder of today and the morning of March 27.

For the second day, enemy incoming fire decreased as a total of 25 rounds were received at Khe Sanh; 12 artillery, 10 mortar and three rocket. There was no ground action in the vicinity. The incoming rounds wounded 17 Marines; 13 were evacuated.

South of the DMZ, seven kilometers southeast of Cam Lo, a third Marine Division Reconnaissance Team observed approximately 250 North Vietnamese Army. Artillery was employed, killing 25 of the enemy.

Early in the morning of March 25, the 1st Air Cavalry Division established heavy contact six kilometers east of Quang Tri City. The enemy force was later identified by a detainee as elements of the K14 Battalion, 5th North Vietnamese Regiment. Gunships supported and the contact was broken at 7:00 p.m. Fifty-two of the enemy were killed. U.S. losses were 10 killed and 26 wounded.

Two hundred forty two tactical air sorties were flown in the Niagara area. Seven enemy were killed. Seven secondary explosions, 14 secondary fires nine bunkers and one mortar position destroyed, and 20 road cuts and two ford cuts were credited to tactical air. Tactical air sorties planned for tomorrow total 314.

FM GEN WHEELER CJCS WASH DC
INFO MR ROSTOW WHITE HOUSE WASH DC
MR RUSK STATE DEPT WASH DC
MR HELMS CIA
GEN JOHNSON CSA WASH DC
GEN MCCONNELL CSAF WASH DC
ADM MOORER CNC WASH DC
Z 291215Z ZYH ZFF-3
FM GENERAL WESTMORELAND COMUSMACV
TO GENERAL WHEELER CJCS
ADMIRAL SHARP CINCPAC
INFO AMBASSADOR BUNKER
ZEM
SECRET MAC 4285 EYES ONLY
SUBJ: KHE SANH REPORT (U)

1. (U) This is report number fifty-four on the Khe Sanh/DMZ/A Shau Valley Area, for the period 280900-290900 March 1968.
2. (U) Weather conditions at Khe Sanh remained good throughout the reporting period. Skies were generally clear with occasional scattered low,

TOP SECRET

middle and high clouds. The forecast for the next 24 hour period is for continued good weather with scattered cloudiness. Isolated thundershowers are predicted in the vicinity of Khe Sanh this afternoon. Visibility is expected to be restricted by haze to seven miles.

3. (S) Aerial resupply increased over the level of the past few days as a total of 217 short tons were delivered. Fifteen airdrops were conducted. Five CH-53 and 32 CH-46 helicopters delivered passengers and cargo. There were 73 replacement personnel delivered.

4. (S) Khe Sanh received 100 artillery, 50 rocket, and 35 mortar rounds, a total of 185 rounds incoming. These attacks killed two Marines and wounded 13 (five evacuated). Friendly actions at Khe Sanh killed 16 enemy, thirteen by tactical air strikes.

5. (S) Along the DMZ, an additional 152 enemy incoming rounds were received. Most fell in the vicinity of C-2 base north of Can Lo where two Marines were killed and 13 wounded.

6. (S) The 1st Air Cavalry Division continued to patrol with one troop of 1st Squadron, 9th Cavalry in the vicinity of Ca Lu as preparations for forthcoming operations vicinity of Khe Sanh progress on schedule. The 101st Airborne Division, carried out deception activities in the vicinity of Dong Ha.

7. (S) Our artillery fired 50 missions in support of Khe Sanh, expending 3,005 (??). Twenty-two of the missions were observed. No COFRAM ammunition was fired.

8. (S) A total of 305 tactical air sorties were

flown in the Niagara area. Of these, 198 were flown in the immediate vicinity of Khe Sanh. Damage observed included seven secondary explosions, eight secondary fires and the destruction of 365 meters of trenches, 31 bunkers and one truck. A total of 258 tactical air sorties are planned for the next reporting period.

9. (S) Five ARC LIGHT strikes, of 30 sorties, were scheduled. Three sorties were diverted to secondary targets. One of the strikes reported observing seven secondary explosions. Six missions are planned for 29 March.

(S) One reconnaissance team was inserted into the A Shau Valley early this morning without drawing fire. Damage assessment from tactical air strikes yesterday in A Shau was four machine gun bunkers destroyed, two secondary explosions. There were no unusual returns or slam missions but 12 emissions at 10 locations were detected on IR flown along Rte. 547, UP-4.

SSO NOTE: DELIVERY DURING DUTY HOURS
500

SECRET

Saturday, March 30, 1968
TEXT OF CABLE FROM
    GENERAL WESTMORELAND

SUBJECT: Khe San Report
This is report fifty-five on the Khe Sanh/DMZ/A Shau Valley area, for the 24-hour period 29 march 1968.

TOP SECRET

Weather at Khe Sanh was generally good yesterday with visibility to seven miles. However, at noon yesterday, fog quickly formed and obscured the sky and reduced visibility to less than one mile. These conditions prevailed during the morning but the fog was expected to lift by 10:00 a.m. Good sky conditions are expected the rest of the day. Heavy fog is again predicted by noon tomorrow to persist until 8:00 p.m.

A total of 233 short tons of supplies and 100 passenger replacements were delivered to the Khe Sanh combat area during the reporting period. Eleven C-130 and three C-123 aircraft conducted airdrops. Forty-five Marine helicopters landed with cargo and passengers. A total of 10.5 tons of air delivery equipment was back-loaded.

Supplies remain at a satisfactory level with 28 days of rations and 23 or more days of large caliber ammunitions on hand.

A total of 55 rounds or enemy indirect fire was received at Khe Sanh, 25 artillery, 25 mortar and six rocket. These attacks wounded five (three evacuated). Ground action occurred when Company D, First Battalion, 9th Marines observed a new enemy trench outside their perimeter. Approximately eight enemy were engaged with small arms and 3.5 inch rockets. The enemy responded with heavy mortar fire. Four enemy were killed and one Marine was wounded.

Along the DMZ, sporadic shelling of friendly bases and installations continued as a total of 63 incoming rounds were received. The only casualties reported were at C3 base north of Cam Lo where five Marines were wounded (two evacuated). Total U. S. casualties were 15 wounded (seven evacuated) and 18 enemy killed (11 by air), one individual and two crew-served weapons captured.

Elsewhere in Quang Tri Province, contact was light with no significant action reported. The First Air Cavalry Division continued reconnaissance near Ca Lu and to the west along Route 9 in preparation for upcoming operations. In a deception maneuver, one Army of the Republic of Vietnam Battalion, one USMC Battalion and one Cav Squadron (reinforced) initiated limited attacks northwest of Dong Ha at 5:00 p.m. last night. Five naval gunfire ships (one cruiser and four destroyers) will support this deception effort.

Artillery fire for Khe Sanh consisted of 82 missions expending 1,626 rounds. Twenty-one missions were observed. No cofram ammunition was fired.

A total of 315 tactical air sorties were flown in the Niagara area. Seven road cuts, 18 secondary fires, damage to two military structures and two trucks and destruction of four military structures and three trucks was observed. Tactical air sorties planned for tomorrow total 255.

There were six arc light strikes (36 sorties) scheduled into the Niagara area. One sortie was diverted to a secondary target. One strike observed five secondary explosions. There were 18 additional secondary explosions reported for the previous period, 8:00 p.m. 27 March to8:00 p.m. 28 March. Eight missions are scheduled for

TOP SECRET

Niagara for 30 March.
   A Shau Valley side-looking air radar and photo missions reported no unusual returns. One reconnaissance team remains in the valley.

SECRET EYES ONLY

1968 MAR 30 12 32

FM GEN WHEELER CJCS WASH DC
INFO MR ROSTOW WHITE HOUSE WASH DC
MR RUSK STATE DEPT WASH DC
MR HELMS CIA
GEN JOHNSON CSA WASH DC
GEN MCCONNELL CSAF WASH DC
ADM MOORER CNO WASH DC
ZEN/GEN CHAPMAN CMC WASH DC
Z 3011297 ZYH ZFF-3
FM GENERAL WESTMORELAND COMUSMACV
TO GENERAL WHEELER CJCS
ADMIRAL SHARP CINCPAC
INFO AMBASSADOR BUNKER AMEMB SAIGON
ZEM
SECRET MAC 4333 EYES ONLY
SUBJ: KHE SANH REPORT (U)

1. (U) This is report number fifty-five on the Khe Sanh/DMZ/A Shau Valley area, for the period 2900029 300900 March 1968.
2. (U) Weather at Khe Sanh was generally good yesterday with visibility to seven miles. However, at 6100 this morning, fog quickly formed and obscured the sky and reduced visibility to less than one mile. These conditions prevailed this

morning but the fog was expected to lift by 1100 hours. Good sky conditions are expected the rest of the day. Heavy fog is again predicted by 0100 hours tomorrow to persist until 0900.

3. (S) A total of 223 short tons of supplies and 100 passenger replacements were delivered to KSCB during the reporting period. Eleven C-130 and three C-123 aircraft conducted airdrops. Forty-five Marine helicopters landed with cargo and passengers. A total of 10.5 tons of air delivery equipment was backloaded.

4. (S) Supplies remain at a satisfactory level with 28 days of rations and 23 or more days of large caliber ammunitions on hand.

5. (S) A total of 56 rounds of enemy indirect fire was received at Khe Sanh; 25 artillery, 25 mortar and six rocket. These attacks wounded five (three evacuated). Ground action occurred when Company D, 1st Battalion, 9th Marines observed a new enemy trench outside their perimeter. Approximately eight NVA were engaged with all arms and 3.5 inch rockets. The enemy responded with heavy mortar fire. Four NVA were killed and one Marine was wounded.

6. (S) Along the DMZ, sporadic shelling of friendly bases and installations continued as a total of 63 incoming rounds were received. The only casualties reported were C3 base north of Cam Lo where five Marines were wounded (two evacuated). Total U. S. casualties were 15 WIA (seven evacuated) and 18 enemy KIA (11 by air), one individual and one crew served weapon captured. (S) Elsewhere in Quang Tri Province, contact was light with no significant action reported. The 1st

TOP SECRET

Air Cavalry Division continued reconnaissance near Ca Lu and to the west along Route 9 in preparation for upcoming operations. In a deception maneuver, one ARVN Battalion, one USMC Battalion and one CAV squadron (reinforced). Initiated limited attacks northwest of Dong Ha at 0600 hours this morning. Five Naval gunfire ships (one cruiser and four destroyers) will support this deception effort.

8. (S) Artillery fire support for Khe Sanh consisted of 82 missions expending 1,626 rounds. Twenty-one missions were observed. No COFRAM ammunition was fired.

(S) A total of 315 tactical air sorties were flown in the Niagara area. Seven road cuts, 18 secondary fires, damage to two military structures and two trucks and destruction of four military structures and three trucks was observed. Tactical air sorties planned for tomorrow total 255.

10. (S) There were six Arc Light strikes (36 sorties) scheduled into the Niagara area. One sortie was diverted to a secondary target. One strike observed five secondary explosions. There were 18 additional secondary explosions reported for the previous period 280900 to 290900. Eight missions are scheduled for Niagara for 30 March.

11. (S) A Shau Valley SLAR and photo missions reported no unusual returns. One recon team remains in the valley.

GP-4

SSO NOTE: DELIVERY DURING DUTY HOURS
650

SECRET EYES ONLY

THE WHITE HOUSE
WASHINGTON

      Saturday, March 30, 1968
      10:45 a.m.

Mr. President:
At Khe-Sanh-DMZ-A Shau:
— 56 rounds enemy incoming;
— 1,626 rounds friendly;
— 223 tons resupply; supplies remain satisfactory level;
— 315 tactical sorties, plus 36 B-52's;
— weather generally good.
You should know Bus Wheeler was a bit annoyed with CIA this morning for calling enemy shelling (56 rounds) heavy.

W. W. Rostow

TOP SECRET

The National Military Command Center again reports on the supply status at Khe Sanh:

SECRET
THE NATIONAL MILITARY COMMAND CENTER
WASHINGTON, D. C. 20301

    3 April 1968
    5:00 AM EST

MEMORANDUM FOR THE WHITE HOUSE SITUATION ROOM
SUBJECT: Supply Status at Khe Sanh as of 8:00 PM EST
2 April (9:00 AM 3 April, SVN time)

1. The Khe Sanh Dump and Ammunition Supply Point (ASP) status as of the above time is as follows:

        Days Supply 8:00 PM 2 Apr EST
        On Hand   (9:00 AM 3 Apr SVN)

Class I (Rations)
    Meal, Combat, Individual   21   2   1 days
    B Rations 6   6 days

Class III (Fuel)
    Aviation Gas (AVGAS)   3   3 days
    JP-4 Fuel (Jet Fuel)   10.6 10 days
    Motor Gasoline (MOGAS)   10.4 1   1 days
    Diesel 21.3 14 days

Class V (Ammunition)
A. High Explosive
60-mm mortar   48   48 days
81-mm mortar   31   31 days
90-mm (tank)   68   68 days
4.2" mortar   28   28 days
105-mm howitzer   22   22 days
155-mm howitzer   32   33 days

B. Antitank

    Rounds On Hand
90-mm AP-T   254
90-mm HEAT   1,089
66-mm rocket (LAW)   2,212
Antitank mines (M-15) 349
Antitank mines (M-19) 469
Antitank mines (M-21) 32
106-mm HEAT   1,557
106-mm recoilless rifle (HEP-T)   1,713
3.5" rocket 2,114

    8:00 PM 2 Apr EST
    (9:00 AM 3 Apr SVN)

C. Antipersonnel

    Rounds on Hand
90-mm BEEHIVE   542
105-mm BEEHIVE 1,090
106-mm BEEHIVE 1,456
90-mm CANNISTER   323

Class V (COFRAM)

TOP SECRET

    105-mm howitzer 1,684
    155-m howitzer   990
    40-mm grenade launcher   6,729
    Hand grenades   2,945

2. On 2 April, Khe Sanh was resupplied with 147 short tons as follows:

Class I	46 tons
Class II	11.5 tons
Class III	14.5 tons
Class IV	40 tons
Class V	31.5 tons
Miscellaneous	3.5 tons

    MARSHALL B. GARTH
    Brigadier General, USA
    Deputy Director for
    Operations, NMCC

SECRET

Wednesday, April 3, 1968, 9:00 a.m.

TEXT OF CABLE FROM
    GENERAL WESTMORELAND

This is report number fifty-nine on the situation in the Khe Sanh/DMZ/A Shau Valley for the 24-hour period of April 2, 1968.

    Weather at Khe Sanh was clear to partly cloudy yesterday with visibility to five miles. Fog and low clouds formed by 9:00 p.m. lowering ceilings and visibility to less than 500 feet and 1/2 miles, respectively. These conditions persisted until 9:00 this morning. Yesterday's pattern is predicted for the next 24 hours.

Operation Pegasus continued with only light contact. All objectives for the day were secured. The air assault of the 2nd Brigade, 1st Cavalry Division to landing zones seven kilometers south southeast of Khe Sanh, which was initially planned for tomorrow, will be initiated today. Cumulative casualties for deception plan and Operation Pegasus since March 30 were: Friendly 41 killed (14 ARVN, 27 US), 271 wounded (80 ARVN, 191 US), nine missing; enemy 402 killed, 29 killed by air, nine detained, 73 infantry weapons and 17 crew-served weapons captured (the bulk of these casualties occurred in the deception operations west of Quant Tri).

The enemy fired 152 mixed artillery and mortar rounds at Khe Sanh Combat Base yesterday. Five Marines received minor wounds.

Artillery fire support for Khe Sanh consisted of 142 missions expending 1,098 rounds, fourteen missions were observed. No COFRAM ammunition was fired.

Resupply for the reporting period amounted to 147 short tons. In addition, 59 passenger replacements were flown to Khe Sanh. Seven C-130 and four C-123 aircraft conducted air drops. Thirty-six helicopters landed and delivered cargo and passengers. Supplies remain at a satisfactory level with 27 days of rations and 22 or more days of large caliber ammunition on hand.

A total of 142 tactical air sorties were flown in support of Operation Pegasus. Of these, 68 were in the immediate vicinity of Khe Sanh. There was no bomb damage assessment. Tactical

TOP SECRET

air sorties planned for tomorrow total 140, with an additional 100 on call. There are 600 additional preplanned sorties that can be diverted into the Pegasus area.

Seven ARC LIGHT strikes (42 sorties) supported Khe Sanh and Operation Pegasus. Ten secondary explosions were observed. Four missions are scheduled for today.

The early morning radar mission in A Shau showed no unusual returns; however, the evening mission revealed returns of 17, 19 and 15 moving target indications in an area northeast and east of A Shau Valley in the vicinity of Route 547. These heavy returns were picked up at different times during the mission. An afternoon photo mission revealed ten probable occupied anti-aircraft defensive positions. There have been twenty-nine ARC LIGHT strike in A Shau Valley since February 24.

SECRET

> Wednesday, April 3, 1968
> 9:40 a.m.

Mr. President:
Khe Sanh-DMZ-A Shau:
— 152 enemy rounds incoming;
— 1,098 friendly rounds;
— 142 tactical sorties, plus 42 B-52's;
— 147 tons resupply;
— weather operable.

W. W. Rostow

This status report is troubling because the enemy is attempting to use MIGs against American B-52s and the enemy is brazen enough to drive resupply shipments at night with truck lights on . . . .

Wednesday, April 3, 1968
9:40 a.m.

MR. PRESIDENT:
1. Herewith, as requested, the reasons why we had to continue bombing up to the 20th parallel: At this time of year, the primary supply routes to the frontiers of South Vietnam run through Laos. Specifically, Route 8 running through the Nape Pass; Route 15 running through Mu Gia, are critical for the enemy's supply of the front against Khe Sanh; A Shau valley, which is a supply route for attack against Hue: and the so-called B-3 front including supplies for attack against Kontum, Pleiku, and Ban Me Thuot.
2. In addition, we have to attack Route 7, which runs northwest from Vinh into the Plans des Jarres in Laos. For Souvanna Phouma, this is critical, notably because an attack is expected in the Plaine des Jarres area at any time by North Vietnamese regulars. It is tactically important to include Thanh Hoa for two reasons;
First, because it is in major concentration and trans-shipment point for both men and supplies going into South Vietnam and Laos;
Second, because it has an airfield which, along with the airfield at Vinh, has recently been active. We have good intelligence that they have

TOP SECRET

been trying to move some MIGs south to attack our B-52's which have done critically important work in breaking up the siege of Khe Sanh and will continue to operate heavily in the northern part of South Vietnam, including the major supply base in A Shau valley.

3. The reason that the President had to take this matter so seriously was because we have the firmest kind of evidence that the enemy is using the supply routes to the South with an intensity we have never seen before, probably in an effort to mobilize forces for a second major wave of attack before the end of the winter-spring offensive. Specifically, Gen. Momyer has told the President that they are for the first time running their trucks at night with their lights on. We have [Redacted] evidence that they are sending down replacement forces to make up their losses before this second wave of attack, perhaps up to 20,000 men (see Tab A).

4. So urgently do they regard this requirement that they are even uprooting and sending South, North Vietnamese Regional Forces normally engaged in local defense (see Tab B).

5. In making a proposal at this time, therefore, the President had to balance the most forthcoming offer possible with his responsibilities as Commander-in-Chief.

W.W.R.

SECRET

       Thursday, April 4, 1968
       9:50 a.m.

Mr. President:
Khe Sanh-DMZ-A Shau;
— 132 enemy rounds;
— 136 tactical support sorties, plus 24 B-52's;
— 97 tons resupply;
— weather favorable.

W. W. Rostow

SECRET

Thursday, April 4, 1968, 9:23 a.m.

TEXT OF CABLE FROM
GENERAL WESTMORELAND

This is report number sixty on the situation in the Khe Sahn/DMZ/A Shau Valley for the 24-hour period of April 3, 1968.

Yesterday at Khe Sanh, low clouds and fog persisted until early afternoon. Weather conditions remained favorable up to 5:00 p.m., when ceilings and visibility lowered to near 500 feet and one mile, respectively. These conditions continued until 9:00 a.m. this morning. A similar pattern is expected today with only slight improvement in conditions predicted.

Resupply for the reporting period amounted to 97 short tons. In addition 21 replacements were flown to Khe Sanh. Five C-130 and three C-123 aircraft conducted airdrops. Nine helicopters landed and delivered cargo and passengers.

The 1st Air Cavalry Division continued to build up artillery assets in the Operation Pegasus

TOP SECRET

area of operation. Six 155mm and four 8 inch howitzers were displaced to a landing zone near Ca Lu. Currently there are 102 tubes supporting the Ca Lu - Khe Sanh complex with 39 additional 105mm howitzers and sixteen 175mm guns supporting from rock pile and Camp Carroll.

The enemy fired 75 artillery and 57 mortar rounds at Khe Sanh Combat Base yesterday. Ten marines were wounded (one evacuated).

In Operation Pegasus, the 1st Cavalry Division continues attacks to the west of Ca Lu toward Khe Sanh. The 2nd Brigade, 1st Air Cavalry Division, air assaulted to positions south east of Khe Sanh yesterday afternoon. Four kilometers south east of the base, Troop "A", 1st Squadron, 9th Cavalry, engaged 200 North Vietnamese Army in a trench complex with gunships. This engagement killed 20 North Vietnamese Army with no friendly losses.

Yesterday afternoon I visited landing zone stud and Khe Sanh. The morale of the troops is very high and they are eagerly assuming the offensive.

Elsewhere in Quang Tri Province, the 3rd Marine Division initiated Phase II of Task Force Kile (Phase I was the deception offensive northeast of Dong Ha). In Phase II the 3rd Battalion, 3rd Marines, in coordination with the 2nd ARVN Regiment sweeps south from Gio Linh with final objectives along the Song Bo Dein river west of Dong Ha.

A total of 136 tactical air sorties were flown in support of Operation Pegasus. Of these, 46 were in the immediate vicinity of Khe Sanh.

Three secondary explosions, damage of one trench, seven road cuts, and destruction of nine bunkers was observed.

Four ARC LIGHT strikes (24 sorties) supported Khe Sanh and Operation Pegasus. No secondary explosions were observed. Six missions are scheduled for today.

Aerial surveillance in A Shau included an early morning radar mission which showed one moving target indicator in the valley. An additional morning photo mission revealed the usual occupied anti-aircraft positions.

This is apparently the last status report on supplies and materiel at Khe Sanh . . . .

THE NATIONAL MILITARY COMMAND CENTER
WASHINGTON, D. C. 20301

    4 April 1968
    0600 EST

MEMORANDUM FOR THE WHITE HOUSE SITUATION ROOM
Subject: Supply Status at Khe Sanh as of 8:00 PM EST
3 April (9:00 Am 4 April, SVN time)

1. The Khe Sanh Dump and Ammunition Supply Point (ASP) status as of the above time is as follows:

                  Previous Status
        Days Supply   8:00 P.M. 2 Apr Est
        On Hand   (9:00 A.M. 3 Apr SVN)

TOP SECRET

Class I (Rations)
    Meal, Combat,
      Individual 21   21 days
      B Rations 7   6 days
Class III (Fuel)
    Aviation Gas (AVGAS) 3   3 days
    JP-4 Fuel (Jet Fuel)   10.6 10 days
    Motor Gasoline (Mogas) 11 days
    Diesel 22.4 14 days
Class V (Ammunition)
A. High Explosive
60-mm mortar   62   48 days
81-mm mortar   30   31 days
90-mm (tank)   68   68 days
4.2" mortar   28   28 days
105-mm howitzer 21   22 days
155-mm howitzer 31   33 days

B. Antitank   Rounds on Hand
90-mm AP-T   254
90-mm HEAT   1,089
66-mm rocket (Law)   2,197
Antitank mines (M-15   349
Antitank mines (M-19)   469
Antitank mines (M-21)   32
106-mm HEAT   1,543
106-mm recoilless rifle (HEP-T)   1,721
3.5" rocket 2,323

C. Antipersonal   Rounds on Hand
90-mm BEEHIVE 542
105-mm BEEHIVE 1,090
106-mm BEEHIVE 1,456
90-mm CANNISTER   323

Class V   (COFRAM)
    105-mm howitzer 1,684
    155- mm howitzer   990
    40-mm grenade launcher   6,729
    Hand grenades   2,945

2. On 3 April, Khe Sanh was resupplied with 97 short tons as follows:
    Class I   29
    Class II   5
    Class III   24
    Class IV   13
    Class V   23.5
    Miscellaneous   2.5

    S. D. CRAMER, JR.
    Rear Admiral, USN
    Deputy Director for
    Operations (NMCC)

INFORMATION

    Friday, April 5, 1968 — 7:50 a.m.

Mr. President:
This [Redacted] instruction to cease firing artillery at the DMZ may (or may not) be the first response to San Antonio.
    We shall follow it closely.
    It is coupled, in today's intelligence, with indications of possible imminent attack at Quang Trio, Hue, and Danang, plus continued intensive efforts elsewhere. It would make sense for them to hurry up attacks in the coastal cities when

TOP SECRET

major U.S. forces are relieving Khe Sanh.

W. W. Rostow

Most dictionaries define denouement as the "outcome or resolution of a doubtful series of occurrences . . ."
Denouement seems to be the perfect word.

The following, "The Analysis of the Khe Sanh Battle" by the United States Military Command marks the beginning of the denouement of Khe Sanh.

(Two charts with this analysis, "Bomb Concentration Pattern" and "Disposition of Enemy Forces" are not clear enough to reproduce in this volume.)

HEADQUARTERS
UNITED STATES MILITARY ASSISTANCE COMMAND, VIETNAM
APO SAN FRANCISCO 96222

MACEVAL   5 April 1968

MEMORANDUM FOR: COMUSMACV
SUBJECT: An Analysis of the Khe Sanh Battle

1. This paper presents an analysis of the effect of friendly firepower on the enemy force positioned in the Khe Sanh area. It was clear by mid-January 1968 that the enemy had concentrated two divisions plus their supporting forces in the vicinity of the allied positions at Khe Sanh. Analysis of his intentions by the MACV Staff, plus intelligence accumulated from many sources, indicated conclusively that the enemy had planned a massive ground attack against the combat base supported by armor and artillery.

TOP SECRET

His initial target date apparently coincided with the TET offensive. Subsequent target dates were:
a. The last week in February. This date would parallel the time schedule followed at Dien Rien Phu. His heaviest attacks by fire at Khe Sanh did occur during the period 21 - 25 February.
b. 13/14 March and 22/23 March. These dates were obtained through intelligence sources.
It now appears that the enemy has abandoned his intentions at Khe Sanh, evidenced by the fact that one of the division forces has been redeployed out of the area and towards Hue.
2. The question demanding an answer is "why?"
3. A massive air campaign known as "Operation Niagara" was initiated in the Khe Sanh area on 15 January 1968. The campaign ended on 31 March 1968. This campaign represented the essential form of offensive power employed by the allied forces. Ground combat action did occur — the battle at Lang Vei is an example. And heavy ground delivered ordnance fires have been employed in the form of light and medium artillery and mortar fires from the Base and heavy artillery fires from Camp Carroll and the Rockpile. But the preponderance of the allied effort was the air campaign waged by tactical and strategic air forces. To illustrate, during the period of the Niagara operation:
MACEVAL   5 April 1968
SUBJECT: An Analysis of the Khe Sanh Battle

    96,000 Tons of air ordnance were delivered
    3,600 Tons of ground ordnance were delivered
        99,600 TONS TOTAL

The air delivered firepower represented 96 of the total. What influence did this air campaign have on the enemy's decision to abandon his attack plans?

Needless to say, a precise measure of the effect of friendly fires on enemy forces is impossible. Some battle results are available but these represent only what has been seen by air observers or reported by pilots during debrief. At TAB A is a summary of this bomb damage assessment. It is fair to say that this data by itself is not conclusive. Further analysis is required.

At TAB B is a graphic portrayal of the area around Khe Sanh.

a. The limits of the Niagara Area of Operations are shown by the grid. These limits specify the geographic boundary of the area in which air ordnance was to be delivered, and was designed to include enemy troop locations as well as lines of communication and logistics complexes.

b. A second area of operations was specified by the ground commander. This was known as "A.O. Scotland" and is depicted in yellow. It is within these limits that the ground commandeer planned his troop movements and controlled the delivery of fires.

c. The area in red represents the geographic concentration of strategic and tactical air delivered fires. While some tactical air fires were delivered external to these limits, this geographic limitation represents the preponderance of fire concentration. At TAB C is a picture of the map overlays showing how these fires were concentrated. The rectangular area with the large circles rep-

TOP SECRET

resent strategic air strikes. The small dots represent tactical air strikes. It is clear that the preponderance of fires were concentrated in the areas represented by the red plot at TAB B.

6. Several assumptions concerning the geographic distribution of enemy forces and the casualty effects of fires must be made.

a. The preponderance of enemy forces were located within the geographical limits of this bomb pattern. The overlay at TAB D plots the known location of enemy battalion size units with reference to this bomb pattern. This area totals 564 Km^2.

b. While not every small enemy unit within the heavy bomb concentration was attacked, an equivalent number in small units was attacked by tactical air strikes outside the heavy concentration.

SECRET

MACEVAL   5 April 1968
SUBJECT: An Analysis of the Khe Sanh Battle

c. The vulnerability of enemy forces within this geographic pattern was similar to that of friendly force sat Khe Sanh.

d. There is a cause and effect relationship between volume of fires and troop dispositions on the one hand and KIA on the other, as represented by this formula.

$$KIA = K \times \frac{Nr\ Troops}{Km^2} \times Tons\ of\ ordnance$$
(see TAB E)

7. In addition to the direct enemy kills, losses to the enemy force also accrued from wounded requiring evacuation. To arrive at this figure, an analysis of US experience in personnel killed and personnel wounded requiring evacuation and hospitalization has been made. From January 1966 to October 1967, for every US soldier killed, 3.44 additional soldiers were wounded severely enough to require hospitalization.

8. In addition, an accounting must be made for enemy killed by ground action. This totals approximately 2000 according to after action reports. Again accounting for wounded/evacuated, an additional 8880 casualties were inflicted by ground forces. That this estimate of wounded/evacuated is valid is attested to by intelligence reports that state that 10% of every NVA unit in the area suffered from concussion type injuries of such severity to require evacuation.

9. A number of different techniques have been considered in order to estimate enemy casualties. Each of these techniques is explained in the following sub-paragraphs.

a. Analysis by cause and effect. The formula for this analysis is discussed in detail in TAB E. The data inputs to this formula are summarized here.

Friendly positions
    Area — 4.8 Km^2
    Enemy delivered fires — 99.25 tons (Khe Sanh experience)
    Friendly forces — 6085

Enemy positions
    Area — 564 Km^2

TOP SECRET

Friendly delivered fires — 99,600 tons (TAB F)
Enemy forces 15 Jan 68   — 20,000
31 Mar 68 — 9,100
Average   — 15,100 (TAB G)

MACEVAL   5 April 1968
SUBJECT: An Analysis of the Khe Sanh Battle

The application of this logic, including casualties inflicted by ground action, yields an estimated 15,760 casualties (3550 KIA + 12,210 wounded and evacuated) from delivered fires plus 8880 casualties (2000 KIA + 6880) from ground action, for a total of 24,640.
b. Estimate based on KBA.
A low side estimate of enemy losses can be computed from the observed KBA figure in TAB A. 1288 bodies plus wounded and evacuated of 4430 yields a minimum personnel loss of 5718 from air operations, plus 8880 from ground action, for a total of 14,600.
c. Estimate based on bomb damage assessment.
A third estimate of enemy casualties can be made by assignment of reasonable personnel losses to the bomb damage assessment at TAB A. A number of KIA has been assigned for each type of bomb damage. Only destroyed facilities were included; damaged facilities were not credited with any KIA. The table at TAB H summarizes such an analysis. Again applying the wounded and evacuated factor, a total of 20,050 casualties were suffered by the enemy as a result of delivered fires plus 8880 in ground contact, or a total of approximately 28,900.

d. The following table summarizes these findings in order of the magnitude of the estimate.

METHOD OF ANALYSIS	KIA	EVAC	TOTAL (ROUNDED)
KBA	3288	11,310	14,600
Cause and Effect	5550	19,090	24,600
BDA	6515	22,410	28,900

10. The magnitude of these losses may appear unreasonable in view of the enemy's average strength of 15,100. However, the evidence suggests that the enemy was able partially to replace his losses. His strength was 20,000 on 15 January and was reduced to 15,200 by 31 March, 6100 of whom were redeployed out of the immediate Khe Sanh area. Therefore his net loss was only 4800, and the total numbers of enemy personnel entering the Khe Sanh area varies between 29,700 on the low side and 44,000 on the high side. This would require a daily replacement rate of between 190 and 380 troops. Because of the importance of the target and the proximity of sanctuaries, these replacement rates are considered reasonable.

MACEVAL 5 April 1968
SUBJECT: An Analysis of the Khe San Battle

11. Therefore it is concluded that:

a. Losses inflicted on the enemy force varied between 49% and 65% of the personnel commit-

TOP SECRET

ted to the Khe Sanh Operation, including replacements.

b. These losses forced the enemy to abandon his plan for a massive ground attack.

c. The magnitude of these losses indicates the enemy forces at Khe Sanh suffered their major defeat of the war.

      DONALD A. GRUENTHER
      COL, USA
      Director

<u>CUMULATIVE BOMB DAMAGE ASSESSMENT — OPERATION NIAGARA</u>

	7AF	B-52	NAVY/MARINE	TOTAL
SECONDARY EXPL	2215	1362	1128	4705
SECONDARY FIRES	1173	108	651	1932
KBA	650	—	638	1288
TRUCKS (DEST/DAM)	204/37	—	49/15	253/52
GUN PSNS (DEST/DAM)	135/18	—	165/25	300/43
BUNKERS (DEST/DAM)	216/19	—	675/80	891/99
STRUCTURES (DEST/DAM)	564/52	—	497/106	1061/158
TANKS (DEST/DAM)	4/0	—	5/4	9/4

<u>CAUSE AND EFFECT ESTIMATE OF ENEMY KIA AT KHE SANH</u>
<u>15 JANUARY - 31 MARCH 1968</u>

Confidential Files on the Siege and Loss of Khe Sanh

1. Methodology: The cause and effect estimate is based on the assumption that the killed by ordnance was proportional to the troop density and tons of ordnance delivered:

$$KIA = K \times \frac{Mr\ Troops}{Km^2} \times Tons\ of\ Ordnance$$

Where K is a constant of proportionality. Data based on the friendly experience at Khe Sanh for the period 27 January through 31 March was used to compute the constant of proportionality:

a. Troop strength = 6085
b. Tons received = 99.25
c. Friendly KIA = 167
d. Area $(Km)^2$ = 4.8
e. K = $\frac{(KIA)\ 167}{(TROOPS)\ (TONS)\ (Km^2)} = \frac{167}{6085 \times 99.25 / 4.8} = .00133$

The estimate of enemy KIA is obtained by applying this formula to the enemy force:

$$Enemy\ KIA = .00133\ \frac{Troops}{Km^2} \times Tons$$

Enemy KIA = (.00133) (15,100) (99,600) = 3547 = 3550
            564

Estimated Enemy KIA = 3550

303

TOP SECRET

FRIENDLY TONS OF ORDNANCE DELIVERED 15
JANUARY - 31 MARCH

I. Air Delivered:
    a. TAC AIR 36,000 TONS
    b. B-52   60,000 TONS
    c. TOTAL   96,000 TONS

II. Artillery:

CALIBER	AVG RDS/DAY	POUNDS/RD	POUNDS/DAY
175	137	147	20,139
155	298	95	28,310
105	1231	33	40,623
4.2	204	27	5,508

TOTAL POUNDS/DAY   94,580
TOTAL TONS/DAY 47.29
TOTAL FOR PERIOD (76 DAYS) = (47.29)(76) = 3594 = 3600

III. Recapitulation:
a. AIR   96,000 TONS
b. ARTY   3,600 TONS
C. TOTAL 99,600 TONS

ENEMY STRENGTH
CHART

AN ESTIMATED KIA FROM BOMB DAMAGE
ASSESSMENT

Confidential Files on the Siege and Loss of Khe Sanh

TYPE	NR KIA	NR DESTROYED	TOTAL KIA
BUNKERS	2	891	1780
TRUCKS	1	253	253
STRUCTURES	.5	1061	531
SECONDARY EXPLOSIONS	.1	4705	470
SECONDARY FIRES		.1	1932 193
KILLED BY AIR	—	—	1288
TOTAL			4515

TOP SECRET

The denouement is complete; U.S. Command announces that Khe Sanh will be abandoned . . .

    Tuesday, June 25, 1968
    3:15 p.m.

MR. PRESIDENT:
Clark did not get to the attached item today: proposed MACV item on changed tactics in Khe Sanh area (western Quant Tri province).
There is some urgency, because of <u>Baltimore Sun</u> leak.
Clark says Westy approved this shift before he left, according to a message from Abrams.
Westy gets into Honolulu tomorrow, I believe.
If we go ahead today we should make sure:
— Westy is informed of this statement;
— he backs it.

W. W. Rostow
TOP SECRET attachment

TOP SECRET

<u>DRAFT OF PROPOSED ANNOUNCEMENT TO BE MADE BY MACV</u>

1. The enemy was engaged at Khe Sanh earlier this year in order to combat him in the hinterlands rather than in the populated areas, to take maximum advantage of our air power and artillery, to prevent him from making a logistical base on the Quang Tri plateau and to sit astride the various potential infiltration routes.

2. General Westmoreland achieved all of these goals. He kept two enemy divisions tied down, destroyed more than half of the 20 to 25,000 troops which the enemy had committed, prevented the establishment of the logistical base and helped block the potential infiltration routes.
3. We now intend to reinforce the successes won by General Westmoreland at Khe Sanh.
4. There have been two significant changes in the situation since early this year. One is an increase in friendly strength, mobility and fire power, so that we are now more capable than we were of conducting both a mobile offense and defense in western Quang Tri. The second is the shift in Communist strength and tactics, necessitated because their earlier tactics resulted in disaster at Khe Sanh.
5. They are now confronting us throughout Vietnam with stand-off mortar and artillery attacks and with small ground attacks, attempting to evade our efforts to fix and destroy their large formations. Additionally, they have increased significantly their strength immediately south of the DMZ — from the equivalent of six divisions in I Corps in January to the equivalent of at least eight divisions today.
6. Because of the increase in our strength, mobility and firepower, and of the change in Communist strength and tactics, we are now in a position to alter our own tactics.
7. During the battle of Khe Sanh, we took maximum advantage of our superior fire power. We now plan to take maximum advantage of our firepower plus our second great asset — our

TOP SECRET

mobility. The concept of our new disposition will be not linear, but mobile. The initiative in western Quang Tri province has been ours since Operation Pegasus. We are now taking steps to assure that it will continue to be ours.

8. We will use mobile forces, tied to no specific terrain, to attack, intercept, reinforce or take whatever action is most appropriate.

9. To take maximum advantage of the change in the enemy posture, we will close down the base at Khe Sanh. Having suffered one debacle with his earlier tactics at Khe Sanh, it is not logical to assume that the North Vietnamese would repeat that debacle. And it is not logical for us to be inflexible under the changed conditions.

10. I obviously am not going to go into details of precisely how we are deploying our forces or how we will utilize the additional maneuverability that we will gain by inactivating the base.

    Wednesday, June 26, 1968 — 9:00 a.m.

Mr. President:
Clark Clifford called this morning with the following points and questions for you.

1. Gen. Johnson retires at midnight July 2 as Chief of Staff of the Army. Clifford is told that it is customary and traditional for the retiring Chief of Staff to be given a Distinguished Service Medal by the President at the White House. His question is: Would you agree to give Gen. Johnson a DSM at a small White House ceremony on July 2?
Yes _____

No _____
Call me _____

2. Westmoreland takes over as Chief of Staff, Army, on Wednesday, July 3, having arrived in Washington on Monday or Tuesday. It is traditional that the Chief of Staff of the Army be sworn in at the Pentagon. But it would also fit custom if you were to award Westmoreland a DSM for his 4 years of service in Vietnam. Clifford recommends that you do this at a small White House ceremony after you return from your 4th of July weekend; say, July 8 or 9. His question, therefore, is: Do you wish to award Westy a DSM at a White House ceremony on July 8 or 9?

Yes _____
No _____
Call me _____

W. W. Rostow

And here the files end.

TOP SECRET

Citizens of the United States (and in fact, concerned individuals throughout the world) have wrestled and agonized with the military and moral aspects of our involvement in Vietnam well before that conflict escalated. The Bibliography cites only a few of the many, many books available about our participation in Vietnam.

Can we summarize our involvement in Vietnam in just a few words? Perhaps even in one sentence?

It haunted us then; it haunts us still.

Appendix

The following are sample pages from these files:

1, 2, 3, 4, 5, 6, 7, 8: typescript pages from the speech by President Lyndon Johnson to the American people about the Tet offensive.

9, 10, 11, 12, 13, 14: typical pages from these formerly-secret files.

TOP SECRET

My fellow Americans:

Nine days ago, the Communist enemy in Vietnam launched the biggest attack of the war. He chose to strike during the heart of the lunar New Year's celebration, which is Vietnam's major holiday. It was as if a widespread assault had been launched against American cities in the early morning hours of Christmas Day. Undoubtedly, the Vietnamese defense forces in the stricken cities were somewhat relaxed. Certainly, the civilian population of the cities was totally unprepared for the savage assault of which they were the victims.

[We should remember that this coordinated and long-planned attack came during the middle of a cease-fire which the communists themselves had announced. We should remember that -- because it tells us so much about the nature of the enemy we are facing.]

I feel that I should report to you on the events of the past nine days -- what the cost has been to us and to our friends -- what the enemy was able to accomplish -- what he was not able to accomplish -- and what we should expect in the days ahead.

The cost in terms of American lives and those of our friends and allies has been grievous. Since January 30, 614 telegrams have gone from this city to American citizens informing them of the death of their son or their husband. The toll among our Vietnamese allies has been even higher -- 1,500 Vietnamese soldiers have died since January 30 defending their cities and their homes. Very many Vietnamese civilians have died and been hurt, although we do not yet know the numbers. The damage in the cities

Confidential Files on the Siege and Loss of Khe Sanh

towns of Vietnam has been heavy, so heavy that we now believe some 200,000 men, women and children have been left homeless as a result of the Communist assault.

There is no gainsaying the fact that we have sustained a heavy blow. I do not wish in the slightest to suggest otherwise. No one, I think, is more aware than I am of the grisly statistics by which we must measure the past few days and their meaning in terms of human grief. I have followed these developments almost hourly -- and with an increasingly heavy heart. The enemy set out to bring home to us the heavy cost of defending freedom. He set out to give us a grim week -- and he has succeeded.

He has also done something else during the past few days. He has learned the cost of aggression. The communist forces which attacked the cities of Vietnam have paid an appalling cost for their boldness. Over 22,000 communist soldiers died since January 30. Another 5,000 have been taken prisoner. In one week, the communists have lost many more soldiers than we have lost during the entire Vietnam war. I take no joy in this carnage. But I think that our sadness about the past week should be mixed with deep pride at the magnificent performance of our men in Vietnam, and of the performance of our allies.

The communist attack was, of course, an assault upon the will of the Vietnamese and American people to continue the fight. Apart from that, the communist attack appears to have had three primary purposes. First, they hoped to cause a general uprising in their favor among the inhabitants of the cities and towns of Vietnam. They told their own troops that

TOP SECRET

happen. Their propaganda broadcasts called upon the Vietnamese people to rise up and end the war. That they were serious in this hope seems clear, for they did not provide any orders to their troops for withdrawal, apparently believing that withdrawal would not be necessary.

They could not have been more wrong. Nowhere did the Vietnamese civilians come to the aid of the communist troops. Nowhere was there an uprising. To the contrary the civilian population of Vietnam's cities appears to view the Communist assault as exactly what it was -- a savage and vicious attack upon civilian populations with a callous and total lack of concern for the welfare of civilian lives.

A second communist purpose appears to have been the destruction of the Armed Forces of the Republic of Vietnam, the ARVN, as a cohesive and disciplined national military instrument. If that was their purpose -- they failed. Everywhere, the ARVN behaved well, and in many places they behaved with outstanding gallantry and professional competence. In the past, a number of prominent Americans have seized every opportunity to criticize the fighting capacity and will of the ARVN. In view of the ARVN performance in the past few days, and in view of the very heavy casualties which they have sustained and the much heavier casualties which they have inflicted -- I suggest it is time for such criticism to stop.

Finally, the communists undoubtedly intended to shatter the government of the Republic of Vietnam by simultaneous assaults on its national and districts centers. The primary communist purpose in South Vietnam is, of course, to destroy the Government of South Vietnam, and to replace

Confidential Files on the Siege and Loss of Khe Sanh

it with a communist government. Thus, throughout Vietnam the communist assault on the cities concentrated on government offices and police stations, on the Vietnam equivalent of the city hall, the county courthouse, and the State Capitol. The communists even announced the creation of a new government in the hope that people would rally to it -- and if not rally to it, then at least accept it as an alternative preferable to a continuation of the fighting. This phony coalition government was treated by the Vietnamese people with the contempt which it deserved.

In these purposes, then, the communists have failed. And they have failed at the cost of 22,000 of their best men slain. The tidings in Washington and Saigon have been heavy this week. But they cannot have been light in Hanoi.

It is a fact that the attacks which began on January 30 were more ambitious in concept, broader in scope, more savage in execution, and more secure in their development than we had thought possible.

It is certain that in the savagery of the past week, the enemy has squandered, for little gain that we can see, a major part of the human and material resources available to him. All of these will be hard for him to replace and some of them may prove impossible to replace. It may be that what we have witnessed the past week is a convulsive effort which he can hardly repeat. But we cannot, in prudence, assume that to be the case.

We know that he has many more forces which were not committed to the assault upon the cities. We believe he is capable of repeating that assault, if he is willing to pay the price.

We also know that the enemy has brought down from the north large and

TOP SECRET

well-trained forces of the North Vietnamese regular army. They have concentrated these forces in the northern part of South Vietnam -- and particularly around our Marines at Khe Sanh. We expect in the very near future that the enemy will attempt to overrun the Marines at Khe Sanh. We expect that he will make a determined effort to do that. We expect that he will fail, and we expect that he will suffer appalling casualties before he discovers that there is not going to be any Dien-Bien-Phu in this war.

I cannot, therefore, hold out to you the prospect of quiet weeks ahead. There will be fierce fighting around Khe Sanh. There may be a recurrence of the assault on the cities of Vietnam. There will be casualties for us and for our friends to mourn.

You may ask, why is it necessary for us to bear this heavy burden. I have discussed with you many times the reasons why we are in Vietnam. This is not the time to discuss those reasons again. There is nothing new to add to the reasons. The only thing that is new is the intensity of the enemy's effort to break our will. He is waiting to see what the effect will be upon the American public -- and upon the Vietnamese public -- of last week's savagery.

I believe that I can tell him what the effect will be. We have known savagery before. And we have known how to deal with it. We still do. Do not look to Iowa, or New York, or Oregon or Alabama for a reward for your deeds of last week. You will not find it.

As for the Vietnamese people, I will let them speak for themselves. They have endured this kind of gangsterism for many years with a fortitude and an endurance which compliment the human race. I will say simply this: We will not let you down. Do not fear that we will cut and run when

Confidential Files on the Siege and Loss of Khe Sanh

gets tough. Neither this administration nor any other elected by the American people will betray you -- or the American soldiers who fight with you. We will be there to the end. And in the end, it will all come out right.

Now -- what is left of the hopes for peace after the events of last week -- and the events we believe will come in the next few weeks. I will tell you frankly that I do not see any prospect for an early peace. At San Antonio I set forth our minimum requirements for peace. We would stop the bombing of North Vietnam if the enemy would assure us, publicly or privately, that prompt and productive peace talks would result, and that they would not take advantage of the cessation of bombing to mount a larger war effort. We set these conditions because we have had some experience with peace talks with communists. At Panmunjon in Korea we talked for 372 days and during that period 12,700 American soldiers lost their lives and almost 49,000 were wounded. I am not interested in such peace talks as that. I have no intention of denying to the American troops in South Vietnam the advantages of American air power if the only purpose of that denial is the well-being of those who are shooting at American troops. That is the meaning of the San Antonio formula. We want peace. We will stop the bombing of the North to get quick and serious peace talks. We will not stop it for any other reason.

I think we have clearly had our answer to our offer of peace talks. I think that the assault upon the cities of Vietnam was the answer. I think that the massive effort the enemy has made to besiege the American garrison at Khe Sanh is the answer -- and incidentally, every man and every pound of material surrounding our men at Khe Sanh came down from North Vi███

TOP SECRET

If it were not for our bombing of the North, our Marines at Khe Sanh would face more enemies and better armed and supplied enemies.

The enemy does not want peace. He wants to try to win a military victory. He expects to defeat us as he defeated France -- by fighting us fiercely in the field and propagandizing us fiercely in our own homes. It was a communist who said that a coffin is better propaganda than a leaflet. They believe that principle, and they are acting upon it in Vietnam.

I repeat to you: they do not want peace at this time. They want to continue the fight. You cannot make peace with a man who is determined to fight you. It is not a question of finding the right words, the right place, the right gimmick. It would be easy to find the formula for peace -- if they wanted peace. It is impossible to find the formula for peace so long as they are determined to have war.

What are we going to do about this? We are going to give them the fight they want -- and more than they want. We are going to mete out the measure they have asked for -- and more than the measure. We will not do this with any joy -- for we are a people who hate war. But we are also a people who are willing - and not for the first time - have always been able to do what is necessary to preserve our freedom and the freedom of our friends.

Peace is available to the communists in Vietnam -- when they want it. The San Antonio terms are reasonable. Indeed, they are more than reasonable. When the enemy wants peace it is available to him. In the meantime, we do not intend to confuse him and to raise his hopes of a cheap victory with constant pleas that he talk peace. He has heard us at San Antonio.

Confidential Files on the Siege and Loss of Khe Sanh

heard him in the mortars that he fired into the heart of the largest cities in South Vietnam. We fully expect to hear him in the fury of the attack upon our Marines. We understand the message. We do not like it -- but we are prepared to accept it. As Winston Churchill put it to another enemy who specialized in savagery, "you do your worst -- and we will do our best."

For that is the way to peace. In this war as in many others, the aggressor will not make peace until he has been convinced that he has no choice. He has chosen to make a supreme effort to obtain victory. That has made the last week a hard one and it is likely to make for other hard weeks to come. If we meet this challenge with fortitude and with unity, then the answer is clear to the enemy. If we meet it with dismay and panic -- if we respond to the enemy attack by calling for our own forces to retreat -- by questioning whether our own forces should be there at all -- by criticizing our friends and our allies -- then the enemy will be succeeding -- and he will see that he is succeeding. He will redouble his efforts, with all that implies for the safety of the American men in Vietnam.

This is a time for steadiness -- and for resolution -- and for determination. I intend to do my best to show all three on your behalf. I ask your help.

MW
2/8/68

TOP SECRET

MEMORANDUM FOR THE PRESIDENT

Subject: The Situation at Khe Sanh

1. You will recall that on 12 January 1968 General Westmoreland informed me that the Khe Sanh position is important to us for the following reasons: (a) it is the western anchor of our defense of the DMZ area against enemy incursions into the northern portion of South Vietnam; (b) its abandonment would bring enemy forces into areas contiguous to the heavily populated and important coastal area; and (c) its abandonment would constitute a major propaganda victory for the enemy which would seriously affect Vietnamese and US morale. In summary, General Westmoreland declared that withdrawal from Khe Sanh would be a tremendous step backwards.

2. At 0910 hours this morning I discussed the Khe Sanh situation by telephone with General Westmoreland. He had just returned from a visit to northern I Corps Area during which he conferred with senior commanders, personally surveyed the situation, and finalized contingency plans. General Westmoreland made the following points:

   a. The Khe Sanh garrison now consists of 5,000 US and ARVN troops. They have more than a battalion of US artillery supporting them, and 16 175 MM guns which can fire from easterly positions in support of the Khe Sanh force.

DECLASSIFIED
Authority JCS 10-10-78 letter
By ___, NARS, Date 3-29-75

TOP SECRET

GROUP 3
Downgraded at 12 year
intervals; not
automatically declassified

Confidential Files on the Siege and Loss of Khe Sanh

b. Among other reinforcing actions, he has moved a full US Army Division into northern I Corps. Within a few days the equivalent of an ARVN airborne division will also reinforce this area.

c. He has established a Field Army Headquarters in the Hue/Phu Bai area to control all forces, both US and ARVN, in northern I Corps. This headquarters is commanded by General Abrams.

d. General Momyer, Commander 7th Air Force, is coordinating all supporting air strikes in the NIAGRA area which constitutes the locale of enemy buildup around Khe Sanh.

e. Air action since 17 January has been remunerative. About 40 B-52 sorties per day and some 500 tactical air sorties per day are being conducted in the NIAGRA area. There have been numerous secondary explosions. It appears that air strikes and our artillery fire have disrupted the enemy's logistic buildup and troop concentration.

3. General Westmoreland stated to me that, in his judgment, we can hold Khe Sanh and we should hold Khe Sanh. He reports that everyone is confident. He believes that this is an opportunity to inflict a severe defeat upon the enemy. Further, General Westmoreland considers that all preparatory and precautionary measures have been taken, both in South Vietnam and here, to conduct a successful defense in the Khe Sanh area.

4. The Joint Chiefs of Staff have reviewed the situation at Khe Sanh and concur with General Westmoreland's assessment of the situation. They recommend that we maintain our position at Khe Sanh.

For the Joint Chiefs of Staff:

EARLE G. WHEELER
Chairman
Joint Chiefs of Staff

TOP SECRET

THE JOINT CHIEFS OF STAFF
WASHINGTON, D.C. 20301

CM-2980-68
19 Feb 1968

MEMORANDUM FOR THE PRESIDENT

SUBJ: TELEPHONE CONVERSATION WITH GENERAL WESTMORELAND

1. You will have received General Westmoreland's 15th report on the situation in the Khe Sanh/DMZ area. Attached hereto is an operations/intelligence summary of events of the past two days. I have also attached a copy of the trip report of General Bruce C. Clarke, U.S. Army (Retired) giving his impressions during his recent trip to South Vietnam. General Clarke was accompanied by Mr. Frank W. Mayborn of Temple, Texas whom I am sure you know.

2. Due to communications difficulties between Washington and Hawaii my telephone conversation with General Westmoreland was not possible until 0830 hours. He provided the following information:

    a. Yesterday an OP-2E aircraft with a crew of 9 was shot down in the MUSCLE SHOALS area while laying sensors.

    b. The ground control approach equipment was knocked out at Khe Sanh yesterday; there is a backup set available and it is being installed.

    c. Light contact continues with the enemy in the vicinity of Dalat.

    d. The stickiest situation at present is at Phan Thiet. The enemy force which penetrated the town, seized the jail and the hospital, still occupies about one-third of the town. It continues to hold the hospital area and occupied bunkers outside of town. Despite the fact the force has lost 103 men killed, the going to clear the town is tough and proceeding slowly.

    e. There continue to be contacts with the enemy north of Saigon and south of Saigon. In a heavy contact south of Saigon Vietnamese Marine Corps units killed 144 enemy.

    f. North of Tay Ninh City an enemy force apparently preparing rocket positions was discovered and attacked, resulting in 60 enemy KIA.

Confidential Files on the Siege and Loss of Khe Sanh

      g. Certain new units of the enemy have been identified near Song Be. These appear to be groups of replacement which have been formed into combat units to continue enemy pressure in the Song Be area.

      h. The enemy has been driven out of Vinh Long. There was some damage to the Cathedral in the town and 58 enemy were killed.

      i. The Riverine force had a contact with the enemy south of Can Tho. Results are not yet known.

    3. He anticipates that there may be additional enemy activity in the Khe Sanh area tonight; however, this is not positive information.

    4. The additional battalion of the First Cavalry Division which I reported yesterday as moving to the Quang Tri area began closing into Quang Tri today.

    5. As a general observation, General Westmoreland stated that the enemy continues to hang in close to the cities. The enemy is apparently attempting to resupply his forces and bring up replacements and reinforcements.

                                      Earle G. Wheeler
                                      EARLE G. WHEELER
                                           Chairman
                                     Joint Chiefs of Staff

TOP SECRET

MEMORANDUM FOR THE PRESIDENT

SUBJECT: Telephone Conversation with General Westmoreland

1. General Westmoreland had little to report beyond the items contained in his report #25 on the situation in the Khe Sanh-DMZ area. Weather was good in the Khe Sanh-DMZ-Coastal area and effective air strikes were made. He made special mention of the B-52 strikes conducted inside the normal three kilometers restraining or safety line from friendly force locations. He expects to continue to target some strikes within this normally restricted area.

2. The logistic situation in I Corps is improving. Seabees have opened the road from the coast to Highway 1 south of the DMZ that can carry one-way traffic and are continuing to make improvements so that the road will handle two-way traffic. Highway 1 is open for one-way traffic from Hue/Phu Bai to Dong Ha. Engineers are working on the road between Ai Van Pass and Hue/Phu Bai so that it is expected to be open for one-way traffic on 1 March. This will make Highway 1 open from Da Nang to Dong Ha for one-way traffic.

3. The 3d Brigade, 82d Airborne Division will complete its move from Chu Lai to Hue/Phu Bai during the next seven days. One battalion is already at Hue/Phu Bai.

4. General Rosson will relinquish command of I Field Force Victor (II Corps Area) to General Peers on 1 March. General Rosson will then overlap with General Abrams at MACV FORWARD for a period of 10 days to 2 weeks preparatory to redesignation as a Provisional Corps Headquarters which will control operations north of Ai Van Pass. General Westmoreland has not yet established a specific date for redesignation to a Provisional Corps Headquarters.

5. General Westmoreland reviewed with General Rosson and General Peers rainy season plans for operations in the II Corps Area, on the assumption that no additional troops will be provided in this geographic area.

6. South of Saigon a Vietnamese Ranger battalion seized an enemy ammunition cache. Quantities have not yet been reported. Some indiscriminate mortar fire was received at Can Tho resulting in 20 civilians killed.

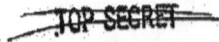

7. Three Popular Force outposts on a canal south of Saigon were attacked. It is General Westmoreland's view that enemy attacks are now shifting to Popular Force outposts in view of enemy failures to seize major population centers.

8. One intelligence team was inserted in the A Shau Valley on 27 February and made immediate contact with the enemy. An effort was made on 29 February to reinforce this team, but General Westmoreland did not have any reports of results.

9. The 3d Brigade, 4th Infantry Division, less one battalion, has relocated from the area south and southwest of Da Nang to Binh Dinh Province to replace the remaining brigade of the First Cavalry Division, which will join its parent unit in the Hue area.

10. General Westmoreland stated that activity was comparatively quiet throughout South Vietnam.

11. I recommend that the daily telephone call to General Westmoreland be discontinued. Information obtained in the daily call is not of sufficient importance or urgency to warrant an additional commitment on the overburdened commander in Vietnam. As an alternative, I suggest a weekly call on Saturday morning to obtain a general assessment and an indication of short-term plans for the 7 to 10 days following the call.

HAROLD K. JOHNSON
CHIEF OF STAFF, U.S. ARMY
ACTING FOR CHAIRMAN, JCS

Bibliography

Selected books about the Vietnam war

Bonds, Ray, ed. *The Vietnam War.* New York, Crown Publishers, 1979.

Braestrup, Peter. *Big Story: How the American Press and Television Reported and Interpreted the Crisis of Tet 1968 in Vietnam and Washington.* Boulder, Col.: The Westview Press, 1977.

Cameron, James. *Here is Your Enemy.* New York: Holt Rinehart & Winston, 1968.

Caputo, Philip. *A Rumor of War.* New York: Holt, Rinehart & Winston, 1977.

Emerson, Gloria. *Winners and Losers.* New York: Random House, 1977.

Fall, Bernard. *The Two Vietnams.* New York: Praeger, 1963.

FitzGerald, Francis. *Fire in the Lake.* Boston: Atlantic — Little, Brown, 1972.

Gabriel, Richard A, and Savage, Paul L. *Crisis in Command.* New York: Farrar, Strauss & Giroux, 1978.

Halberstam, David. *The Best and the Brightest.* New York: Random House, 1972.

———. *The Making of a Quagmire.* New York:

Random House, 1965.

Herr, Michael. *Dispatches*. New York: Knopf, 1977.

Johnson, Lyndon. *The Vantage Point: Perspectives of the Presidency, 1963–1969*. New York: Holt, Rinehart & Winston, 1971.

Just, Ward. *To What End?* Boston: Houghton Mifflin, 1968.

Kalb, Marvin & Abel, Elie. *Roots of Involvement*. New York: W. W. Norton, 1971.

Kearns, Doris. *Lyndon Johnson and the American Dream*. New York: Harper & Row, 1976.

Kinnard, Douglas. *The War Managers*. Hanover, N.H.: The University Press of New England, 1977.

Kissinger, Henry. *The White House Years*. Boston: Little, Brown, 1975.

Kovic, Ron. *Born on the Fourth of July*. New York: McGraw-Hill 1976.

Maclear, Michael. *The Ten Thousand Day War: Vietnam, 1945–1975*. New York: St. Martin's Press, 1981.

Manning, Robert and Janeway, Michael. *Who We Are: An Atlantic Chronicle of the United States and Vietnam*. Boston: Atlantic Press — Little, Brown, 1965.

Oberdorfer, Don. *Tet: The Turning Point in the Vietnam War*. New York: Doubleday, 1971.

Pisor, Robert. *The End of the Line: The Siege of Khe Sanh*. New York: W. W. Norton, 1982.

Prados, John. *The Hidden History of the Vietnam War*. Chicago; Ivan R. Dee, 1995.

Schandler, Herbert. *The Unmaking of a President*.

Princeton: Princeton University Press, 1977.
Schell, Jonathan. *The Military Half*. New York: Knopf, 1968.
———. *The Village of Ben Suc*. New York: Knopf, 1967.
Sheehan. Neil. *A Bright Shining Lie*. New York: Random House, 1989.
Shore, Moyers S. *The Battle for Khe Sanh*. Washington, DC: USMC History Branch, 1969.
Szulc, Tad. *The Illusion of Peace*. New York: The Viking Press, 1978.
Westmoreland, William C. *A Soldier Reports*. New York: Doubleday, 1976.
Wicker, Tom. *JFK and LBJ: The Influence of Personality Upon Politics*. New York: Morrow, 1968.

Index

Abrams, Gen. Creighton, 62, 121, 139, 144, 161, 164, 170, 173, 181, 183, 191, 193, 209, 231, 267
Alsop, Joseph, 10-13, 38
"Analysis of the Khe Sanh Battle," 295-305
Associated Press, 42, 67-68, 71

Baltimore Sun, The, 42, 306
Bundy, William, 10-11
Bunker, Ellsworth, 8, 21, 32, 63, 65, 121, 122, 258, 267, 273, 278

Chapman, Gen., 65
Churchill, Winston, 51
Clark, Evert, 42
Clark, Gen. Bruce, 147
Clifford, Clark, 306, 308
Corddey, Charles W., 42
Cramer, Rear Ad. S.D., 293
Cushman, Gen. Robert E., 16, 19, 24, 119-120, 191-193, 228, 231

Davis, Bg. Gen. Oscar, 162
Davison, Col., 137
Diem, Bui, 7-8
Don, Tran Van, 7

Eckhardt, Gen., 165, 171
Economist, The, 29-34, 51
Eisenhower, Dwight, 29-34, 51

Garth, Bg. Gen. Marshall B., 284
Giap, Gen. Vo Nguyen, 5, 58-59
Ginsburgh, Gen. R., 51
Goodpaster, Lt. Gen. A.J., 29-34
Gruenther, Col. Donald, 302

TOP SECRET

Helms, Richard, 66, 273, 278
Hidden History of the Vietnam War, The, 1-2
Hoover, Adm, 267

Johnson, Gen. Harold K., 65, 155, 170, 173-175, 180, 191, 203-204, 208-211, 267, 273, 278, 308
Johnson, Lyndon Baines, 2, 10-13, 14-15, 35, 51, 53, 67, 68, 69, 72, 76, 78-82, 83-85, 86, 88, 91-101, 102, 103, 105, 106, 108, 112, 115, 118, 124-126, 129, 130, 133, 136, 141, 144, 147, 150, 153, 155, 161, 170, 176, 180, 185, 188-190, 191, 197, 202, 208, 216, 223, 231, 237, 238-239, 242, 245, 247, 253, 256, 261, 269, 271, 281, 286, 287, 289, 293, 306, 308
Johnson, Lyndon Baines Presidential Library, 6

Karnow, Stanley, 4-5
Kennedy, Robert, 10-11
Kerwin, Gen. Walter, 203
Khang, Gen. Nguyen, 193
Koster, Gen., 228-229
Ky, Nguyen Cao, 8, 175, 182

Lam, Gen. Hoang Xuan, 119-120
Loc, Gen. Vinh, 121
Lodge, Henry Cabot, 8, 101-102

Maclean, Michael, 7-8
MACV, 1-2
Martin, Graham, 8
Mayborn, Frank, 147
McCafferty, B., 157, 167
McConnell, Gen., 65, 267, 273, 278
McNamara, Robert, 10-11, 21-22, 42, 124
Momyer, Gen. Robert, 25, 40, 122, 138
Moorer, Adm. Thomas, 65, 273, 278

"Navy to Aid Hunt For Four H-Bombs," 42
Newsweek, 144
"New Tonkin Inquiry to Call McNamara," 42
New York Times, The, 42
NMCC, 150, 291-293

Palmer, Lt. Gen. Bruce, 166, 172
Peers, Gen. William R., 183, 210
Prados, John, 1-2, 51

Rommel, Gen. Ervin, 58

330

Confidential Files on the Siege and Loss of Khe Sanh

Rosson, Lt. Gen., 47, 121, 193, 209-210, 231
Rostow, W.W. "Walt," 3, 10, 14-15, 21-22, 32-33, 35, 54, 59, 69-70,
    72, 83, 86, 101, 103, 105, 112, 115, 118, 124-126, 129, 133,
    136, 141, 144-145, 150, 153, 161, 170, 176, 180, 185-187,
    191, 197, 208, 211, 216, 231, 238-239, 242, 247-248, 253,
    256, 261, 264-265, 267, 271, 273, 278, 281, 286-288, 289,
    293-294, 306, 308, 309
Rusk, Dean, 21-22, 65, 273, 278

Shannon, Bg. Gen. James A., 253
Sharp, Adm. U.S. Grant, 16, 23, 46, 49, 63, 66, 258, 267, 273, 278
Smith, Bromley, 108
Sorenson, Ted, 12

Taylor, Gen. Maxwell D., 3, 8
Ten Thousand Day War, The, 7-8
Tet offensive, 4, 91
Thieu, Gen. Nguyen Van, 8, 21, 32, 121, 173, 175, 181, 182
"This Is It," 58-59, 69

"U.S. Keeping Close Tabs on Enemy Drive," 42
"U.S. Recaptures Embassy in Saigon in 6-Hour Siege," 42
"U.S. Reports Saigon Was in Contact," 42-43

Vien, Gen. Linh Quang, 21, 35, 151, 175, 182, 190, 237
Vietnam: A History, 4-5
"Vietnam Roundup," 38

Washington Post, The, 42
Westmoreland, Gen. William, 3, 13, 16-20, 21-22, 23-26, 27-28, 35,
    39-41, 43, 44, 49, 56, 62, 63-65, 66-67, 69-70, 83-85, 86, 88-
    89, 103-105, 107, 108-112, 1112-114, 115-118, 118-123, 125,
    126, 127-129, 130, 131, 132, 133-136, 136-139, 139-140,
    144, 147-149, 150-152, 153-155, 156-157, 158-159, 161-163,
    164-166, 167-169, 170-172, 173-175, 176-179, 180-183, 185-
    187, 191-193, 197-198, 199-202, 203-204, 204-208, 208-210,
    211-216, 223-227, 231, 237-238, 239-241, 242-244, 248-250,
    253-255, 256-258-, 258-260, 261-264, 265-267, 272, 273, 275-
    278
Weyland, Gen. Frederick C., 47, 86, 171, 193
Wheeler, Gen. Earle, 3, 16, 23, 33, 39-41, 44-48, 49-50, 52, 53-57,
    59-62, 63-65, 66-67, 69-70, 72-75, 76-77, 86-87, 103, 106-108,
    118, 123, 125, 129, 130-132, 136-139, 144, 147-149, 150-152,
    155-1`57, 174, 180-183, 190, 237-238, 260, 267, 273, 278,
    281, 284-286, 289-291, 306-307, 309
White, Edwin Q., 71

TOP SECRET

About the Editor . . .

Thomas Fensch is the author or editor of over 20 books of nonfiction. He is the publisher of New Century Books and editor of the Top Secret series.

His previously-published books include:

Steinbeck and Covici:
    The Story of a Friendship
Conversations with John Steinbeck
Conversations with James Thurber
Of Sneetches and Whos and the Good Dr. Seuss:
    Essays and on Writings and
    Life of Theodor Geisel
The Man Who Was Dr. Seuss:
    The Life and Work of Theodor Geisel
The Man Who Was Walter Mitty:
    The Life and Work of James Thurber
Writing Solutions:
    Beginnings, Middles & Endings
Associated Press Coverage of a Major Disaster:
    The Crash of Delta Flight 1141

He has a doctorate from Syracuse University and lives near Houston, Texas.

www.ingramcontent.com/pod-product-compliance
Lightning Source LLC
Chambersburg PA
CBHW022049160426
43198CB00008B/174